Brazilian Industrialists and Democratic Change

Brazilian Industrialists
and Democratic Change

Leigh A. Payne

The Johns Hopkins University Press
Baltimore and London

© 1994 The Johns Hopkins University Press
All rights reserved
Printed in the United States of America on acid-free paper

The Johns Hopkins University Press
2715 North Charles Street
Baltimore, Maryland 21218-4319
The Johns Hopkins Press Ltd., London

Library of Congress Cataloging-in-Publication Data

Payne, Leigh A.
    Brazilian industrialists and democratic change / Leigh A. Payne.
        p.   cm.
    Includes bibliographical references and index.
    ISBN 0-8018-4648-X (hc:acid-free paper)
    1. Industrialists—Brazil—Political activity.   2. Business and politics—
Brazil.   3. Brazil—Politics and government—1964–1985.   4. Brazil—
Politics and government—1985–   5. Industry and state—Brazil.   I. Title.
JL2429.B8P39   1993
322′.3′0981—dc20   93-974

A catalog record for this book is available from the British Library.

To Stephen E. Meili

Contents

Tables

x   Tables

Acknowledgments

I am greatly indebted to many individuals and institutions for making this research possible. This study had its early beginnings as a Ph.D. dissertation for the Department of Political Science at Yale University. While numerous professors, students, and staff members in the department provided invaluable assistance, the dissertation committee's chair, Juan J. Linz, and a key member of the committee, Margaret E. Keck, deserve special gratitude for the countless hours they spent working with me on the project.

I am also grateful to the following institutions for their financial support for both the field research in Brazil and the preparation of the final book manuscript: the Social Science Research Council; the Fulbright Commission; the Inter-American Foundation; the Helen Kellogg Center for International Studies at the University of Notre Dame; and the University of Wisconsin-Madison.

While in Brazil, I found an intellectual home at the Centro de Estudos de Cultura Contemporânea (CEDEC), in São Paulo. I also benefited from discussions with, and insights generously shared by, numerous Brazilian scholars, too many to try to thank by name. Furthermore, the project would not have been possible without the cooperation of members of the Brazilian business community and labor movement. Those I interviewed are listed in the Bibliography.

Over the years I have also received research assistance from the following individuals: Judith Pann, Ruthanne Deutsch, Aurelio Eduardo Nacimento, Miguel Fadul, and Katy Wolitsky. I would also like to thank Kathy Kruger for her speedy clerical assistance at various stages of the writing project, and Darren Hawkins and Mara Conner for their editorial assistance.

I extend many thanks to my colleagues at the University of Wisconsin-Madison. They have generously helped me through the various stages of publishing the manuscript. I especially thank Michael Schatzberg for his thoughtful comments on the manuscript.

I am also indebted to the editors and reviewers at Johns Hopkins University Press. Henry Tom's interest in the book motivated me to revise it even after I thought I had grown weary of revisions. I also thank Miriam Kleiger for her meticulous, patient, and speedy copy editing; Barbara Lamb for her editorial guidance;

and Carol Zimmerman for her support and assistance in the final production process. In addition, I am grateful to William Smith for his helpful review of the manuscript.

Finally, I extend my thanks to my parents and siblings, my children, and my friends. Without their reassurances and humor, I would not have endured this process. I have dedicated this book to my husband, however: he is the only person other than myself who has suffered through, and celebrated, all the various stages of this project.

Introduction

In 1978 Brazilian newspapers reported that business leaders had begun to oppose the military regime and endorse democratic change. These reports contradicted everything that students of Latin American politics thought they knew about business elites. After all, business leaders had actively supported the 1964 military coup against democratic president João Goulart, which ended the last democratic era in the country and ushered in twenty-one years of repressive military rule. They had also been the only mainstay of civilian support for the successive military governments. Moreover, they were the only civilian sector that had benefited from the military regime, especially during the so-called economic miracle of 1968–73, when industrial growth rates soared, averaging 13 percent per year.

This phenomenon of private sector acceptance of democratic change also occurred in other parts of Latin America. Like their Brazilian counterparts, business elites in Argentina and Chile had endorsed and bolstered military coups and military regimes. Yet, they too appeared to reverse their political positions and accept democratic change during the 1980s and 1990s.[1] And business leaders in Mexico and Bolivia, although they experienced a form of authoritarianism distinct from that in Brazil and the Southern Cone (Argentina, Chile, and Uruguay), also became active proponents of democratic rule.[2]

Business elites' acceptance of democracy indicated a positive movement toward democratic stability in Latin America. That stability, after all, depends on support from the business community. Since business elites proved in the 1960s and 1970s that they could help undermine democratic regimes, their commitment to democracy would eliminate at least one threat to stability. In addition, business elites are in a unique position to sustain the economic health of democratic regimes, thereby providing increased stability. Latin American business elites, like their counterparts in advanced industrial capitalist systems, provide jobs, goods and services, and government revenues essential to national survival. During the current international trend toward economic liberalization and reduced state intervention in national economies, the Latin American private sector will play an increasingly salient role as the engine for national development. Thus, business cooperation is increasingly important to the survival of democratic regimes in Latin America.

xiii

Despite Latin American business elites' obvious importance to democratic stability in the past, and their increased potential in the current redemocratization process, there have been few analytical approaches to explain their political attitudes and behavior. Moreover, the few theoretical approaches to Latin American politics which include a discussion of business elites would not have predicted those elites' recent acceptance of democratic change. Delayed development approaches and *dependencia* approaches, for example, suggest that business elites lack the political and economic power to compete in liberal democracies and would, therefore, rely on capitalist authoritarian regimes to protect their interests.[3] The theory of the bureaucratic-authoritarian state implies that the dominant sectors of the Brazilian and Southern Cone bourgeoisie view authoritarian rule as necessary because it alone can implement the economic policies essential for capitalist development and repress popular protest against those policies.[4] In an attempt to reconcile the contradictions in business elites' political behavior, one recent approach to the transitions from authoritarian rule suggests that business elites are not likely to maintain their acceptance of democracy.[5] This approach contends that once they are confronted by the challenges of open democratic rule, they will, as in the past, endorse an authoritarian reversal. Contrary to these theories, however, business elites' acceptance of democratic change has occurred concurrently with a resurgence of labor conflict, a reemergence of the left, and economic decline.

This failure to predict business elites' current political attitudes and behavior is not surprising. After all, the approaches mentioned above were designed to explain not business elites per se, but broad political and economic development in the region. While these theories certainly include business elites, they are not based on empirical analysis of those elites. Instead, their assumptions about business elites' political attitudes and behavior are derived from their observations of these elites' political actions during unique historical moments, or from their interpretations of these elites' political and economic goals. These assumptions are inadequate to explain business elites' political attitudes and behavior. Yet in the absence of empirical research or alternative theoretical frameworks, they have dominated the general understanding of Latin American business elites.

The adaptive actor approach set forth in this study overcomes the weaknesses in the existing analytical approaches to business elites. It is a framework exclusively devoted to explaining business elites' relationship to political change. It is derived from empirical research, and explains the apparent inconsistencies in business elites' support for the overthrow of democracy in one historical period and their acceptance of democratic change in another. In addition, the adaptive actor approach challenges the underlying assumptions about business elites which appear in the literature on dependencia, delayed industrialization, the bureaucratic-authoritarian state, and transitions from authoritarian rule. Those four approaches tend to exaggerate business elites' preference for authoritarian rule, misconstrue their motivations for engaging in collective action, and ignore the limitations on their collective political power. As a result, those approaches cannot account for Latin American business elites' ability to adapt to various types of political systems, especially democratic rule.

Chapter 1 develops the adaptive actor approach in detail. This approach makes three broad contributions to the study of business elites and political change. First, business elites have limited, but potentially significant, political power. Their unique role in the economy and in society provides them with substantial political resources. However, the business community's innate characteristics (e.g., diversity and fragmentation), its subordinate and dependent relationship with the state, and its defensive and individualistic style of political action often prevent it from maximizing those resources.

Second, business elites overcome these constraints on their political power and engage in collective action when they perceive that their investments are threatened. The perceived threats must be extensive enough to have an impact on the diverse members of the business community. Moreover, the threats must be too great for firms to overcome them through individual political action. In such situations, members of the business community believe that the cost of ignoring the threats is greater than the cost of collective action. However, they rarely engage in such collective action, owing to their individualistic and competitive natures and the availability of individual or indirect means of influencing political outcomes from within the political system.

Third, business elites are indifferent to political regimes, while being concerned about the capacity of particular governments to protect their investments. Neither democratic nor authoritarian governments are inherently better able to protect investments. Similarly, both types of regime are capable of promoting policies that threaten business investments. Thus, business elites are not naturally inclined to endorse either form of political system.

To protect their investments, business elites require both political stability and political inclusion. Political stability, in industrialists' view, includes government legitimacy (i.e., the government can command obedience and maintain order) and competence (i.e., the government formulates and enforces coherent and predictable political and economic rules and effectively manages the economy). Political inclusion ensures the private sector either direct or indirect influence over the government's decisions affecting business, thereby protecting investments. While the absence of these factors is necessary to mobilize business elites against a government, it is not sufficient in and of itself to produce effective collective action. In addition to these factors, business elites must also have support for their political goals from other social sectors. Propitious domestic and international conditions may increase the likelihood that other social sectors will share business elites' anti-government position. Thus, while business elites may mobilize against either a democratic government or an authoritarian one, their rejection of that government is neither a rejection of that political system per se nor an endorsement of a particular alternative; they simply seek political stability and business influence and adapt to whatever government provides those conditions.

After chapter 1 introduces the adaptive actor approach, chapters 2–5 apply it to explain Brazilian business leaders' political attitudes and behavior from 1964 to 1989. These chapters draw on survey material gathered from 155 interviews I conducted with Brazilian industrial leaders. The industrialists interviewed do not represent a random sample. Instead, they are industrial leaders or key opinion shapers identified as such in newspaper or news magazine articles, public opinion polls, business association documents, secondary literature, and interviews with other industrialists. More details on my selection criteria and research methodology are provided in the Appendix. The Appendix (and the list of interview subjects provided in the Bibliography) also illustrates that the group of industrialists interviewed possessed significant social status and political power within the business community and Brazilian society. In addition, this group is highly heterogeneous in terms of the size, sector, technology, and nationality of the firms they represent.

Chapters 2–5 follow the chronological order of regime changes from 1964 to 1989: the 1964 military coup, the military regime (1964–74), the military government's transition to democracy (1974–85), and the civilian government's transition to democracy (1985–89). In the remainder of this introduction, I provide a concise summary of my research findings for each political period, and for those readers unfamiliar with Brazilian political history, I provide a concise background for each period.

Chapter 2 describes industrialists' involvement in the 1964 coup. It identifies factors motivating them to support the coup which are overlooked in the theory of the bureaucratic-authoritarian state. In particular, it emphasizes industrialists' concern with political instability and with their loss of influence within the Goulart government. It further stresses the role that international opinions and trends played in shaping business leaders' perceptions of the Goulart government.

The 1964 coup marked the end of a highly fragile democratic experiment in Brazil. It cannot be said that democracy had been consolidated in Brazil, because authoritarian residues remained.[6] The democratic credentials of the first president during this short democratic interregnum, Getûlio Vargas (1951–54), were tainted owing to his earlier presidency. He had risen to the presidency after a military coup in 1930 and remained in power until 1945. During that time he established an authoritarian state, the Estado Nôvo (1937–45), which centralized economic and political control in the hands of the state bureaucracy and used repression and censorship to silence its opponents. During his second term, Vargas invested heavily in infrastructural development and stimulated public and private investments in economic development. While he laid the groundwork for future economic expansion, Vargas also faced a serious economic crisis. This crisis, along with increasing attacks from his opponents, scandals in the government, and corruption, led to calls for his resignation. Vargas committed suicide, leaving a note attributing his act to pressure from multinational corporations and foreign governments.

An enduring legacy of Vargas's government was the semicorporatist state adopted during the Estado Nôvo, particularly the labor controls enacted in the Consolidated Labor Code (CLT) of 1943.[7] The CLT has survived every subsequent government and political regime. And since the basic tenets of the CLT are referred to throughout this study, it merits some preliminary explanation. The CLT organized workers into a hierarchically ordered semicorporatist structure. At the local level, workers were represented by *sindicatos,* or unions, defined by specific trades (or occupational categories) and regions. For example, the São Paulo Metalworkers' Union represented all of the workers in metalworking plants in the city of São Paulo. These local unions were then grouped into state-recognized trade federations, such as the Federation of Metalworkers for the State of São Paulo. The federations then formed part of nationwide sectoral confederations, such as the National Confederation of Workers in Industry (CNTI). Although the CLT did not specifically recognize plant-level representation for workers, it did not proscribe it. In addition, although the CLT prohibited statewide and nationwide autonomous unions, this restriction was not always enforced during the democratic period. Other constraints that the CLT imposed on trade union autonomy included: state control over union elections and finances (through compulsory union dues); restrictions on the right to strike (strikes were allowed only when the employer failed to comply with contractual obligations); and constraints on collective bargaining (the CLT allowed individual, rather than collective, contracts, and instituted a labor court system that supervised contracts and arbitrated labor conflicts). The CLT has been called the "clothing for all seasons" because it was adopted by the authoritarian Vargas government and survived all the governmental and political regime changes over the next four decades. Whereas the populist democracies ignored many of the restrictions on labor, the military regime strengthened them.[8]

The CLT also organized business associations.[9] Business groups, however, successfully limited the state's control of their organization, autonomy, and leadership. Under the CLT, industrialists retained their preexisting multisector federations, such as the Federation of Industries of the State of São Paulo (FIESP), thus preventing Vargas from fragmenting the broad federation of industries into statewide federations for each narrow industrial category (e.g., the metalworking industries, the chemical industries, and the textile industries). Industrialists also won the right to form small, specialized syndicates as part of the multisector federations. Thus, FIESP represented syndicates of groups as diverse as the cane and umbrella manufacturers, and the automobile manufacturers. In other words, despite Vargas's original intention, the employers' syndicate and federation structure did not mirror that imposed on workers. Industrialists also retained significant autonomy from the state in that, to defend the specialized or technical needs of their constituents, they were allowed to create associations parallel to the state-organized ones. Moreover, the business community also derived benefits from the official incorporation of some of their organizations into the state structures. The official status of these organizations granted them a permanent source of revenues (through compulsory dues) and formal representation in government.

President Juscelino Kubitschek (1956–61) eventually succeeded Vargas, and is the only democratically elected Brazilian president to have completed his term. Kubitschek did not have broad support when he was elected. However, his political skills enabled him to negotiate with, and to diffuse opposition from, potential enemies. His creation of the new national capital in Brasília provided a compelling national symbol of new direction and hope for the future. His motto, "Fifty years of progress in five," accurately describes his monumental success in modernizing and developing the economy. All of these factors gave Kubitschek unexpected popularity. Moreover, his term ended before Brazilians had to pay the price of development: high rates of inflation, balance-of-payments deficits, and debt repayments plagued his successors.

Jânio Quadros, a political outsider and maverick, was elected president in 1961. The future of Brazilian politics would most certainly have followed a different course if Quadros had served his entire term. However, only eight months after taking office he resigned, leaving the government to his vice-president, João Goulart.

Goulart had made enemies among powerful conservative forces while serving as Vargas's labor minister. He was identified with Brazilian populist, leftist, and labor groups. Conservative forces allied with anti-Goulart factions of the military attempted to stage a coup to prevent Goulart from assuming the presidency but were thwarted by the military officers loyal to constitutional rule. Nonetheless, Goulart was only permitted to assume office after he accepted a reduction of his presidential powers and the establishment of a parliamentary system. His full presidential powers were restored in 1963, but he was ousted one year later in a successful military coup.

Goulart's government faced opposition from sources other than the conservatives. Radical popular movements became disenchanted after unsuccessfully lobbying Goulart's government for social reforms, which it could ill afford given the economic crisis inherited from the Kubitschek era. The United States government, distrustful of Goulart's alliances on the left, pressured his government and offered assistance to those conspiring against him. Goulart's own ineffective leadership also reduced his already weak base of support. Eventually, the coup conspirators exploited the increasing discontent with Goulart, overcame resistance from loyal military officers, and toppled the government. After ousting Goulart, the military remained in power until 1985.

Chapter 3 analyzes business leaders' attitudes and behavior during the height of the military dictatorship (1964–74) and provides evidence suggesting that the industrialists who supported Goulart's overthrow did not necessarily endorse authoritarian rule. Their primary motivation was to protect their investments by restoring political stability and business influence. The first military government, under General Humberto de Alencar Castello Branco (1964–67), provided much of the stability that business leaders desired, and reversed many of the Goulart reforms that had threatened their interests. And through a series of decrees called Institutional Acts, Castello Branco and his successors eliminated many political freedoms and granted the regime nearly unlimited powers. Individuals identified as threats to national security (those in the political center as well as on the left) were forced into retirement and stripped of their political rights. Castello Branco abolished all existing political parties and replaced them with the military regime's party, the Alliance for National Renovation (ARENA), and a loyal opposition party, the Brazilian Democratic Movement (MDB). The president was also empowered to disband Congress when he deemed it necessary. Castello Branco dismissed members of Congress, called arbitrary recesses, and deployed the military around the congressional chambers. He also instituted a system of indirect elections (through an electoral college controlled by the military) for presidential and gubernatorial contests.

The highly repressive aspects of the military regime began with General Artur da Costa e Silva (1967–69) and General Emílio Garrastazú Médici (1969–74). In 1968 the military violently crushed strikes and protests. The regime imposed tight restrictions on labor, including control over union leadership. It removed union leaders, barred candidates from running in union elections, and "intervened" in unions by appointing delegates or juntas to run them. The union leaders who were selected by the government or cooperated closely with it were termed *pelegos*.[10] Guerrilla uprisings (1969–73) were effectively repressed by the military, and these uprisings intensified the government's commitment to authoritarian controls and repression. The number of individuals arrested, jailed, exiled, tortured, and killed by the military regime increased exponentially. Between 1964 and 1978, the military regime removed 4,582 individuals from office and deprived them of their political rights; arrested, jailed, and tortured thousands of political prisoners; expelled 245 students; killed three hundred people; and forced ten thousand others into exile.[11]

The regime also adopted a strategy of economic expansion based on the repression of labor, on direct foreign investment, and on the expansion of state enterprises. Between 1968 and 1973, the economy grew by an average annual rate of 10 percent. Exports increased dramatically, and diversified so as to include manufactured goods as well as Brazil's traditional coffee exports. This economic surge has been widely referred to as "the economic miracle."

Although business leaders obviously benefited from the economic miracle and from political order, they also protested certain aspects of the regime. Many industrialists who had never endorsed the coup opposed the regime. Others, who had supported the coup but had believed that the military would restore order and call new democratic elections, became disenchanted with the military's decision to impose authoritarian rule. Still other business leaders opposed the exclusionary aspects of the regime, particularly the limits on business influence. However, these disgruntled individuals never mobilized an opposition movement. Indeed, most business leaders remained satisfied with the military regime.

Chapter 4 analyzes industrialists' attitudes and behavior during the first phase of the transition from authoritarian rule, the phase guided and controlled by the military regime (1974–85). General Ernesto Geisel (1974–79) called for a "political decompression," a slow, gradual, and stable transition to democracy. When General João Batista Figueiredo (1979–85) took office, he announced a political *abertura* (opening). The military had hoped to keep control over the political transition beyond Figueiredo's term, but it miscalculated the level of opposition. Political liberalization fostered massive protests from a variety of social groups. The opposition party prevailed in direct elections. And although the military controlled the electoral college that appointed the new government in 1985, that college actually elected the opposition's ticket rather than the military regime's. Thus, the military regime ended with Figueiredo.

Although industrialists faced serious problems during the early phase of the transition, they did not derail it, contrary to what one would expect on the basis of existing analyses of the transition to democracy. A significant minority would have liked to do so but lacked sufficient support, either within the business community or from other social sectors, to build an effective opposition movement. In contrast, a small but important group of business leaders advocated a more rapid and extensive democratic opening than that initiated by the military regime, and played a significant, albeit largely symbolic, role in the transition. Most industrialists, however, neither wholeheartedly endorsed nor attempted to disrupt the transition to democracy; they simply learned to accept and make the most of it. They tolerated the gradual and restricted transition controlled by the military regime, because its slow pace enabled them to adapt to changes by developing their own negotiating methods and forming employers' associations. And although the liberalization forced industrialists to face new challenges (e.g., renewed strike activity), restrictions on that liberalization allowed them to retain some of the protections they had enjoyed under the military regime (e.g., government intervention in strikes, and the right to dismiss workers for any reason).

Chapter 5 analyzes the second phase of the transition, the "New Republic" (1985–89). The elected president, Tancredo Neves, had been a leader of the opposition political party the MDB, and the party that succeeded it in 1979, the Party of the Brazilian Democratic Movement (PMDB), throughout the twenty-year military rule, and he enjoyed broad support from the opposition movement in Brazil in the mid-1980s. But Neves died before he could assume office, leaving this second crucial phase of the democratic transition in the hands of his vice-president, José Sarney. Optimism over the first civilian government since 1964 quickly faded. Sarney had been head of the military regime's political party ARENA, and the party that succeeded it in 1979, the Social Democratic Party (PDS),[12] and lacked the popular support that Neves had had. Indeed, Sarney's government suggests parallels with Goulart's ill-fated rise to office in 1961, since in addition to assuming office because of a power vacuum, Sarney, like Goulart, was plagued by economic decline, leftist resurgence, and labor conflict.

Despite these parallels to the conditions prevailing at the time of the earlier coup, industrialists did not attempt to undermine the transition to democracy. This was due in part to a general perception within the business community and other social sectors that problems could be resolved within the political system. Although they were not always successful in their endeavors, business leaders had developed, and were permitted to use, both individual and collective strategies to improve business conditions. Their success was limited by a lack of consensus within the business community, by business representatives' firmly entrenched patterns of accommodation to the government, by competition from other social groups, and by the government's preoccupation with resolving the economic crisis. Nonetheless, because the regime granted business leaders at least a limited degree of influence over policies, protected private property, and held open the possibility of political change through democratic elections, the business community tolerated the New Republic government.

The two chapters on the transition period offer convincing evidence that industrialists tolerate democratic governments even during periods of economic crisis, and in spite of an assertive political left, and labor conflict. The differences with the 1964 period suggest that certain conditions permit business elites to constitute a loyal opposition rather than a disloyal one. First, during the New Republic business leaders retained influence over government policies within the existing political structure. Second, the government guaranteed the protection of property rights. Third, international trends reinforced democratic transitions and assuaged business leaders' fears of an end to capitalism. In sum, although there were still industrialists who espoused authoritarianism, they were not an organized element within the business community, the government, or society at large, and their views were not reinforced in the international environment. Thus, by the end of the New Republic, industrialists did not pose a threat to the emerging democracy.

Chapter 6 explores the implications that Brazilian industrialists' political attitudes and behavior between 1964 and 1989 have for democratic change in the region. It argues that the events that motivated business leaders to derail the democratic government in 1964 are unlikely to be reproduced, at least in the short term. Those events were unique to a particular historical period. Negative experiences under authoritarian rule, and the propitious international and domestic political environment today, suggest that business elites will adapt to, rather than overthrow, democratic governments. Moreover, these democratic governments also have protections from business elites' political power. Business elites' diversity, their weak collective spirit, and their dependence on the government and on other social sectors generally prevent them from developing a coherent blueprint for an alternative government. Nonetheless, in their successful efforts to protect their essential interests, they are often capable of limiting political liberalization and social and economic redistribution.

Chapter 6 further tests the findings on Brazilian business leaders by presenting comparative case studies on Argentina, Chile, and Spain. While these cases emphasize different features of the adaptive actor approach, they generally reinforce it. Moreover, they highlight the factors that differentiate certain business elites' political attitudes and behavior from those of their counterparts in other countries.

The Conclusion explores the implications of this study for democratic stability in Latin America. It identifies reasons why business elites are unlikely to successfully mobilize against the new democracies in the region. It also suggests strategies through which governments can simultaneously limit opposition from the business community and strengthen democracy. Specifically, governments should respect the business community as an important political actor, recognize its need to have access to information on—and participation in—government decisions, and establish channels of communication with it. Increased communication with business will strengthen the democratic goals of broad societal participation. It will also increase production, sales, jobs, revenues, and therefore, overall political stability. One reason that many are concerned with greater business influence in government is the belief that this would lead to the elimination of economic redistribution programs. However, evidence suggests that business elites, because of their inability to reach consensus, their self-interest, and their competition with other social groups for government favors, have rarely, if ever, achieved political hegemony over public policy. Instead, when business elites perceive that they have influence over government decisions, they have proven highly adaptable to different kinds of governments—even, as in the Spanish case, socialist ones. Therefore, while it is not easy, democratic governments can simultaneously satisfy business elites' genuine political preferences, implement social and economic redistribution programs, and strengthen democracy.

Portuguese and Spanish Acronyms

AAB Aliança Anticomunista Brasileira (Brazilian Anticommunist Alliance)
ABI Associação Brasileira da Imprensa (Brazilian Press Association)
ADCE Associação de Dirigentes Cristãos de Empresas (Association of Christian Entrepreneurs)
ADEP Ação Democrática Popular (Democratic Popular Action)
ADP Ação Democrática Parliamentar (Parlamentary Democratic Action)
ANAPEMEI Associação Nacional das Pequenas e Médias Empresas Industriais (National Association of Small and Medium-Sized Industries)
ANFAVEA Associação Nacional dos Fabricantes de Veículos Automotores (National Association of Automobile Manufacturers)
AP Alianza Popular (Popular Alliance)
ARENA Aliança de Renovação Nacional (Alliance for National Renovation)
ARTE Assessoria das Relações Trabalhistas das Empresas (Labor Relations Consultants to Business)
BNDE Banco Nacional de Desenvolvimento Econômico (Bank for National Economic Development)
CCOO Comisiones Obreras (Workers' Commissions)
CEDEC Centro de Estudos de Cultura Contemporânea (Center for Studies of Contemporary Culture)
CEOE Confederación Española de Organizaciones Empresariales (Spanish Confederation of Business Organizations)
CGT Central Geral dos Trabalhadores (General Workers' Command)
CIESP Centro das Indústrias do Estado de São Paulo (Center of Industries of the State of São Paulo)
CLMD Cruzada Libertadora Militar Democrática (Liberating Cross of Military Democracy)
CLT Consolidação das Leis do Trabalho (Consolidated Labor Code)
CNI Confederação Nacional das Indústrias (National Confederation of Industries)
CNTI Confederação Nacional dos Trabalhadores na Indústria (National Confederation of Workers in Industry)
CONCLAP Conselho Nacional das Classes Produtoras (National Council of Producing Classes)

CUT   Central Única dos Trabalhadores (Central Workers' Organization)
DAP   Departamento de Assistência à Média e Pequena Indústria (Department for Assistance to Small and Medium-Sized Industry)
DIEESE Departamento Intersindical de Estatística e Estudos Sócio-Econômicos (Interunion Department of Statistical and Socioeconomic Studies)
DOI-CODI Destacamento de Operações e Informações–Centro de Operações de Defesa Interna (Information Operations Detachment–Center for Internal Defense Operations)
ESG   Escola Superior de Guerra (Superior War College)
FIERGS Federação das Indústrias do Estado de Rio Grande do Sul (Federation of Industries of the State of Rio Grande do Sul)
FIESP Federação das Indústrias do Estado de São Paulo (Federation of Industries of the State of São Paulo)
FNLI   Frente Nacional da Livre Iniciativa (National Front for Free Enterprise)
IBAD   Instituto Brasileiro de Ação Democrática (Brazilian Institute for Democratic Action)
IDB   Instituto Democrático Brasileiro (Brazilian Democratic Institute)
IPES   Instituto de Pesquisas e Estudos Sociais (Institute for Economic and Social Research)
IUPERJ Instituto Universitário de Pesquisas do Rio de Janeiro (University Research Institute of Rio de Janeiro)
MAC   Movimento Anticomunista (Anticommunist Movement)
MDB   Movimento Democrático Brasileiro (Brazilian Democratic Movement)
MSD   Movimento Sindical Democrático (Democratic Union Movement)
OAB   Ordem dos Advogados do Brasil (Organization of Brazilian Lawyers)
OBAN   Operação Bandeirantes (Operation Bandeirantes)
OPAC   Organização Paranaense Anticomunista (Anticommunist Organization of Paraná)
PCB   Partido Comunista Brasileiro (Brazilian Communist Party)
PCdoB Partido Comunista do Brasil (Communist Party of Brazil [Maoist])
PDS   Partido Democrático Social (Social Democratic Party)
PDT   Partido Democrático Trabalhista (Democratic Labor Party)
PFL   Partido da Frente Liberal (Liberal Front Party)
PL   Partido Liberal (Liberal Party)
PMDB   Partido do Movimento Democrático Brasileiro (Party of the Brazilian Democratic Movement)
PNBE   Pensamento Nacional de Bases Empresariais (National Grassroots Business Association)
PP   Partido Popular (Popular Party)
PSOE   Partido Socialista Obrero Español (Spanish Socialist Labor Party)
PT   Partido dos Trabalhadores (Workers' Party)
SINFAVEA Sindicato Nacional dos Fabricantes de Veículos Automotores (National Syndicate of Automobile Manufacturers)

SNI   Serviço Nacional de Informações (National Intelligence Service)
TFP   Tradição, Familia, e Propriedade (Tradition, Family, and Property)
UBE   União Brasileira de Empresários (Union of Brazilian Businesses)
UCD   Unión del Centro Democrático (Union of the Democratic Center)
UDR   União Democrática Ruralista (Rural Democratic Union)
UGT   Unión General de Trabajadores (General Workers' Union)
UNIAPAC   União Internacional dos Dirigentes Cristãos de Empresas (International Union of Christian Entrepreneurs)

Chapter One

The Adaptive Actor Approach
to Business Elites

Students of Latin American politics are naturally skeptical about the region's democratic future. We applaud the transitions from authoritarian rule under way since the late 1970s, yet question whether those transitions will inexorably lead to long-term political stability or to social and economic redistribution and broad political freedoms. The region's political history is not reassuring: only three of the twenty-one countries in the region (Costa Rica, Colombia, and Venezuela) have sustained any semblance of democratic procedures. Social and economic redistribution is even more rare. Moreover, previous attempts by Latin American democratic regimes to expand political rights and social and economic redistribution, in the 1960s and 1970s, ended in a chain reaction of military coups and authoritarian regimes. What are the chances that democracy will survive today? What kind of democracy will evolve?

There are some auspicious signs for the future of democracy in the region. The new post–Cold War environment has reduced the internal security pressures that led to authoritarian regimes in the past and has increased national and international support for democratic change. In addition, the failure of authoritarian regimes to bring economic stability and political order, and the widespread discrediting of such regimes, has lessened their appeal as alternative political models. Finally, well-organized social movements excluded and persecuted under authoritarian rule are likely to become democratic watchdogs, protecting the region against authoritarian reversals.

Despite these advances, most students of Latin American politics doubt that the authoritarian legacy has ended. Studies of the political attitudes and behavior of the military and the technocrats, who were two of the three main groups behind the military coups of the 1960s and 1970s in Brazil and the Southern Cone,[1] reveal that despite their responsibility for repression and economic decline during the military regimes, these groups continue to wield substantial political influence, albeit often behind the scenes. Moreover, these studies characterize the political influence of these groups as antidemocratic.

The third pillar of the Latin American coup conspiracies in the 1960s and 1970s—business elites—has been largely ignored by scholars analyzing recent

1

political change in the region, but these elites promise to play a more overt role in the current political process than they have in the past. They are not as implicated in the economic failures and political repression as their military and technocratic allies are. Moreover, political and economic changes under way in the region have enhanced their potential political influence. The emphasis on reduced state intervention in the economy will increase the private sector's role in national development. And political liberalization has created new and more effective channels of participation for various social groups, including the private sector.

The heightened role of business elites in contemporary Latin American politics highlights the scarcity of studies analyzing these elites and their political attitudes and behavior. The absence of empirically derived theoretical frameworks regarding business elites has led students of Latin American politics to adopt the assumptions about business elites which are found in the preeminent theoretical literature on political and economic development in Latin America, primarily the theory of the bureaucratic-authoritarian state.[2] As discussed below, this literature, while it considers business elites, was never intended to explain their political attitudes and behavior. And although nearly every other aspect of the theory of the bureaucratic-authoritarian state has been criticized,[3] its assumptions regarding Latin American business elites have remained untested and widely used.

The recent literature on the transitions from authoritarian rule in Latin America (hereafter referred to as the "transitions literature"), provides the most striking example. The most significant study within the transitions literature takes its assumptions about business elites' behavior from the theory of the bureaucratic-authoritarian state.[4] It assumes that business elites' attitudes have not changed over time, and that they are likely to repeat their actions, that is, undermine the transition and restore authoritarian rule.

Preliminary evidence of Latin American business elites' role in transitions from authoritarian rule contradicts that prediction. Despite the challenges that economic crises, labor conflict, and a resurgent left have posed to their interests, business elites have not mobilized behind an authoritarian reversal. Instead, they have appeared to adapt successfully to the democratic change underway in the region.

In light of the failure of existing approaches to explain contemporary Latin American business elites' attitudes and behavior, an alternative framework is imperative. I have developed the adaptive actor approach to provide that alternative and overcome the weaknesses in the theory of the bureaucratic-authoritarian state and the transitions literature. The adaptive actor approach focuses exclusively on business elites' political attitudes and behavior and their impact on political change. It is based on empirical findings—specifically, research on Brazilian business leaders' political attitudes and behavior between 1964 and 1985. Finally, it provides an explanation for the apparent contradictions between business elites' support for the authoritarian regime in the 1960s and 1970s and their acceptance of democracy in the 1980s.

The Adaptive Actor Approach

The adaptive actor approach identifies business elites' true political power, preferences, and motivations. It contends that business elites possess substantial political resources but are often incapable of using those resources effectively, and it identifies the conditions that either constrain or enhance their collective power. The adaptive actor approach further argues that business elites are indifferent to political regimes; they are neither inherently authoritarian nor inherently democratic. Rather, they adapt to governments that create a minimally stable investment climate, and reject those that do not. This approach, therefore, challenges the assumptions about business elites' power and preferences which appear in the theory of the bureaucratic-authoritarian state and in the transitions literature.

Business Elites' Political Power

The theory of the bureaucratic-authoritarian state characterizes Latin American business elites' political power in a contradictory manner. It suggests that business elites are politically and economically weak. Consistent with delayed, or "late-late," industrialization approaches and dependencia approaches, the theory attributes Latin American business elites' weakness to the region's delayed industrialization, which subordinated the business class to the demands of international capital.[5] The elites' weakness led them to support the authoritarian coups and regimes during the 1960s and 1970s. Too weak to defend their interests against other social forces in a competitive democracy or to promote economic expansion, they supported an authoritarian regime driven by capitalist interests. Thus, the theory asserts that although business elites are too weak to defend their interests under democratic rule, they are nevertheless sufficiently strong to help undermine that rule, replace it with an authoritarian regime, and sustain the regime by providing its only base of civilian support.[6] The theory attempts to resolve this contradiction by isolating one faction within the business class which possesses both political and economic strength: the transnational faction. This faction is defined as those entrepreneurs engaged in the most complex and technologically advanced set of business organizations in the region, and those which have the closest links to international capital.[7] However, this attempt at clarification still fails to explain why such a powerful faction was unable to influence political change within the democratic system.

The transitions literature perpetuates an ambiguous view of business elites' political strength. It assumes that Latin American business elites are strong enough to undermine the transition from authoritarian rule if that transition threatens business interests. While the literature recognizes that business elites' destabilization efforts will prove successful only if supported by other social sectors, it assumes that such sectors share business elites' political sentiments. It thus implies that although business elites are powerful enough to undermine democratic regimes, they are not powerful enough to safeguard their own interests within democratic political systems.

The contradiction regarding business elites' political power is understandable. Latin American business elites are intermittently weak and strong, depending on the interplay of various forces. Because business elites can effectively limit and reverse democratic change, and have done so, it is imperative to understand the conditions that enhance or diminish their power. Those conditions are not explained by the four main assumptions regarding business elites' political power which appear in the theory of the bureaucratic-authoritarian state and the transitions literature.

First, the assumption that business elites' political impotence results from delayed industrialization is only partially true. Because business elites in advanced industrial countries have also demonstrated political weakness at times, factors inherent to any business community must be considered in evaluating Latin American business elites' political strength.

Second, the assumption that Latin American business elites are too weak to defend their interests in competitive democracies and therefore resort to military coups offers little understanding of business elites' political power in "normal" circumstances. Coups occur relatively infrequently and are thus not particularly helpful in understanding what conditions enhance or undermine the collective power of the business class. To understand business elites' behavior we need information about that behavior both during coups and during "normal" political periods. There is evidence to suggest that business elites possess significant political resources that allow them to adapt to a variety of systems of government during "normal" periods. However, business adaptability is ignored in the theory of the bureaucratic-authoritarian state and in the transitions literature.

Third, the assumption that transnational elements of the bourgeoisie provide Latin American business elites with political strength overlooks the potential weakness inherent in a fragmented business class. The theory of the bureaucratic-authoritarian state assumes that the transnational bourgeoisie is sufficiently powerful to influence the government on its own, and that the government can use its power to grant certain favors to induce the rest of the business community to accept its policies.[8] The adaptive actor approach argues that divisions within the business community often weaken the political power of business.

Fourth, the assumption in the transitions literature that business elites enjoy sufficient support from other social sectors to achieve their political demands ignores a fundamental weakness in business elites' collective power: business elites oı lack societal support for their interests. Indeed, if they possessed such support th would become a hegemonic class, capable of consistently winning their demands from either democratic or authoritarian regimes, and overthrowing any regime that fails to act in the express interest of the business class. Critics of the neo-Marxist structuralist and functionalist approaches have argued against such a narrow interpretation of capitalists' power. The government may jeopardize individual capitalists' interests in order to protect the long-term stability of the capitalist system.[9] Moreover, business elites and their allied governments have frequently proven powerless against popular social movements for change.[10] Business elites simply do not have sufficient power to achieve their demands consistently, and are forced to adapt to the prevailing political and economic system.

The adaptive actor approach identifies the factors that enhance and constrain business elites' power. The strength of Latin American business elites results from their significant resources. Like their North American and Western European counterparts, these elites possess extensive political resources that they can use to influence political outcomes in a wide range of areas.[11] Indeed, so great are these resources that scholars sometimes consider the business sector more important than the electorate to the functioning of democracy.[12] For example, members of the business community have substantial financial resources generated from their personal wealth, their firms' profits, and business organization's budgets. The business community also possesses organizational resources, such as the staff, expertise, technology and materials provided by business associations. Business leaders also have social resources—contacts, connections, and prestige—that they have obtained as a result of their education, wealth, social background, friendships, and professions. These social resources give them access to government officials and, therefore, influence over political decisions. Business leaders travel in the same social circles as many policy makers. They often attend the same schools, parties, or social clubs. They also tend to trade occupations: business leaders often pursue political careers, and public officials often retire to jobs in the private sector.

Business elites' political activities and sanctions also influence political outcomes in Latin America as in advanced industrial countries. Specific political acts used by business elites to influence policies and political appointments include lobbying, both by individual firms and by business associations; preparing and publishing position papers; advertising; managing campaigns in support of, or in opposition to, particular policies; helping to elect candidates to public office, influencing political appointments, sponsoring debates and speeches, training and financing political activists, and meeting (both formally and informally) with politicians and activists. The sanctions used by business elites to influence political outcomes include threats (which may or may not be carried out) to reduce production and investment or to engage in capital flight. The results of these sanctions are slow growth, increased levels of unemployment, and reduced public revenues.[13] In addition, business elites may punish politicians for supporting unfavorable policies by withdrawing support for their reelection campaigns. Because capitalist governments, whether authoritarian or democratic, depend on business elites to supply goods for the domestic market, provide jobs, and pay taxes, and individual politicians rely on business elites to finance their electoral campaigns, politicians take business sanctions seriously and try to avoid them. Therefore, even if governments do not grant business elites a direct role in decision making, they generally consider the impact their policies will have on business and act accordingly.

Despite these sources of potential political power, business elites in Latin America, like their counterparts in advanced industrial countries, are often unable to effectively use their resources to influence political outcomes.[14] Among the obstacles that business elites face in turning their significant political resources and potential power into effective political power are the inherent characteristics of the business community, the pattern of business-state relations, and the nature of political action by business.

Inherent Characteristics of the Business Community.   Fragmentation within the business community prevents effective collective action.[15] It results from competition, individualism, and diversity. Whether by habit or by nature, businesspeople are inclined to withhold information from their competitors rather than uniting and cooperating with them.[16] Moreover, because businesspeople are concerned primarily with how policies or governments affect their individual firms, they will not generally forego their specific or short term needs to make collective demands.[17] In addition, firms vary in size; location; vulnerability to economic fluctuations; and access to credit, subsidies, and incentives. As a result, government policies affect businesspeople unequally, which leads them to evaluate those policies differently. In addition, the varying ages, personalities, backgrounds, experiences, and ideologies of businesspeople create diverse interests and opinions.[18] As a result of this fragmentation, businesspeople are caught in a vicious cycle. They avoid collective action because it rarely satisfies their individual needs, yet without collective action their political power is limited.[19]

Business-State Relations.   In order to influence government policies, business elites must be taken seriously by the government. Latin American business elites, however, have not always enjoyed this kind of respect from their governments. This results from their lack of social prestige, their narrowly self-interested goals, and their dependence on the state.

Of the explanations for Latin American business elites' limited social prestige,

Albert Hirschman's is the most persuasive. He contends that because of the timing of Latin America's industrial development, its business elites achieved less prestige and influence than did their North American or Western European counterparts. The late timing of Latin America's industrialization, and of its incorporation into the global market, meant that Latin American entrepreneurship was dominated by immigrant producers who lacked national prestige. Moreover, these industrialists primarily copied foreign products; imported ideas, processes, and technology; and manufactured light consumer goods for domestic markets which were small. Their foreign counterparts, in contrast, achieved national prestige and international recognition for innovation and for the production of heavy consumer or producer goods that were exported throughout the world.[20] Thus, Latin American industrialists lacked the social and economic power to wield the same level of influence over politics that their foreign counterparts did.

Latin American business elites' national prestige and political power is also limited owing to the widespread popular perception that these elites lack commitment to national development goals and aspirations.[21] Businesspeople are perceived as pursuing their own narrow self-interest, producing and investing only to make profits and increase their personal wealth. They are seen as indifferent both to national growth and development (except insofar as their own firms benefit from it) and to the negative public costs of economic expansion (e.g., environmental degradation). They are further perceived as united against public programs to redistribute wealth and deliver social services. Thus, while capitalist governments depend on private businesses for the reasons discussed above, few governments want to be perceived as operating solely in the interests of capital.

Latin American business elites' political influence is also stymied by their dependence on the state. For example, they lack an autonomous base of power. In Latin America and southern Europe, in particular, the state often organizes business associations, officially recognizes them, and defines their functions, thereby limiting competition between them. This form of corporatist control limits business elites' autonomy and impairs their ability to defend their interests against adverse government policies.[22]

In addition, Latin American business elites often rely on governments and public enterprises for their economic survival. The public sphere provides businesses with, among other things, subsidies, incentives, credit, technology, and a market for their goods. As a result, industrialists are unlikely to challenge government policies, for fear that their protests may provoke the government to reduce their subsidies, incentives, or loans; withhold payment for goods or services; audit their firms and impose fines; close their business associations; or—in extreme cases, under authoritarian regimes—detain, arrest, exile, or even torture them.[23]

To reduce the risks of government reprisals under authoritarian regimes, businesspeople will often avoid public confrontation and restrict their political activities to direct contacts with the head of state or members of the cabinet in closed, private meetings.[24] Although in democratic systems businesspeople feel freer to pursue a wider variety of political activities, this freedom does not necessarily lead to greater influence in government. For example, if they rely heavily on the government for favorable policies, they may limit the severity or the nature of their public criticisms. The heads of business associations may feel that they will best serve their constituents by maintaining amicable relations with the government and thereby gaining more access to decision makers. Moreover, this reliance on the government for favorable policies may also fragment the business community, and some individuals (especially the heads of business associations and large businesses, who have more access to governments) will exchange acquiescence for personal favors or political rewards from the government, thereby diminishing the collective power of the business community.[25]

The Nature of Political Action by Business.   Latin American business communities have on occasion overcome their inherent weakness and created forceful and autonomous movements against national governments. This kind of mobilization generally occurs when government policies threaten private sector investments, and individual defensive actions against those threats are ineffective. A generalized threat compels businesspeople to overcome their fear of government retaliation. If the threat is sufficiently serious, they will have nothing to lose by public protest and may even achieve favorable policy changes. Although businesspeople may prove successful in uniting to defeat certain government policies, their diversity, competition, and individualism prevent them from reaching the consensus necessary to formulate alternatives to those policies. In other words, rather than working toward an agreed-upon ideal, the business community is often motivated to take collective action by the desire to avoid worst-case scenarios. The business community's collective action is normally limited to vetoing government policies and practices. It relies on other social sectors to develop and implement alternatives.

Business Elites' Political Preferences and Motivations

The theory of the bureaucratic-authoritarian state suggests that Latin American business elites endorsed authoritarian rule because they believed that it would eliminate obstacles to economic expansion. The theory assumes that in the 1960s and 1970s Latin American business elites, particularly the transnational faction, joined with the military and the technocracy for the express purpose of overthrowing democratic systems and replacing them with authoritarian systems. According to the theory, because of the exhaustion of the "easy phase" of import-substitution industrialization (the domestic production of manufactured consumer goods that had previously been imported), Brazilian and Southern Cone business elites faced a number of bottlenecks to economic expansion. These bottlenecks included high balance-of-payments deficits, substantial foreign debt, and high inflation rates.[26] To overcome these economic problems, stabilize the economy, and encourage industrial investment and expansion, technocrats and business elites advocated "orthodox" economic policies.[27] However, they did not believe that democratic governments would willingly adopt such policies, which would undermine the social and economic redistribution programs these governments needed to maintain popular electoral support. Therefore, to achieve their economic objectives, business elites and technocrats needed a different—authoritarian—political regime.

According to the theory, authoritarian rule also appealed to Latin American business elites because it would restore social order. They believed that the democratic governments of the 1960s and 1970s had encouraged the mobilization of the left and the working class. Radical labor unions threatened industrial expansion and foreign investment, and the radical left threatened private property.[28] The theory asserts that the Cuban Revolution "confirmed" business elites' view that political activation of the popular sector would lead to an overthrow of the capitalist system.[29]

The transitions literature further develops the view that Latin American business elites distrust democratic rule. It suggests that they will accept only a highly restricted democracy, because a full democracy would threaten the private sector. Thus, the closer a transition moves toward full democracy, the more likely it is that business elites will again undermine democratic rule and help to install a new authoritarian regime.[30]

The adaptive actor approach rejects these assumptions as exaggerations of business elites' authoritarian preferences and economic motivations. First, the assumption that business elites prefer authoritarian rule to democratic rule presupposes that they are sufficiently concerned about broad political questions to form a consensus around regime preferences. Given their narrow self-interestedness, however, they are generally indifferent to broad political questions, being primarily concerned with how specific policies affect their firms. As a result, business elites adapt to various types of regimes as long as those regimes provide an acceptable business climate.

Second, the assumption that business elites engage in political action to bring about economic expansion is inconsistent with the inherent characteristics of the business community, namely, competition, individualism, and diversity. Natural competition prevents each firm from engaging in collective action that might benefit its adversaries. Individualism leads investors to increase the profits of their own firms rather than working toward a collective good. Diversity of opinions and needs within the business community prevents business elites from formulating a consensus on alternative policies and implementing those policies. In addition, business elites might prove capable of "vetoing" a specific government or its policies, but they would rely on other social sectors to identify alternatives. Collective action is thus limited to defending the business community against threats, rather than promoting economic expansion.

The Preference for Investment Stability.   As noted above, business elites on the whole are indifferent to political regimes but are concerned with how well particular governments protect business interests. Their pragmatic approach to politics leads them to endorse governments that protect the conditions essential to their survival—their ability to produce, to invest, and to make profits.[31] In other words, they seek a stable investment climate and will accept any government as long as it does not threaten their investments.[32] The best conditions for ensuring that protection include the following three overlapping factors: government legitimacy, government competence, and business influence over government decisions.

Government legitimacy—the general belief in society that "in spite of shortcomings and failures, the existing political institutions are better than any others that might be established"—is crucial to investment stability because it enables the government to command obedience from the population and endure periods of difficulty.[33] Legitimacy can be derived from the personal charisma of an authoritarian head of state or from adherence to traditional norms, as well as from legal authority.[34] Therefore, both democratic and authoritarian regimes are potentially legitimate.

Govenment competence sustains a government's legitimacy and provides investment stability. It reassures members of the business community that the government has the capacity to implement the policies formulated and to attain the desired results.[35] In contrast, government incompetence will undermine investment stability, because it is likely to weaken a government's authority and legitimacy, cause divisions and competition within the policy-making arena, provoke frequent changes in policies and policy makers, and lead to unpredictable policies or "decisional paralysis." Neither democratic nor authoritarian regimes are inherently more likely to be competent; thus, neither is necessarily more capable of providing investment stability.[36]

One factor essential to government competence is predictability, or a government's capacity to reassure members of the business community that the economic and political rules will not suddenly change, possibly threatening their investments.[37] Businesspeople rely on a certain amount of predictability and coherence in economic policies to enable them to make investment and production predictions with a modicum of accuracy.[38] They fear revolutionary change or the enactment of legislation that might threaten property rights and employers' traditional prerogatives, or dramatically increase the costs of production. Latin American policy makers, both democratic and authoritarian, have been known for "cultivating unpredictability and distance" from business leaders, frequently changing fiscal, monetary, and foreign-exchange policies, and failing to communicate these changes to business groups, thus undermining investment stability.[39] In other words, neither democratic nor authoritarian regimes are better suited to providing the predictability that business elites demand.

Although members of the business community desire predictability, they are capable of adapting to change. They will embrace rapid change if it produces policies more favorable to business, and they will even adapt to changes that challenge their rights and privileges, as long as those changes are gradual and consistent with long-term political stability. The slow pace of change provides them with time to make adjustments to protect their interests, and to negotiate compromises in which they may sacrifice their less pressing needs, in order to protect their most vital interests.

A stable investment climate also gives business leaders some form of influence over the government decisions that affect their ability to produce, invest, and make profits. Business leaders hope to use their influence to ensure predictable and favorable economic policies and protect themselves from deleterious ones. They demand not only access to information about economic decisions but also participation in, and influence over, the final outcome of those decisions. Business leaders will accept a variety of forms of influence, such as formal consultation roles in appropriate ministries; informal consultation with the executive branch; and representation in the legislature, in political parties, and in pressure-group politics. They also accept indirect forms of influence whereby government policies merely reflect the demands and needs of the business community. In light of the variety of types of influence they accept, it is clear that both democratic and authoritarian regimes can satisfy their demands.

In short, neither an authoritarian regime nor a democratic one is inherently better able to provide business elites' primary political demand: a stable investment climate. As a result, most businesspeople do not naturally endorse a particular type of regime. Instead, they will adapt to governments that are legitimate and competent, and that provide business with influence. Competent and legitimate political leadership has played an important role in many studies of the breakdown of democracy and of transitions from authoritarian rule,[40] but it has not been examined as a factor in business elites' attitudes toward political change.

While business elites' demands for investment stability are consistent over time, their regime preferences may change because of new perceptions. As sophisticated versions of rational choice theory argue, individuals' preferences and actions are determined not by pure choice but by contextual factors.[41] As the context changes, the same actors may face a different set of options. They may select an option other than one chosen in the past—not because they are irrational, but because the new option seems to be a better means to satisfy their desires within the current context.[42]

Some important contextual factors include (1) time, experience, and information; (2) social norms; (3) international and domestic opinions and trends; and (4) institutional changes. For example, if actors have had negative or positive experiences in the past, they may avoid or select certain options that would reproduce these experiences. Past experience provides new information with which actors may modify their preference structure. In addition, individuals typically shape their preferences and actions according to social norms (e.g., habit, tradition, custom, and duty).[43] As social norms change, so too will individuals' views.[44] Individuals' perceptions are also shaped by the prevailing domestic and international views and experiences, or by the zeitgeist—"a feeling shared across national boundaries, that a particular type of political system is the most desirable or the most questionable."[45] Finally, the emergence or disappearance of institutions will increase or limit the number of options available. In some cases those institutional changes— and the resulting changes in the options available—are brought on by the actions of the very same individuals who are developing their political preferences.[46] In short, business leaders' decisions are based on their assessment of the existing set of options, and thus their political preferences and actions may be inconsistent over time.

Defensive Motivations.   There is no doubt that Latin American business elites, like their counterparts in North America and Western Europe, desire economic expansion, as the theory of the bureaucratic-authoritarian state assumes. They do not, however, unite collectively to pursue such an end. As mentioned above, the inherent competition, individualism, and diversity within the business community prevent such collective action. But under certain extreme circumstances Latin American business elites will unite to veto a government or its policies, without effectively endorsing an alternative.

The use of this veto capability is most likely when business elites collectively perceive that a government or its policies severely threaten them. Such mobilization, however, is contingent upon a number of factors. For example, businesspeople will overcome their competitive nature only if the cost of remaining inactive is greater than the cost of acting collectively. In addition, they will only act collectively if the threat to their investments is one that affects the business community as a whole. Only when solutions specific to individual firms are unavailable to offset the threat will business leaders mobilize collectively.

Business elites' use of the veto demonstrates that they generally act defensively.

They engage in collective action only to sustain, or to prevent dramatic decreases in, profits. Although this is not the best strategy for any one firm, it may be the best strategy for all firms collectively.[47] This notion of collective defense contradicts some prominent theories of collective action. It assumes that business leaders will engage in collective action—at least, the defensive type of collective action—even in the absence of individual sanctions or social or economic payoffs.[48] Moreover, business elites' collective defense, as the Latin American coups demonstrated, can have a great impact on political outcomes.[49]

Collective defense is consistent with the "maxi-min" or "second-best alternative" calculations identified in sophisticated versions of rational choice theory. In a "maxi-min" calculation, actors attempt to minimize the negative outcomes. They choose the option whose worst consequences are better than the worst consequences of any other option. This contrasts with selecting the option with the "best-best consequences."[50] Applying a "maxi-min" calculation to Latin American business elites' political activities during the 1960s and 1970s would lead one to conclude that business elites did not support the military coups in order to achieve economic expansion (a "best-best consequence") but believed that the democratic governments' policies were far worse than any imaginable alternative. During the transition from authoritarian rule, a "maxi-min" calculation would have led business elites to conclude that accepting democratic change would have fewer negative consequences than resisting it.

In "second-best alternative" calculations, rational actors pursue achievable, rather than ideal, options.[51] Thus, although business elites ideally desire economic expansion, they pursue goals that they believe to be more realistic. They try to defend their interests against threats, rather than attempting to design a regime that will act in their interests.

The Brazilian Business Elite as an Adaptive Actor

Brazilian business leaders' political attitudes and behavior are analyzed in detail in subsequent chapters. However, the broad application of the adaptive actor approach (see table 1.1), and its challenges to the theory of the bureaucratic-authoritarian state and to the transitions literature, are outlined below.

Brazilian business leaders have rarely engaged in collective action. Their involvement in the overthrow of democratic president João Goulart in 1964 was an exception. They engaged in collective action in 1964 because they perceived both that the Goulart government posed severe threats to their investments, and that individual action would prove ineffective in defending their firms against those threats. They considered Goulart a threat because of his government's questionable legitimacy, its incompetence, its unpredictable policies, the threats it

Table 1.1.   Summary of the Adaptive Actor Approach

I. Business elites have potential, but limited, political power.
  A. Their political power is based on their
     1. financial resources;
     2. organizational resources; and
     3. social status.
  B. Limitations on their power result from
     1. inherent characteristics within the business community: competition, individualism, and diversity;
     2. subordinate and dependent business-state relations; and
     3. defensive political capacity (veto) rather than offensive capacity.
  C. They engage in collective action (i.e., collective defense) to protect investments. However, they will only do so if
     1. the threats are severe and affect most businesses;
     2. individual actions are ineffective at eliminating the threat to firms; and
     3. the cost of inaction is greater than the cost of collective action.
II. Business elites are indifferent to political regimes, being neither inherently authoritarian nor inherently democratic. Instead, most business elites evaluate governments on the basis of their protections of investments. Those protections include
  A. government legitimacy;
  B. government competence; and
  C. business influence over government decisions affecting business.

posed to the private sector, and its exclusion of business from decision making. While business leaders' perceptions were based in part on their observations of the Goulart government and their experiences under it, those perceptions were also shaped by Cold War propaganda and the Cuban Revolution. Because of their perceptions of extreme threat and the ineffectiveness of individual political action, industrialists proved capable of overcoming their natural competitiveness, parochialism, and diversity and emerged as a formidable political force behind Goulart's overthrow.

Although business leaders engaged in collective action against Goulart, they did not necessarily desire the end of democracy or the installation of an authoritarian regime. Indeed, their opinions about the authoritarian regime established by the military and the technocrats after the coup were divided. Most business leaders benefited from the high levels of economic growth and industrial expansion during the "economic miracle." However, these were temporary positive results of the military regime's policies, not the goals underlying business leaders' support for the coup. Moreover, the military regime was unable to sustain these favorable economic policies. And as business leaders began to perceive that the regime had lost legitimacy, had proved incompetent in managing the economic crisis, and had implemented unpredictable policies, closed off opportunities for domestic private sector investment, and excluded business influence in its decision making, they could no longer trust the authoritarian regime to protect the investment climate. As a result, they began to withdraw their support.

Although business leaders were not universally behind the transition from authoritarian rule, they generally accepted it owing to the reassurances that the transitional government provided to the private sector. The legitimacy of that government resulted from the new post–Cold War international climate, the failure of authoritarian regimes, and widespread domestic support for democratic change. And although the transitional government was not competent in managing the economic crisis or producing predictable policies, it did guarantee protections for private property. Finally, it allowed for new channels of influence for business leaders. Thus, in contrast to what happened during 1964, the problems of the political liberalization—the economic crisis, the resurgence of the left, and renewed labor conflict—did not mobilize business leaders against the transition. The business community did not universally fear the transitional government, and individual businesspeople possessed the means to overcome threats to their firms without engaging in collective action against the state.

Thus, whereas Brazilian business leaders' actions with respect to the coup and the democratic transition appear to be inconsistent, their overall attitudes and preferences remained constant during both political periods. They were consistently indifferent to the political regime but concerned about investment stability. Different domestic and international contexts shaped their perceptions and made their behavior seem inconsistent.

Chapter Two

When Industrialists Rebel

There is no doubt that Brazilian industrialists played an important role in the 1964 military coup. Some even claimed sole responsibility for the coup. According to Paulo Ayres Filho, of Universal Consultores, "the 1964 Revolution was made in my living room" [22 Oct. 1987]. The Brazilian president of a multinational corporation's large Brazilian operation said, "The 1964 Revolution was made by me. The military didn't want to come in. They did it because they were begged by the business community. I know, because I begged them. It isn't that the business community supported the military in their coup, but that the military supported us in our coup" [6 Oct. 1987]. Although these claims are certainly exaggerated, the São Paulo industrialists played such a prominent role that journalists even referred to the coup as the "Paulista revolt."[1]

The details of business leaders' political activities in the 1960s which are provided in this chapter confirm one assumption in the theory of the bureaucratic-authoritarian state: business leaders formed part of the coup conspiracy that toppled President Goulart. However, the data presented here challenge other assumptions in that theory. Specifically, interview data suggest that investment instability and business's loss of influence, rather than economic expansion and authoritarian control, were the primary motivations behind business leaders' support for the coup. The data further question the theory's assumption regarding the transnational character of the business rebellion against Goulart. The theory underestimates the importance of domestic opposition to Goulart and overlooks forms of international influence other than economic relations.

In addition to refining these assumptions in the theory of the bureaucratic-authoritarian state, this chapter provides new insights into factors shaping business elites' political perceptions and power.

Industrialists and the Coup

The major organizing force behind business leaders' support for the coup was the Institute for Economic and Social Research (IPES), which was formed on 29 November 1961.[2] Although there was no formal relationship between IPES and

16

preexisting business organizations, some of IPES's members were also directors of key business associations, including the Federation of Industries of the State of São Paulo (FIESP), the Center of Industries of the State of São Paulo (CIESP), the National Confederation of Industries (CNI), the National Council of Producing Classes (CONCLAP), and the American Chamber of Commerce. IPES also coordinated the activities of, and received funds from, existing broad-based pressure groups such as the Brazilian Institute for Democratic Action (IBAD).[3] IBAD was formed in 1959 to "defend democracy," but it mainly united several industrial, commercial, military, Catholic, and middle-class groups to fight what its members perceived as the growing threat of communism in Brazil.[4]

When I did my interviews with Brazilian business leaders in 1987–88, few of IPES's founders were still alive. Fortunately, one of IPES's most active founders, participants, and defenders, Paulo Ayres Filho, agreed to be interviewed and described the organization's formation. This chapter relies on Ayres's account, which has been confirmed by the other founders I interviewed, as well as the few documents that were produced at the time of the coup. An industrialist from a São Paulo pharmaceutical firm, Ayres had written numerous anticommunist and pro-free trade articles during the 1950s. He circulated these publications to many people throughout Brazil, including his friends and colleagues in Rio de Janeiro. Thus, when a group of businessmen from Rio de Janeiro began discussing the possibility of forming a business group that would oppose the Goulart government, Ayres's name came up. He was considered the ideal person to lead such an organization. Gilberto Huber, Jr., a Brazilian businessman of North American origin who owned a company called Yellow Pages in Rio de Janeiro, had never met Ayres. Nonetheless, he telephoned him to discuss the possibility of such a movement. Ayres was enthusiastic, and Huber flew to São Paulo that afternoon. He arrived at Ayres's house at 4:00 P.M. and talked with Ayres until 3:00 A.M. During the course of that meeting, the São Paulo and Rio de Janeiro branches of IPES were formed.

Initially, IPES's membership consisted of ten businessmen in Rio de Janeiro and São Paulo who were concerned with the "leftist tendency in political life" in Brazil[5] and were anxious to find "democratic solutions" to the country's problems.[6] Despite its clear anticommunist bent, the group attempted to remain apolitical. It recognized that a "radical right" image would prevent it from gaining support within the Brazilian population.[7] Thus it professed to study the "reforms proposed by João Goulart and the left, from a free enterprise, technical, business point of view" rather than from a particular ideological perspective. Furthermore, by advocating open political participation and endorsing "moderate reform in the existing political and economic institutions,"[8] it broadened its appeal to include individuals in the political center.

Despite these attempts, Ayres accused the "communist press" of labeling IPES "reactionary" and calling it an agent of "imperialism" [22 Oct. 1987]. According to Ayres, these press attacks initially hindered IPES's recruitment efforts. Ayres stated that members of the business community were reluctant to become members of an overtly anticommunist organization. They feared that such membership would be held against them by the government if it were to adopt leftist ideas and programs. Ayres contended that the reprisals feared by some business leaders included the denial of government credits and subsidies. Others worried about their personal security, since Ayres and other IPES members claim to have received threatening telephone calls from the "communists."

Fear generated by these threats prompted IPES to carry out most of its initial recruitment efforts and political activities underground.[9] The organization's newsletters, which evaluated the political situation, analyzed public opinion, and contained anticommunist articles, were circulated discreetly:

> Shopkeepers wrapped the revealing leaflets in packages, or dropped them into shopping bags. Elevator operators quietly handed them to passengers overheard complaining about conditions. Shoeshine boys slipped them into pockets while brushing customers. Taxi drivers left them on the seats of their cabs for casual pick-up by fares. Barbers inserted them in magazines being perused by waiting clients. One printer in Rio secretly ran off 50,000 posters with cartoons depicting Castro lashing his people, and the caption, "Do you want to live under the whip of communism?" At night, squads of helpers posted them in public places.[10]

By the time IPES emerged from underground, it had become a strong organization. By 1963, it claimed the support of five hundred enterprises in São Paulo and Rio de Janeiro and of key business leaders, including twenty-seven of the thirty-six directors of FIESP, twenty-one of the twenty-four directors of CNI, and "a large number" of members of the American Chamber of Commerce and other business associations.[11] In addition, it had branches in Rio Grande do Sul, Pernambuco, Minas Gerais, Paraná, and Amazonas.

The addition of new members, as well as the dues they contributed, enabled IPES to expand its activities. It organized an intelligence division, which had investigators within and outside of the government, "to collect, classify and correlate information on the extent of Red infiltration in Brazil."[12] IPES allegedly admitted to spending between two hundred thousand and three hundred thousand dollars on this intelligence-gathering and distribution network,[13] which derived its information from press clippings, transcripts from wiretapping operations, and data gathered from informants at all levels. IPES used the data gathered from this division to warn the Brazilian public of the spread of communism and thereby increase anticommunist sentiment among the public.

IPES engaged in other activities to shape public opinion. For example, it employed famous actors, writers, journalists, and public relations companies to promote its views. It also sponsored speeches, symposia, conferences, public debates, films, theater performances, interviews, books, pamphlets, magazine and newspaper articles, and television and radio programs. In addition, it ran letter-writing, telegram, and telephone campaigns to increase the circulation of its ideas.[14]

IPES also targeted particular groups in society which it hoped to influence. Those groups included politicians, the armed forces, the church, the middle class, workers, students, and the business class. For example, to increase business influence in the government IPES extensively lobbied Congress and the executive branch on various economic policies and provided generous financial contributions to candidates for political office who were committed to free market principles and anticommunism. IBAD and Democratic Popular Action (ADEP), another pressure group that coordinated its activities with those of IPES, allegedly spent $12.5 million in October 1962 (funneled through an advertising agency called Sales Promotion, Inc.) to elect eight governors, fifteen federal senators, two hundred fifty federal deputies, six hundred state deputies, and various candidates to municipal office.[15] Individual industrialists apparently regarded these electoral efforts as extremely important. For example, during the Goulart administration, CIESP sent a written questionnaire on the role of business in government to its 427 members. Of the 395 respondents, 95 percent believed that business should have representatives in government (2% felt that this was unnecessary, and 3% were indifferent), and 96 percent believed that only individuals with firsthand knowledge of industry could adequately represent industrialists' interests.[16]

IPES extended its ties to technocrats and the military through personal connections. Many IPES members had attended the Superior War College (ESG), which trained military officers and technocrats. This bond facilitated IPES's efforts to recruit members of the armed forces. For example, General Golbery do Couto e Silva joined IPES and directed the organization's intelligence-gathering operations. IPES also used its personal and ideological links with conservative Catholic groups, such as Opus Dei, to influence members of the Catholic Church.

In addition, IPES financed the creation of new organizations and trained leaders for them, as well as for groups that already existed. For example, it helped establish middle-class organizations such as women's groups.[17] IPES claimed to have trained twenty-six hundred individuals and supported them both financially and materially to win elections in business associations, student organizations, and trade unions.

To win support from urban workers, IPES realized that it was necessary to improve the image of private enterprise. To that end, IPES promoted the idea of the "social function and responsibility of private property," as well as providing its standard courses on leadership and waging its anticommunist and pro–private property campaign. IPES became involved in a variety of social welfare projects. It launched literacy campaigns. It provided legal, medical, dental, and hospital assistance. It established consumer, credit, and housing cooperatives. And it set up schools to provide job training in fields such as typing, industrial design, art, publicity, architecture, business skills, chemistry, tailoring, home economics, and agronomy.

Much of the organization and financing of IPES's labor activities came from the American Institute for Free Labor Development (AIFLD), a group that was affiliated with the AFL-CIO and had connections to the Central Intelligence Agency; and many of the union leaders whom IPES supported had been trained in the United States.[18] These leaders defended material gains for workers and opposed labor militancy. They denied the existence of, and hoped to avoid, class struggle. Instead, IPES advocated the idea that industrialists and workers could both benefit from fighting together to promote their mutual interests, particularly industrial growth. IPES supported the Democratic Union Movement (MSD), which used as its slogan "God, private property, and the free market."[19]

Paulo Ayres Filho explained [22 Oct. 1987] the process of training union leaders. He said that IPES leaders identified workers who they thought would be receptive to IPES's goals. If those workers were interested in training, IPES took them to a country house for a seminar on leadership skills. They taught the workers orthodox economic theory, how to run a meeting, how to combat leftist union leaders (who were better prepared, Ayres contended), and how to undermine a meeting through the practice of "minority domination." Then each of the targeted workers identified other workers who they thought would join the program. By the end of 1964, IPES's officials claimed that the organization had trained two thousand workers, many of whom had been elected to head important trade unions.

IPES enjoyed extensive contacts within the business community. Its organizers claimed that developing these contacts had not been easy, because few business leaders had initially shared IPES's views. An article in one of the IPES-funded publications divided the Brazilian business community into six ideological groups, and indicated that IPES could only draw from one of them: the so-called "conscious elements." The six groups were defined as follows:

1. Communists (1%). Destructive members who are either seduced into supporting activities against their own class, or whose political ambition drives them to do so.

2. Criminals (3%). Members who passively accept the actions of opposing classes as long as they can maximize their returns. They neglect the broad interests of their class.

3. Useless Innocents (10%). Liberal members who support social-economic projects due to their naiveté or their good intentions.

4. Reactionaries (12%). Those members who consider all modernizing projects "communist." They will not accept change, and fossilize the country in order to protect their interests.

5. The Unconscious (70%). Members who are only part of the class because of their economic objectives, but who have no political or ideological interests.

6. The Conscious Elements (4%). Members willing to lead the class against the "communist threat." Their interests go beyond the narrow terrain of their business, and enter into politics.[20]

Hence, one of IPES's main tasks was to increase the percentage of "conscious" members of the business community. It focused on educating business leaders about the threats they were facing under the Goulart government, and encouraging them to participate in the anti-Goulart movement. Eventually IPES won support from a broad base of business leaders. However, this was only partially due to the organization's efforts. Goulart's policies and practices, discussed in detail below, provoked fear in most industrialists, prompting them to join IPES in order to find solutions to their problems.[21]

By far the most important of IPES's activities was its role in the 1964 coup. IPES, Ayres contends, never planned to participate in a military coup. Its initial aim was only to create a broad-based opposition movement that would pressure the Goulart government to modify its radical posture. Some IPES members, however, felt constrained by the organization's emphasis on education and information, as well as its lack of direct action. One such industrialist from the São Paulo IPES group allegedly "organized vigilante cells to counter left-wing hecklers at anti-Communist meetings with 'intellectual methods—like a kick in the head.'" A group of industrialists carried this further; they set up a hand grenade factory and launched guerrilla operations against leftists.[22]

According to the president of a multinational corporation's large Brazilian operation, IPES altered its tactics to include direct involvement in the coup conspiracy after two events that occurred in March 1964: Goulart's 13 March rally, and the 25 March navy mutiny. This industrialist stated that those events frightened business leaders. He explained: "We were on the eve of a communist takeover . . . We mobilized in the factories. We armed ourselves against communism. We went to ask the military to help us. 'Something has got to be done,' we said. I'm telling you this from my personal experience. I was there" [6 Oct. 1987].

At the 13 March rally, Goulart announced that he had signed a decree expropriating specific lands and nationalizing privately owned oil companies. He also announced plans to carry out additional reforms, which included legalizing the Communist Party, enfranchising illiterates, raising taxes, and stabilizing rents. He also called for additional constitutional reforms that would end the injustices in society. His adviser, Leonel Brizola, went even further and called for the immediate dismissal of Congress, and for new elections to increase the representation of popular sectors in government. These proposals indicated to industrialists that Goulart's radical tendencies could not be modified through normal democratic procedures. Indeed, in their view, Goulart threatened those very procedures.

A little more than one week later, on 25 March, more than one thousand sailors and marines occupied the metalworkers' union headquarters in Rio de Janeiro. These noncommissioned officers and enlisted men protested the navy minister's arrest of a sailor who had tried to organize a sailors' association. They also demanded certain political privileges (e.g., the right to run for public office) and improved living conditions. Goulart dismissed the navy minister and replaced him with an admiral recommended by the General Workers' Command (CGT), a trade union confederation allied with the Communist Party. The new navy minister granted the mutinous sailors amnesty. Industrialists saw this act as an attack on the hierarchy of the armed forces, an indication of the significant influence that labor and the left had over Goulart's decisions, and of the erosion of the traditional structure of authority in the country.

After these events, IPES and the armed forces began to mobilize. According to Ayres, an IPES group met with all three branches of the armed forces.[23] It strengthened "long cultivated friendships" in the military services, convincing the various branches to carry out the "revolution" and reinstate "morals and justice, freedom and democracy."[24] It called on the armed forces to help carry out "a revolution to depose Goulart, re-establish the hierarchy and discipline in the Armed Forces, and make the economy . . . follow a normal course again."[25] It is clear, however, that after the navy mutiny, few military officers needed to be "convinced" to oust Goulart.

Contacts between members of the business community and the military increased. General Castello Branco prepared a manifesto stating that Goulart's threats to constitutional order provided legal justification for military intervention, because it was the duty of the armed forces to defend the Constitution. Castello Branco's manifesto was circulated among other top military personnel in order to persuade them to adopt this viewpoint. Members of the business community acted as the conduit: "They carried copies in their breast pockets, [and] put the manifesto into the proper hands."[26] Once sufficient consensus had been established within the military, the coup took place. One of the founders of IPES, the president of a multinational corporation's large Brazilian operation, described the events leading up to, and following, the coup:

> General Amaury Kruel, commander of the Second Army in São Paulo [and former Goulart ally], called Goulart twice, asking him if he would change his position. He [Kruel] didn't want to be disloyal to the government. Then the revolution occurred. No one got hurt. I was ready to take my gun and head into the street to help out the revolution, but fortunately Goulart gave up easily, and there was no violence. I went to the club the next day and visited with my friends. It was a day like any other. But there was a great sense of relief. [6 Oct. 1987]

Not for Ayres; he argued [22 Oct. 1987] that the struggle against radicalism had only begun. Despite the success of the coup, he felt that industrialists should remain vigilant against the threat of communism in Brazil. To this end, he tried to convince his colleagues that IPES's work must continue. However, much to his disappointment, few industrialists shared his view. They were not willing to continue paying dues or to participate in activities to keep the organization alive. Thus, IPES ceased operations shortly after the 1964 coup.

Clearly, responsibility for the coup does not rest primarily with industrialists. Alternative theories are more compelling. For example, changes in the military's interpretation of their role in society and threats to military hierarchy were instrumental in mobilizing the armed forces to seize power.[27] In addition, Goulart undermined support from the left, as well as the center and the right, helping to bring about his own demise.[28] Also, the role of the United States government in destabilizing Goulart and supporting the conspirators was a key impetus behind the coup.[29]

Nonetheless, industrialists' mobilization efforts, implemented by IPES, were instrumental in building opposition groups against Goulart. IPES used its extensive political resources to shape public opinion in favor of its goal of ousting Goulart. It also used its social ties with members of the armed forces to achieve that goal. However, the opposition groups, although often organized by business leaders, joined the movement not to defend business interests but to protect broader national interests, such as economic recovery, social order, and the hierarchy of the armed forces. As explained in more detail below, even business leaders who endorsed the coup had diverse motivations for doing so. Before analyzing their motivations, however, I will identify the groups of business leaders who supported the coup.

Who Supported the Coup?

Consistent with the theory of the bureaucratic-authoritarian state, the original leaders of IPES had significant ties to foreign, particularly United States, capital.[30] Although all of IPES's founders were Brazilian, they had strong links to United States businesses: they managed subsidiaries of United States firms, received technical assistance or investment capital from United States corporations, sat on the boards of United States corporations, or belonged to the American Chamber of Commerce.[31] This is not surprising. After all, Goulart seriously threatened multinational corporations with his controls over profit remittance, and his expropriation and nationalization plans. In addition, the United States government had made its opposition to Goulart obvious by discontinuing foreign aid except to the "islands of administrative sanity," namely, the conservative state governments that opposed Goulart.[32] In other words, industrialists with ties to United States capital organized IPES because they were immediately threatened by Goulart's policies; and their fears were shared—and their efforts supported—by a strong ally: the United States government.

However, this view downplays IPES's appeal among private domestic businesses that lacked ties to foreign capital. Goulart's strategies also hurt these businesses. For example, Brazilian entrepreneurs owned all of the oil companies that would have been nationalized under Goulart's 13 March decree. In addition, IPES attacked the Goulart government on a wide range of political and economic issues of concern to private domestic businesses and other social groups, and defended some democratic reforms. Thus IPES was able to build a strong pressure group to defend the interests of business and other national interests, as well as the interests of foreign capital.[33]

My research confirms that the overthrow of Goulart received support from a large number of industrialists with diverse backgrounds. I asked 132 of the industrialists I interviewed whether they had supported the 1964 coup. Although I did not expect industrialists to admit their support for the coup, a majority (64%) stated that they had supported it. Moreover, analysis of these responses reveals a number of statistically significant variables, which are summarized in table 2.1.[34]

As one would expect, age played an important role in business leaders' support for the coup: 74 percent of those who were at least twenty years old at the time of the coup supported it. However, a more significant factor than age in determining support for the coup was whether the individual was in business in 1964. Of my interview sample, 82 percent of those who had been in business at the time of the coup admitted that they had supported it. Thus, my data confirm that an overwhelming majority of industrial leaders supported the coup.

The nationality of the firm also proved significant in determining industrialists' support for the coup. However, the data do not support the hypothesis that multinational firms and firms with extensive ties abroad were the strongest supporters of the coup. Neither the percentage of foreign capital in a firm, the percentage of the firm's products that were exported, nor industrialists' experience abroad proved

Table 2.1.   Percentage Distribution of the Industrialists Interviewed, by Support and Nonsupport of the 1964 Coup, and Several Statistically Significant Variables

	N	Supporters of Coup (%)	Nonsupporters of Coup (%)
All respondents[a]	132	64.4	35.6
Industrialist's age			
Born before 1945	108	74.1	25.9
Born after 1944	24	20.8	79.2
Industrialist's earliest business experience			
Before 1965	79	82.3	17.7
After 1964	53	37.7	62.3
Nationality of firm			
Brazilian	97	71.1	28.9
Multinational	35	45.7	54.3
Brazilian industrialist's self-defined ideology[b]			
Rightist	48	79.2	20.8
Centrist	28	67.9	32.1
Leftist	16	43.7	56.3

[a]Only 132 of the 155 interview subjects were asked this set of questions.
[b]Only Brazilian industrialists are included in this analysis because responses for non-Brazilian industrialists did not prove statistically significant.

statistically significant in determining industrialists' support for the coup. The nationality of the firm proved significant; but the data challenge rather than confirm the transnational hypothesis elaborated in the theory of the bureaucratic-authoritarian state. As illustrated in table 2.1, 71 percent of the industrialists from Brazilian firms whom I interviewed supported the coup, as opposed to 46 percent of the industrialists from foreign firms.

However, before rejecting the transnational hypothesis altogether there are several factors one must consider. For example, because of host governments' sensitivity toward multinational corporations' involvement in domestic political affairs, executives (especially non-Brazilians) at foreign firms were probably more reluctant to admit that they supported the coup. It is possible that executives from multinational firms concealed their support when I interviewed them, thus skewing the results. In addition, owing to turnover, many foreign executives may not have been in Brazil or may not have had ties to Brazil in 1964, in which case they could not have supported the 1964 coup. Indeed, the data indicate that multinational executives who were still working for the same firms that had employed them in 1964 (and who therefore may have had ties to Brazil in 1964) were stronger supporters of the coup than were those who had changed jobs since 1964 (and who therefore might not have had ties with Brazil in 1964). Of those industrialists from multinational corporations who were still with the same firm, 67 percent said that they had supported the coup, compared to only 38 percent of those who had changed firms. In other words, like Brazilian executives, a majority of the multinational executives who had business ties in Brazil in 1964 supported the coup. Thus I argue that the data, rather than confirming the hypothesis that international ties determine support for the coup, suggest that business involvement in Brazil (whether with a multinational or a Brazilian company) is the stronger determining factor.

The data further indicate that ideology played an important role in determining industrialists' support for the coup. Industrialists' self-identification on an ideological scale proved statistically significant, although only for executives at Brazilian firms. Those Brazilian industrialists who identified themselves as being on the right were most likely to state that they had supported the coup (79% of this group did so), followed by those who defined themselves as centrists (68%), and lastly by those who defined themselves as left of center (44%). It is not surprising that those who associate themselves with the right and even with the center supported the coup. However, such significant support from those who consider themselves left of center was surprising. It may indicate either that support for the coup was shared by reactionary and progressive elements within the business community, or that reactionary industrialists who had supported the coup in 1964 altered their political views (and became progressive) during the twenty-year dictatorship. This study provides evidence to support both of these hypotheses.

In short, while transnational industrialists assumed leadership positions within the business movement, the vast majority of industrialists from both foreign and multinational corporations supported the coup. And although the strongest support came from politically conservative members of the business community, some of those who considered themselves to be on the left also supported the coup.

Why Industrialists Supported the Coup

The theory of the bureaucratic-authoritarian state suggests two primary reasons why business leaders supported the coup: economic stagnation, and social (particularly labor) conflict. Although those two factors were important, most of the industrialists I interviewed considered political instability and the rise of the left to be the most important reasons for their support of the coup. As table 2.2 indicates, in the aggregate far more interviewees cited political stability and leftist subversion as motivating factors. Moreover, most cited only one or two motivations for their support for the coup.[35] And among the single explanations, political instability and leftist subversion ranked the highest: twenty-six (23%) listed political instability alone, and twenty-three (21%) listed the left alone, while only three (3%) mentioned the economy alone, and two (2%) mentioned labor alone. Moreover, more

Table 2.2.   Interviewees' Reasons for Supporting the
1964 Coup

	Interviewees Citing Reason	
	No.	%
Political instability	54	64
Leftist subversion	51	60
Labor unrest	20	23
Economic problems	18	21
Other	4	5

$N = 85$.

Note: Because some interviewees provided more than
one answer to this question, the responses add up to more
than 85, and the total percentage is higher than 100%.

than half (59%) of the industrialists I interviewed mentioned political instability
and/or leftist subversion as their reasons for supporting the coup, and excluded other factors. However, as explained below, there is a great deal of overlap between
these motivating factors.

Political Instability

The following excerpts from three interviews—with the director of a very large
Brazilian firm, the president of a medium-sized Brazilian firm, and the director of a
medium-sized Brazilian firm—illustrate industrialists' concerns with the political
climate under President Goulart.[36]

> I supported the revolution not because of the left, but because of anarchy. The law was not
> respected. Subversion of order was occurring. Even a military mutiny. Economic prob-
> lems also. If I had to pick which problem is worse, between lack of respect for authority,
> widespread hunger, and economic problems, I'd pick lack of respect for authority be-
> cause the other two can be solved. [9 Dec. 1987]

> I supported the coup because of the disorder, not for ideology at all. It [the Goulart admin-
> istration] was a good example of disgovernment. Goulart could not administer the crisis,
> and it created social chaos . . . I prefer military intervention to social chaos. [30 Oct.
> 1987]

> João Goulart managed the masses. He wanted an independent group of support, a political
> force. But then he couldn't control this force, and they started acting against him. The
> revolution was a natural consequence of this lack of control and the undermining of the
> military system. We couldn't live under that system; it couldn't survive. It was much more

a movement against the disorder and lack of organization . . . It was a good movement
. . . There wasn't really a threat from the left, it was just against disorganization. [24 Nov.
1987]

These statements, and other discussions with industrialists concerned with political
instability, suggest three aspects of the Goulart government which business leaders
perceived as threatening, and which the theory of the bureaucratic-authoritarian
state overlooks: the loss of government legitimacy; unpredictable economic and
political rules; and the exclusion of business interests from government decision
making. (A fourth factor, Goulart's mismanagement of the economy, is considered below in the discussion on industrialists' economic motivations for supporting
the coup.)

First, the industrialists I interviewed remarked that Goulart's legitimacy had
been challenged before he took office. A near-civil war had erupted when President
Jânio Quadros had resigned, leaving his widely disliked vice-president, Goulart, to
govern. A political collapse had only been avoided when Goulart accepted a parliamentary, rather than a presidential, political system, thereby greatly reducing his
political power.[37] While the right had never supported Goulart, key leaders on the
left now began to suspect him of attempting to co-opt them and turning his back on
social reforms.[38] Some of my interview subjects, citing spontaneous antigovernment protests in major cities, also claimed that middle-class groups had mobilized
against Goulart.[39] Moreover, as business leaders saw it, violence from the left and
the right had escalated under Goulart, who was incapable of, or uninterested in,
ending it. Indeed, one of Goulart's closest advisors, Leonel Brizola, even advocated
the use of "grupos de onze," or clandestine groups of eleven armed revolutionaries,
to force political change. In short, industrialists claimed that Goulart's base of support, which was never strong to begin with, continually eroded during his administration, gave rise to a groundswell of popular opposition, and undermined his
legitimacy. Goulart neither represented the wishes of the people nor ruled with their
consent. As a result, he could not command obedience or maintain order within
society.

Goulart's legitimacy was further undermined by charges of internal corruption.
According to industrialists, individuals both within and outside Goulart's government had obtained kickbacks and payoffs. Moreover, they argued that Goulart not
only tolerated corruption but benefited from it. Industrialists claimed that Goulart
and Brizola had amassed personal fortunes during their terms in office and had used
this wealth to buy extensive tracts of land in Brazil and Uruguay. In addition, industrialists asserted that Goulart used personal loyalty, rather than seniority or merit, as
his criterion for promoting military officers.[40] Finally, they cited certain aspects of

Goulart's personality as unbefitting to a national leader. In particular, they believed that Goulart could not command respect while rumors of his wife's extramarital affairs abounded.[41]

Second, Goulart threatened business leaders by ignoring established economic and political rules. Specifically, industrialists charged that when Goulart attempted to take control and carry out reforms, he did so by decree rather than by democratic and constitutional means. The reforms he announced at the 13 March rally were just one example of his efforts to bypass the legislature in order to promote his agenda. Industrialists also believed the widespread rumor that Goulart would ignore his constitutional mandate, postpone the October 1965 presidential elections, and remain in office.[42] They also cited his autocratic response to the naval mutiny as another example of his flouting of traditional authority structures, and as a national security threat.

Third, industrialists opposed Goulart because of his exclusion of business interests from government decisions. In part, this perception resulted from Goulart's attempts to bypass Congress, since industrialists had traditionally enjoyed significant influence within the legislature. Business leaders also felt that if Goulart postponed elections they would be unable to use their electoral power to replace him. Another sign of industrialists' lack of influence was Goulart's expropriation and nationalization programs. Although these programs would not have affected the majority of industrialists, Goulart's antibusiness rhetoric led many to fear that his nationalization program would not end with the 13 March reforms. Just two days after the rally, Goulart announced his intention to "fight the privileged."[43] Business leaders further believed that Goulart was using antibusiness rhetoric to sway public opinion against the private sector, thereby reducing their social status. In short, they felt that Goulart had closed off the institutional mechanisms that they employed to directly influence political outcomes, and that he had attempted to reduce their indirect influence by reducing their social status and economic power.

In sum, in the view of business leaders and other social sectors, Goulart lacked legitimacy, created political and economic instability, and excluded business interests from decision making.[44] Although other Brazilian governments that the business community has supported could be similarly characterized, Goulart lacked the personal charisma, the sense of mission, and the overall popularity to command obedience without legal or traditional authority. Moreover, unlike other government leaders, Goulart abandoned the existing rules of the political and economic game and set out on his own path. That path excluded both direct and indirect forms of business influence.

In analyzing these political motivations behind industrialists' support for the coup, it is obvious that business leaders were not motivated by a desire for economic expansion alone. Indeed, their desire to create or maintain sufficient political stability to protect their investment and production decisions and minimize their losses was a much stronger motivation.

Leftist Subversion

Most industrialists recognized that the Brazilian Communist Party was weak in 1964. Moreover, few industrialists considered President Goulart a communist. Ayres, for example, believed that Goulart had extended ties to the Communist Party not because he was himself a communist, but in order to guarantee his own power. Ayres called Goulart "a demagogue and, politically speaking, an ambitious man who wanted personal absolute power."[45] According to Ayres, the Communist Party, with its organizational structure and populist appeal, aided Goulart in preparing his platforms and winning popular support. Other industrialists echoed the opinion that Goulart was not a leftist but merely an opportunist. Several pointed to Goulart's extensive landholdings as an indication that he was not a communist but was merely using his appeal to the left to gain political power. Others offered that Goulart was a capitalist who acted and spoke like a communist. Indeed, several industrialists even considered Goulart to be on the right. When the industrialists I interviewed were asked to place Goulart on a 10-point ideological scale, they put him, on average, just left of center (at position 4). As illustrated in table 2.3, this opinion of Goulart was consistent regardless of the industrialists' position on the coup.[46]

Nonetheless, industrialists believed that under Goulart the appeal of communism was growing. Paulo Ayres Filho expounded on the claim that an international communist conspiracy was under way in Brazil.[47] This conspiracy, he contended, was organized by the "Russian Communist Party," had been initiated in the 1930s, and by 1964 had deeply infiltrated "practically all professional and political organizations," including those of workers, students, university professors, newspaper editors and columnists, radio and television personalities, political leaders, members of the armed forces, and even executives and managers at foreign and national businesses.[48] Most of these individuals could not be called communists, Ayres argued, because they were unaware that they were participating in movements "inspired and animated by the Communist Party"; they had uncritically adopted leftist slogans, becoming useful dupes for the communists.[49] In addition, some industrialists claimed that the Communist Party did not need broad support to overthrow the country. Because of the Cuban Revolution, which had culminated just five years prior to the events in 1964, industrialists felt that "only a dedicated few are needed to accomplish the downfall of a country."[50] Moreover, industrialists felt that the Communist Party had controlled key positions in the government and would continue to gain power as a result of Goulart's plan to legalize the party. One self-proclaimed anticommunist put the number of communists in the country at "800 at

Table 2.3.   Ratings of Goulart's Ideology by the Industrialists Interviewed

Rating[a]	All Respondents		Supporters of Coup		Nonsupporters of Coup	
	No.	%	No.	%	No.	%
Extreme left	29	23.9	16	23.5	5	14.7
1 or 1.5	9	7.4	6	8.8	1	2.9
2 or 2.5	20	16.5	10	14.7	4	11.8
Moderate left	55	45.4	32	47.1	17	50.0
3 or 3.5	28	23.1	14	20.6	8	23.5
4 or 4.5	27	22.3	18	26.5	9	26.5
Center						
5 or 5.5	19	15.7	10	14.7	8	23.5
Moderate right	17	14.0	9	13.2	4	11.8
6 or 6.5	9	7.4	4	5.9	4	11.8
7 or 7.5	3	2.5	3	4.4	0	0.0
8 or 8.5	5	4.1	2	2.9	0	0.0
Extreme right	1	1.0	1	1.5	0	0.0
9 or 9.5	0	0.0	0	0.0	0	0.0
10+	1	1.0	1	1.5	0	0.0
Total	121	100.0	68	100.0	34	100.0

Note: Average ratings of Goulart's ideology by "all respondents," "supporters of coup," and "nonsupporters of coup," respectively, were 3.8, 3.9, and 3.9.

[a]Although the scale did not include decimals, at times respondents placed themselves between the integers on the scale. These responses are represented by the decimals.

the hard core, with some 2,000 supporters in government agencies."[51] Several industrialists I interviewed repeated a statement that they attributed to Luís Carlos Prestes, head of the Brazilian Communist Party, during his exile in East Germany. Prestes had allegedly remarked, "We're in power [in Brazil], though not in government." Consciously or not, Ayres contended, the Goulart government was turning Brazil into a "super Cuba," and it had to be stopped.[52] Industrialists' particular concerns about Goulart's socialist tendencies centered on his plans to expropriate private land and oil refineries, and establish rent controls and ceilings. One director of a small firm remarked that in 1964 he would drive toward his factory and wonder if it would still be his when he arrived [21 Sept. 1987].

Objective analysis of the Brazilian left in the 1960s does not bear out these industrialists' fears. First, Goulart's nationalization and expropriation plans were extremely limited. Second, the left in Brazil in the early 1960s was weak and disorganized, and lacked commitment to revolutionary change.[53] At least in hindsight, most of the industrialists I interviewed recognized how weak the left had been in the 1960s. Therefore, one can only understand the strong fear of the left, and of Goulart's expropriation and nationalization plans, if that fear is viewed in the context of the 1960s. Industrialists' fears were undoubtedly fueled by the Cuban

Revolution and by Cold War propaganda. They were convinced that a leftist revolution was not only possible but probable, and would have grave results for private enterprises. Industrialists would lose their firms, their livelihoods, and perhaps even their lives. One director of a medium-sized Brazilian firm whom I interviewed expressed this fear, stating, "A communist revolution existed. The communists had prepared lists of names of members of the business community to be killed" [26 Apr. 1988].

Analysis of data on the backgrounds of the interviewees who cited leftist subversion as a motivation behind their support for the coup provides further evidence of the impact of international opinion on Brazilian industrialists' views of the left. Industrialists' experience abroad proved statistically significant in determining which of them feared the left in 1964.[54] For example, 51 percent of those with substantial experience abroad supported the coup because of the threat of the left, compared with 38 percent of those with some experience abroad, and 19 percent of those with no such experience. Those who had extensive experience abroad would have had more exposure to anticommunist and Cold War ideology, which provides a plausible explanation for their heightened fears of the left.

Labor Unrest

Although in 1964 nearly all industrialists recognized that the labor movement was weak, a minority believed that the left was infiltrating the labor movement and radicalizing it. For example, some cited the CGT, a trade union confederation, as an example of labor's ties to the left. Many of the trade union leaders involved in the CGT were also members of the Brazilian Communist Party (PCB). In addition, some industrialists believed that the Goulart government was inciting workers to rise up against employers. They perceived that strikes were occurring with increasing frequency, workers were making outrageous demands, and firms were being forced to close as a result of this outside agitation of the labor movement.[55] The following excerpts from interviews—with Paulo Ayres Filho, with the director of a very large Brazilian firm, and with the director of a small Brazilian firm—illustrate this viewpoint:

> The government was threatening the country. The workers were not. They didn't have any leaders. But the government was inciting the workers. The workers didn't understand what was going on. The government was lying to workers to mobilize them. We had to get rid of the politicians. [22 Oct. 1987]

> It got to the point that there were strikes in São Paulo every day. Solidarity strikes. And absurd ones. There would be, for example, a strike in the Santos Port, and a strike in solidarity by nurses in São Paulo. Unions were demanding too much. They demanded extra payment for certain kinds of work. So, they have to carry toilets to their ship, and they say,

"This is embarrassing work," and so we have to pay an extra rate for "embarrassing work." The [Communist] Party controlled workers. I saw it. A boy would ride up on his bicycle with a note saying the party was calling a strike. Within hours the entire firm was paralyzed. No one asked why. No one questioned. They just stopped work on the orders of the party. And the party was carrying out purely political and ideological strikes. We just kept wondering what they were going to come up with next. We would read the paper each morning to see what they were going to do next. What new thing they'd come up with. We were desperate. And the government supported the activity; there was no way to get any judgment on it. The unions were completely infiltrated by the Communist Party, and so was the government. [3 Nov. 1987]

We were going to have to shut down the plant because we couldn't work with all the strikes. [6 May 1988]

The statistics provided in table 2.4 demonstrate that industrialists faced more strikes in 1963 than in the prior two years. Between 1962 and 1963, the number of strikes nearly doubled. Even if, as one scholar suggests, these strikes occurred primarily in the public sector (e.g., state-run corporations, the transportation sector, and the docks) rather than in private industry, they nevertheless affected private industry.[56] For example, strikes in the communications sector could paralyze an entire firm's shipping and receiving operations. In addition, a bank workers' strike (like the one in October 1963) would affect industrialists' operations by keeping them from drawing funds and conducting other financial business.[57] Moreover, a general strike (like the one in July 1962), although not aimed at particular industries, would obviously affect shipping, receiving, and other aspects of individual firms' production.[58]

However, claims of revolutionary infiltration of the labor movement are not consistent with objective analyses of the period preceding the coup. Those analyses suggest that in the 1960s the PCB, rather than endorsing revolution, demanded "nationalist and democratic" reforms of the existing political structure.[59] They also contend that most of the radical labor activity was dispersed and disorganized, occurred in the rural and public sectors, and has often been overestimated.[60] Indeed, as the figures provided in table 2.2 suggest, most industrialists recognized that labor was not radical, was not controlled by the Communist Party or by the government, and was not a threat to business interests. In fact, some industrialists stated that the working class had joined them in their struggle against communism. For example, the director of a small Brazilian firm remarked, "In 1964 the communists tried to take power. Workers and employers worked together to free society of this communist takeover" [14 Oct. 1987]. An executive of a large Brazilian firm said [19 May 1987] that the workers in his firm had asked him to provide them with arms to defend their jobs. He said that they took up sticks to fight off radicals. Similarly, the

Table 2.4.   Strikes in São Paulo, 1961–63

Year	Number of Strikes
1961	180
1962	154
1963	302

Source: Kenneth Paul Erickson, *The Brazilian Corporative State and Working Class Politics* (Berkeley and Los Angeles: University of California Press, 1977), 159.

president of a multinational corporation's very large Brazilian operation remarked that "leftism was only in the government, in the military, and in public enterprises, not in private enterprises. There was little politicization. Those workers were just barely able to survive, and weren't concerned with politics" [1 June 1988]. In addition, only two of the industrialists I interviewed isolated labor unrest from the other factors that might have motivated them to support the coup. The majority of those who feared labor unrest saw it as part of a general climate of fear, combining it with threats from the left, political instability, and economic crisis.

Those who perceived labor as a threat were no doubt influenced by international opinions. For example, two variables proved statistically significant in determining which industrialists feared labor in 1964: the nationality of the firms at which these individuals worked, and their experience abroad.[61] For example, 30 percent of the executives at United States-based firms whom I interviewed supported the coup because of labor unrest, compared to 18 percent of those at Brazilian firms, and 7 percent of those at non–United States multinational firms. Finally, 27 percent of those who had had a significant amount of experience abroad listed labor as a central reason behind their support for the coup, compared to 11 percent of those with less experience abroad. Of the industrialists who had never been abroad, not one mentioned labor as a reason for supporting the coup. These variables suggest that those who had been exposed to Cold War propaganda were more sensitive to labor unrest and its threats to industry than those who had not been so exposed.

Economic Problems

As the theory of the bureaucratic-authoritarian state contends, the threat posed by economic conditions under Goulart was among the factors that motivated industrialists to help undermine his government.[62] Clearly, the business community faced problems resulting from soaring inflation, balance-of-payments deficits, debt payments, and deteriorating terms of trade, which were aggravated by the United States government's reduction in the amount of aid it gave to Brazil.[63]

However, industrialists' primary concerns about Goulart's management of the economy were based on their perceptions of antibusiness bias in his decisions, and his ineffective administration. Two of my interviewees, the president of a multinational corporation's very large Brazilian operation and the director of another such corporation's large Brazilian operation, confirmed industrialists' fears about the economy:

> I was a member of a right-wing student group at the time [of the coup]. We used to fight with the left-wing students. So, I supported this [anti-Goulart] movement. But it was mainly because of Goulart's inefficiency and the economic crisis—90 percent inflation. And his style—populism. [2 June 1988]

> Goulart was not on the left, but he was an incapable president. He had tried to use the same formula as Vargas—social legislation, labor rights, and so on. But he wasn't able to court the business class. He had no support from them. That created an economic crisis. [6 June 1988]

Industrialists criticized Goulart's poor leadership skills, which they believed prevented him from resolving the economic crisis. Specifically, they criticized his constantly changing policies and policy makers, and his radical economic reforms, which reduced business confidence in the future of the economy. Reacting to these conditions, private businesses allegedly deposited $2 billion in foreign bank accounts during the first few months of 1964.[64] Moreover, most multinational corporations stopped investing in Brazil because of the government's threats to limit profit remittances and nationalize firms.[65] Furthermore, given their belief that Goulart would disband Congress, postpone elections, and rewrite the Constitution, industrialists felt that they had no means of influencing the direction of the economy. They feared that Goulart's unchecked power might lead to a collapse of the entire free enterprise system.

As noted in table 2.2, industrialists considered the economy a prime, though not the foremost, motivation for supporting the coup. When they mentioned the economy, they usually listed it among other factors—mainly political instability, the leftist threat, and labor unrest—as part of a general climate of fear. Only three mentioned the economy as their sole motivation for supporting the coup.

In sum, the theory of the bureaucratic-authoritarian state exaggerates the amount of concern that industrialists felt for the economy in 1964. It overemphasizes industrialists' fear of the economic crisis and their desire for economic expansion, while ignoring the most obvious economic reasons for industrialists' support of the coup: namely, their perception that Goulart was excluding business influence in his policy making, threatening the private enterprise system, and incompetently managing the economic crisis.

Adaptive Industrialists and the 1964 Coup

This analysis of business leaders' involvement in the 1964 coup provides new insights into (1) Latin American business elites' collective political power, and the conditions that enable them to effectively use that power; (2) the impact of international factors on business mobilization; and (3) business elites' political motivations and demands. These insights are all consistent with the adaptive actor approach.

IPES's movement against Goulart provides evidence that business leaders can, at least temporarily, overcome their traditional political and economic weakness. While innately competitive, individualistic, and fragmented, they suppressed those tendencies during the Goulart government and acted collectively. They effectively mobilized their rich reserve of financial, organizational, and social assets to achieve their political ends: specifically, they undermined the Goulart government. Thus, they demonstrated the potential political power of Latin American business elites.

The combination of circumstances and factors that mobilized business leaders in 1964 is rare, as the adaptive actor approach suggests. The perception of threat to private sector investments was so great that industrialists who differed from each other in their ideological perspectives and in their needs were nevertheless alike in fearing the Goulart government, although they had different specific reasons for their fears. Moreover, because they considered these threats too serious to ignore, they could not adopt their customary quiescent attitude toward the government. And whereas business leaders typically use individual political pressure to eliminate threats to their firms, their perception of the extent and severity of the threat, and Goulart's apparent indifference to their needs, convinced them that they had little individual leverage over the government. Finally, their perception that Goulart would postpone elections and disband Congress eliminated (in their eyes) the possibility that he could be replaced, or collectively influenced, via democratic methods. Thus, business leaders perceived that their only defense against Goulart's threats was to overthrow him. In other words, the costs of tolerating Goulart's government were much greater than the costs of collective action against it.

In their view, involvement in the coup conspiracy had few costs. They did not fear government reprisals because they perceived Goulart's prejudicial economic policies and political exclusion as more harmful. Furthermore, the coup had broad societal support, which ensured a successful outcome. Other social sectors, particularly the military, shared business leaders' ultimate goal of ousting Goulart, although they did not necessarily share their specific motivations for it.

International factors also played an important role in mobilizing business leaders in 1964. While the theory of the bureaucratic-authoritarian state does not ignore these factors, it emphasizes the role that transnational business leaders played in the coup coalition. Empirical evidence verifies the leadership function of transnational elites but also suggests that domestic entrepreneurs with few or no international links were even more likely to support the coup. Evidence further suggests that business leaders exposed to Cold War ideology either through travel or through business arrangements tended to mobilize against Goulart because of their perception of threats from labor and the left, while business leaders without significant international experiences tended to fear political instability and economic crisis. In other words, transnational economic relations influenced motives but did not necessarily determine support for the coup. Consistent with the adaptive actor approach, additional forms of international influence, particularly the prevailing international fear of socialist revolution, also shaped business leaders' perceptions.

An examination of business leaders' involvement in the 1964 coup also refines our understanding of their political motivations and preferences. Industrialists were not primarily concerned with economic growth or an end to social unrest, as the theory of the bureaucratic-authoritarian state suggests; rather, their primary motivations were the desire for political stability and the fear of leftist subversion. They perceived that Goulart lacked legitimacy. His popular support, weak from the beginning, eroded over time as he lost support from his constituents. He undermined traditional and legal forms of authority but lacked the charisma or social support to rule without them. He was also incompetent at resolving the nation's economic problems. Indeed, the problems that the country faced in 1961 (e.g., the mounting foreign debt, high rates of inflation, and balance-of-payments deficits) intensified under Goulart. And whereas Goulart did not cause these problems, and his policies were often constrained by external factors (e.g., reduction in United States aid to Brazil), he nonetheless proved incapable of managing the economy. Goulart's attempts to carry out reforms proved ineffective: they heightened the perception of government incompetence, intensified opposition to the government, empowered the antigovernment conspirators, and increased political instability. Business leaders felt that Goulart's proposed reforms dramatically altered the status quo, and that they could no longer depend on the government to defend free enterprise. Their fears were shaped as much by Goulart's reforms, however, as by the prevailing international fear of socialist revolution. They believed that Goulart intended to transform the entire political and economic system, and would make these changes without guaranteeing business leaders direct and indirect influence over the direction of change.

In sum, the political game in which business leaders were engaged did not involve deciding whether a particular political system—democracy or authoritarianism—would maximize their profits. Instead, they were engaged in the defensive game described in the adaptive actor approach: they were protecting their investments against perceived threats. While ideally elections and peaceful democratic succession would have protected their investments, business leaders opted for the military coup as the only feasible way of ending an unstable situation that denied them influence. As the following chapter explains, however, their support for the 1964 coup does not necessarily imply endorsement of the military regime installed thereafter.

Chapter Three

Industrialists and Dictatorships

Consensus within the business community broke down shortly after the 1964 coup. Although business leaders had generally agreed that Goulart should be ousted, their opinions on the installation of the military regime, and the appropriateness of the regime's policies and practices diverged. While some clearly endorsed the regime, others opposed it. The majority passively accepted the regime and benefited from some of its policies while criticizing others.

Business leaders' attitudes toward the military regime thus challenge assumptions in the theory of the bureaucratic-authoritarian state. Indeed, passive acceptance of the regime is distinct from the kind of active endorsement that the theory attributes to business elites. Moreover, business leaders' ambiguous relationship to the regime contradicts the assumption that these leaders endorsed the coup in order to install an authoritarian regime. In other words, their support for the military coup did not necessarily translate into endorsement of the authoritarian regime that followed.

After the "Revolution"

Shortly after the 1964 coup, a military regime was installed in Brazil; it lasted until 1985. The first decade of military rule saw the height of the dictatorship, under the leadership of General Humberto de Alencar Castello Branco (1964–67), General Artur da Costa e Silva (1967–69), and General Emílio Garrastazú Médici (1969–74). The military crushed political freedoms through its use of arbitrary decrees, intimidation, exile, imprisonment, torture, and murder. Simultaneously, economic growth skyrocketed during the so-called "economic miracle" of 1968–73.

Given business leaders' support for the military coup, their involvement in the coup conspiracy, and their natural interest in restoring social order and stimulating economic growth, one would naturally assume that they endorsed the regime. Some scholars have even suggested that business leaders involved in IPES developed the blueprint for the military regime, including specific educational reforms, foreign investment strategies, and labor legislation.[1] But as yet these scholars have not produced the blueprint, or provided any evidence that it in fact existed.

Indeed, the postcoup links between the industrialists in IPES and the military regime are at best tenuous. Members of IPES replaced many of the government officials ousted by the military regime, and assumed positions in ministries, advisory committees, government-owned banks and credit institutions, and other government agencies. The IPES members appointed to political offices in the military regime, however, were economists or military personnel.[2] There is no evidence that industrialists were appointed to political positions. Clearly, the IPES members who assumed such positions represented some of the interests of the private sector and shared that sector's goals. But the claim that business leaders themselves had a direct role in constructing the new regime or defining its policies and practices is unsubstantiated. Nonetheless, IPES members cooperated with the military regime and supported its policies and practices.

Although they did not directly influence the military regime, business leaders nonetheless enjoyed highly favorable government policies. In particular, the regime's strategy for economic growth and its control over labor and the left benefited industrialists, at least in the short term.

One of the central goals of the military regime was economic growth, and the regime initially succeeded in achieving this goal, stimulating industry by providing subsidies and credits to the industrialized south-central region of Brazil.[3] Inflation dropped to 55 percent in 1965 and continued to fall until it reached 18 percent in 1972 (table 3.1). Inflation was controlled by wage repression, by a reduction in public expenditures, and by a closing of loopholes in corporate and personal income tax laws. The government also encouraged foreign investment by relaxing profit remittance laws, developing basic infrastructures (e.g., transportation), extending credit, and implementing devaluations and tax concessions to stimulate exports. These measures, coupled with extensive borrowing from international banks, led to the high growth levels seen during the "economic miracle" years, 1968–73. Industrialists clearly benefited from the "miracle," because the industrial sector grew at an average annual rate of 13 percent.

The economic miracle rested on the military regime's wage repression. As table 3.2 indicates, real wages fell steadily during the first decade of the regime. One would expect that employers would have applauded the regime's wage controls, because these controls kept production costs low and increased sales. Initially, however, this was not the case. The industrial federation FIESP objected to the wage controls on the grounds that they violated the constitutional provision for collective bargaining. Eventually, however, when the trade unions' statistics-gathering organization, the Interunion Department of Statistical and Socioeconomic Studies (DIEESE), called for higher wages to compensate for the decline in real wages, FIESP reversed its position. It immediately issued a statement praising the regime's wage policy, labeling it "rational, because under it relative stability of prices, and

Table 3.1.   Inflation and Growth of the Industrial
Sector, 1963–74

Year	Inflation (%)	Rate of Growth (%)
1963	78.0	0.2
1964	87.8	5.2
1965	55.4	−4.7
1966	38.8	9.8
1967	27.1	3.0
1968	27.8	13.3
1969	22.3	12.1
1970	19.3	10.4
1971	18.8	14.3
1972	18.5	13.4
1973	21.2	15.8
1974	32.9	9.9

Source: Maria Helena Moreira Alves, *State and
Opposition in Military Brazil* (Austin: University of
Texas Press, 1985), 107, 268.

Table 3.2.   Wage Repression under the Military
Regime, 1964–73

Year	Real Wages Index
1964	100
1965	88
1966	75
1967	74
1968	75
1969	77
1970	82
1971	81
1972	79
1973	69

Source: "DIEESE: Maior produtividade não se reflete
nos salários," *Gazeta Mercantil,* 26 December 1974.

adequate and medium-level wages were achieved." FIESP argued that although the
wage controls had initially created difficulties, such as reduced buying power for
workers, these distortions had been corrected by 1968. The statement added that,
contrary to DIEESE's claims, workers' living standards had not declined: "They

live comfortably and have more services, although they, of course, have the right to live a better life." FIESP rejected DIEESE's claim that workers should receive bonuses for the loss in wages they had suffered.[4] In short, industrialists objected not to wage controls but to the military regime's usurpation of the power to set wages.

The regime's draconian efforts against alleged subversives also clearly bene-fited business leaders. The military's repressive apparatus swiftly and effectively removed the threat of revolution and expropriation of private property. IPES's lead-ers appeared to support state repression, since reports suggest that a former member of the organization gave the regime's intelligence apparatus the dossiers IPES had created on alleged subversives during the Goulart government. These dossiers were apparently used by the regime to identify many of the individuals whom it detained, stripped of political rights, fired, imprisoned, tortured, and killed.[5]

The regime's controls over labor also benefited business leaders. After two ma-jor strikes in 1968, the Costa e Silva government virtually outlawed strikes. As a result, the military regime successfully eliminated production stoppages due to strikes during its first fourteen years in power (see table 3.3). Some industrialists publicly praised and defended the regime's strike restrictions. One member of the business community stated, "We all know where we would be today if the new right-to-strike law had not been enacted. Certainly we would be facing chaos. Thanks to the good sense of the current government, which brought the protection of law, today we enjoy tranquility in society . . . without which the productive work of industry and industrialists would not be possible."[6] Individual industrialists and their associations further argued that control over strike activity was essential to national security and the common good.[7] Business leaders applauded the regime's harsh repression of one major strike in 1968. The National Confederation of Indus-try expressed this view in a letter to President Costa e Silva:

> It is time to put an end to disorder before it results in total subversion . . . Under the pretext of bringing about a renovation of the structures in society, groups of agitators have infil-trated the schools of our youths and the souls of our workers, looking to confuse them, in truth, confusing them, instigating them to abandon dialogue, and instead imposing con-cepts and formulas that do not include the democratic option that the nation is promoting. [Such agitators] try, through underground criminal acts, to corrupt the institutions of fam-ily, society, and regime . . . Brazilian business—adept at the inalienable right to criticize—reaffirms its faith in the broad and peaceful debate of ideas, the only democra-tic process that will bring an end to the large problems of the country.[8]

In short, the business community derived significant benefits from the regime's economic strategies, and from the elimination of labor conflict and of the Goulart government's revolutionary goals. However, as demonstrated below, despite these benefits business leaders never fully endorsed the military regime.

Table 3.3.   Strikes in Brazil, 1963–77

Year(s)	Number of Strikes
1963	302
1965	25
1966	15
1970	12
1971	0
1973–77	34

Source: Kenneth Paul Erickson, *The Brazilian Corporative State and Working Class Politics* (Berkeley and Los Angeles: University of California Press, 1977), 159; and Alves, *State and Opposition in Military Brazil,* 52.

Note: Prior to the existence of DIEESE, strike data were not gathered in any systematic fashion. Thus, strike figures are available for only a few select years during the 1960s and 1970s.

Industrialists' Political Preferences

When I asked the industrialists I interviewed to identify the best president in Brazilian history, the largest group (48%) named military presidents. The resulting data, set forth in table 3.4, suggest that business leaders tend to prefer authoritarian rule rather than democratic rule. Yet careful analysis reveals factors that contradict that view. Rather than forming strong commitments to a specific type of political system, business leaders have diverse preferences that are contingent upon historical contexts and practical (e.g., investment-related) criteria.

The data presented in table 3.4 demonstrate the diversity of industrialists' opinions. Neither authoritarian political systems nor democratic ones received endorsement from a majority of the industrialists interviewed. While the largest group (48%) endorsed military presidents, a significant minority (30%) endorsed democratically elected presidents. Thus, one cannot claim that business leaders universally prefer one type of political system to another.

Analysis of the data further reveals that different types of industrialists prefer different types of political regimes. Consistent with the theory of the bureaucratic-authoritarian state, table 3.5 demonstrates that a vast majority (89%) of executives from multinational firms preferred authoritarian governments to democratic ones. Brazilian industrialists, on the other hand, were more evenly divided between the two types of governments: 49 percent endorsed authoritarian governments, and 40 percent endorsed democratic ones.

Table 3.4.   Governments Preferred by the Industrialists Interviewed

	Interviewees Expressing Preference	
Type of Government, and President(s)	No.	%
Civilian-democratic governments	29	29.9
Kubitschek	24	24.7
Quadros	5	5.2
Military-authoritarian governments	47	48.4
Castello Branco	37	38.1
Geisel	6	6.2
Médici	3	3.1
Geisel and Médici	1	1.0
Both democratic and authoritarian	9	9.3
Kubitschek and Castello Branco	8	8.3
Quadros and Castello Branco	1	1.0
Other	12	12.4
Vargas	3	3.1
None	7	7.2
Do not know	2	2.1

Note: N = 97. The total adds up to more than 97 and the percentages add up to more than 100% because some respondents provided more than one answer to this question.

Table 3.5.   Percentage Distribution of the Industrialists Interviewed, by Nationality and Business Experience, and Government Preference

	Type of Government Preferred		
	Democratic	Authoritarian	Both
Nationality			
Brazilian	40.28	48.61	11.11
Foreign	00.00	88.89	11.11
Earliest business experience[a]			
Before 1964	30.43	60.87	8.70
After 1964	57.69	26.92	15.38

[a]The figures given here are for Brazilian industrialists only.

Business experience was the only other factor that proved to be statistically significant in determining industrialists' political preferences, although this was only true for industrialists at Brazilian firms, not foreign ones. As table 3.5 illustrates, those individuals whom I interviewed who became industrialists after the 1964 coup tended to support democratic rather than authoritarian governments. In contrast, those individuals who were already industrialists at the time of the coup tended to support authoritarian governments. Ironically, this means that the industrialists who strongly supported democratic presidents were those who had never conducted business under a democratic regime.

Both of these variables—the nationality of the firm, and business experience—suggest that those industrialists who had had most to fear from the Goulart government were more likely to endorse authoritarian presidents. Multinational firms in general were more vulnerable to Goulart's expropriation policies than were domestic firms. And domestic entrepreneurs who had experienced business instability under Goulart were obviously more sensitive to the threats posed by Goulart's government than those who had not. Thus industrialists' political preferences are no doubt shaped by their own or their firms' past experiences.

Historical context also limits business leaders' political preferences. I asked industrialists to identify the best government in Brazilian history, not their ideal political system. Therefore, since military presidents have dominated recent history, it is logical that the best president many industrialists could remember was a military president—Castello Branco, for example. In addition, the scarcity of democratically elected presidents in Brazilian history limited the respondents' choices: there were few democratic presidents from which to choose. Moreover, only one of those presidents—Juscelino Kubitschek—completed his term. Brazilian industrialists thus had little exposure to, or experience with, democratic governments.[9] Indeed, given the limited democratic history in the country, democratic governments arguably received a greater endorsement—and consequently, military governments received a lesser endorsement—than one would expect on the basis of their relative duration in Brazilian history. In other words, in light of the Brazilian military's dominance over Brazilian politics during the prior two decades, the military did not make a very strong showing among business leaders.

These data further suggest the criteria on which industrialists base their political preferences. Although the industrialists I interviewed strongly preferred Castello Branco to any other president in Brazilian history, few of them endorsed other military presidents. It is especially surprising that Médici, the military president in power during the economic miracle, did not receive more endorsements. This finding indicates that industrialists do not always evaluate governments on the basis of economic criteria alone. Furthermore, the low level of endorsement for the other military presidents suggests that whereas industrialists tended to support Castello Branco's government, they did not necessarily endorse the military regime as a whole.

Industrialists' lack of commitment to authoritarian regimes is further confirmed by cases in which certain industrialists endorsed both democratic and authoritarian presidents. Their choices demonstrate that they did not prefer one type of regime over another; rather, they evaluated individual governments, the policies of those governments, and the impact of those policies on business. In addition, the policies

on which industrialists base their opinions appear to have included not only economic measures (since otherwise Médici would have received more support) but
also policies influencing investment stability and the influence of business on the
government's decision making. The two presidents who received the highest endorsement are Castello Branco (38%) and Kubitschek (25%). These presidents did
not promote the highest levels of economic growth or social order. However, they
were arguably best at protecting investment stability: that is, they had legitimacy,
managed the economy competently, protected private property, and responded to
business needs.[10]

In short, industrialists are not inherently authoritarian. While those I interviewed
strongly approved of the Castello Branco government, they did not endorse the military regime as a whole. Moreover, a majority of the newer industrial leaders indicated a strong preference for the democratic government of Kubitschek. At the
same time, however, industrialists are also not strongly democratic. Not only did
those I interviewed fail to automatically eliminate military presidents from consid-
eration when evaluating the best governments in Brazil, but they showed a strong
preference for at least one of those governments.

These aggregate data provide a glimpse of the great diversity of opinion in the
business community toward the military regime. Rather than uniting behind the regime, the business community was divided into three groups. Some, the democrats,
opposed the regime and its policies on principle. Others, the uncommitted, accepted the military regime as they would have accepted any other political system
that provided a modicum of investment stability, but criticized some of its specific
policies affecting business. Indeed, the military regime only enjoyed strong support
from a small group of reactionary business leaders.

The Democrats

The democrats were a minority within the business community. While committed to democratic rule, these individuals had divergent attitudes toward the military
coup. One faction of democratic industrialists, for example, accounted for the small
number of business leaders who opposed the military coup. Given their political
commitment, they could not justify the overthrow of a democratic president,
despite the problems he presented. Not surprisingly, they opposed the military regime implanted after the coup.

The other faction of democratic industrialists had supported the coup. Their si-
multaneous support for the coup and for democracy was not, in their view, contradictory. They had supported the coup because they believed that Goulart
threatened democracy and that military intervention was necessary to restore
democratic order. While this view appears naive now, these industrialists expected
the military to play its historical role in Brazilian politics: namely, they expected

that the military would intervene to defend the Constitution, and remain in power only long enough to restore order and call elections. They did not suspect that the military would install an authoritarian regime.[11] Thus, once it became clear to these industrialists that the military planned to stay in power and impose authoritarian rule, they withdrew their support. One businessman described the conversion that was typical among democratic business leaders who had supported the coup. He stated that he had been a "militant" supporter of the 1964 "revolution," as the coup is called by its supporters, because he believed that Goulart was undermining democracy in Brazil. However, because of his commitment to democracy he became disenchanted when the military regime that had replaced Goulart imposed its own brand of dictatorship on the country rather than calling new elections and restoring democratic rule.[12]

Whether or not these democrats supported the coup, they all opposed the military regime despite the economic boom it brought to industry. They had a principled objection to military-authoritarian rule, and to the loss of human and civil rights, political participation, and freedom of expression and association that accompanied it. Several of these individuals claimed that they had voiced opposition to the military regime during its early years. However, the military effectively used intimidation, threats, and reprisals to silence them. Some industrialists even went into exile owing to their fear of retribution from the military government. Thus, the democrats within the business community played virtually no role during the first decade of the military regime. As described in subsequent chapters, however, during the political opening these industrialists publicly voiced their opposition to the regime and its authoritarian practices.

The Reactionaries

The reactionary industrialists, also a minority within the business community, argued that authoritarian rule was necessary. They included some of the founders and members of the defunct IPES. Their primary reason for endorsing the coup and the military regime was to protect national security. They believed that without authoritarian control, the left would take over the country, undermine the existing capitalist order, and carry out violence against the population. The president of a multinational corporation's large Brazilian operation summarized this view:

Castello Branco came to office. He was the best president Brazil has ever had. He was a consensus president. Everyone wanted him. Then, after 1968, with the terrorist acts such as Araguaia [a guerrilla uprising], and the communist leader Carlos Marighella, who opened fire on an American captain as he was leaving his house with his wife and child watching, and who did it just because he was American, and putting bombs in the American Chamber of Commerce, they forced the military regime to stay on even longer. Institutional Act 5 was adopted to combat these acts of terrorism. Who could consider a return to democracy when this kind of violence was going on? It wasn't possible. The twenty-year military rule was good for Brazil. Some people talk about torture, but there was only violence against the terrorists. In what country isn't there torture? Do you think that if they found someone in France putting a bomb in a shop, and after a series of these bombings, they are not going to torture those people to find out who they work for? It is an invisible enemy and you are forced to use these tactics. [6 Oct. 1987]

Indeed, reactionary business leaders' fear of subversion was so great that it was the basis of one of their only criticisms of the regime. They believed that Castello Branco's government did not carry his political program far enough. As a result, they believed that subsequent regimes were forced to extend and intensify repression, an outcome that would not have occurred if Castello Branco had eliminated subversion. The director of a multinational corporation's large Brazilian operation stated, "After the coup, Castello Branco didn't bring any of the changes that people hoped for. He was supposed to end all of the subversion. But he was weak. He allowed for too much liberty. There were strikes again in 1968, and they were violent. Workers went into the streets breaking things. There were guerrilla groups. And the regime had to end all of this. Médici and the Institutional Act No. 5 ended it" [16 Sept. 1987]. Similarly, Paulo Ayres Filho believed [22 Oct. 1987] that the Castello Branco government was too reluctant to crack down on subversives; this, in his view, enabled the subversives to continue threatening the nation even after the military took over.

Castello Branco's rhetoric certainly advised moderation in efforts to eliminate subversion. In his words: "The extreme right is reactionary; the extreme left is subversive. Brazil must steer an honest middle course . . . The answer to the evils of the extreme left does not lie in the birth of a reactionary right."[13] Moreover, he criticized wealthy industrialists and large landowners for pressing him for self-interested gains. However, despite his rhetoric, Castello Branco took measures that went well beyond eliminating the "extreme left." The antisubversive net he cast covered individuals who could hardly be considered extreme leftists or subversives, including former presidents Kubitschek and Quadros.[14]

Because of their fear of subversion, reactionary industrialists embraced the military regime and cooperated with it. However, they also bolstered the regime's repressive practices. These industrialists assisted the military regime in its efforts to eliminate subversion. Specifically, they helped finance and implement the regime's torture apparatus, through Operation Bandeirantes (OBAN), and formed anticommunist vigilante cells such as the Brazilian Anticommunist Alliance (AAB).

OBAN was a semiclandestine organization founded by the regime in September 1969 to consolidate civilian and military efforts to fight subversion. OBAN, and its

1970 successor the Information Operations Detachment–Center for Internal Defense Operations (DOI-CODI), detained labor leaders, urban guerrillas, and other "subversive" individuals, and tortured and sometimes killed them. It is widely believed, and has been confirmed by businesspeople, that the deceased São Paulo executive Henning Albert Boilesen coordinated support from members of the business community for OBAN and even participated in torture sessions from 1969 until 1971.[15] He allegedly collected funds, equipment, and other resources from businesses to establish the torture center and to reward torturers after they had eliminated subversive leaders considered particularly dangerous.[16]

Some claim that business contributions to OBAN were entirely voluntary. An executive at a United States multinational corporation claimed that a United States consular official encouraged members of the business community to make these contributions.[17] The multinational firms rumored to have contributed to OBAN include Nestlé, General Electric, Mercedes Benz, Siemens, and Ford.[18] Large Brazilian firms and their directors were also allegedly important donors to OBAN. The domestic firms and directors rumored to have contributed include an enormous São Paulo agribusiness firm, Copersucar; an extremely successful construction company, Camargo Correia; and Paulo Maluf, a politician in the military regime's party and the director of his family's wood and pulp firm, Eucatex.[19] Funding also came from certain social groups to which business leaders belonged, including the ultraconservative Catholic lay organization Tradition, Family, and Property (TFP), which was run by Adolpho Lindenberg, the founder of a large civil engineering and construction firm.[20]

Others contend, however, that their contributions were not voluntary but were obtained through a form of extortion. They stated that members of the business community were first asked to contribute, but that if they refused, they were threatened. One industrialist whom I interviewed recounted that his firm's bank account at the Banco do Brasil was closed and he was threatened with physical harm when he refused to contribute.

Still others suggested that industrialists realized that they had something to gain (e.g., control over radical social movements) if they did contribute, and much to lose (because of financial constraints imposed on them by the regime, physical harm from right-wing forces within the regime, and increased subversion) if they did not. Regardless of their motivations, most industrialists provided the funds or equipment OBAN requested.[21]

Reactionary industrialists have also been implicated in the formation of the AAB in November 1974. The AAB issued death threats to key individuals on the left, and claimed responsibility for planting bombs in the headquarters of the Brazilian Press Association (ABI) and the Organization of Brazilian Lawyers (OAB).[22]

There is no incontrovertible proof that any of the industrialists rumored to have financed OBAN or formed the AAB actually did so. Lists of contributors and founders do not exist. Moreover, those accused of financing or forming these groups deny any involvement. A journalist investigating OBAN argues that secrecy has prevailed partly because of the illegality of the operation, but more importantly because industrialists feared retribution from the left for participating, even indirectly, in torture.[23] Their fears were apparently justified, for Boilesen was murdered by urban guerrillas in 1971.[24] Another plausible argument is that these businesspeople have been falsely accused of promoting torture and repression. This is highly unlikely, however, since some of the industrialists I interviewed, while denying their own involvement, acknowledged that businesspeople had indeed contributed funds, cooperated with the regime's repressive apparatus, and formed anticommunist vigilante groups.

The clandestine and morally reprehensible nature of reactionary business leaders' involvement in the military regime impedes the development of an accurate portrayal of these industrialists. Only a few of the individuals I interviewed confessed, and some others hinted, that they had endorsed the regime and its authoritarian practices in the ways described above. On the basis of reports from industrialists who attributed various activities to other business leaders, this number appears to be artificially low. Little public information exists about strident advocates of authoritarianism who engaged in violence against "subversives," because the media did not consider them newsworthy. Most observers of Brazilian politics saw an authoritarian political attitude as the norm among industrialists. Nonetheless, as indicated both by rumors and by admissions, the industrialists involved in these repressive groups were diverse. They were drawn primarily from multinational firms but also from domestic firms. They were engaged in diverse sectors of the economy, including industry, construction, and agribusiness. And while some were active in conservative religious organizations, others were not religious.

The Uncommitted

The majority of industrialists within the business community fall into the "uncommitted" category. They supported the coup and accepted the military regime and most of its policies. Despite their generally supportive attitude, however, they cannot be labeled authoritarian. Indeed, most of their comments about the military regime suggest that they simply ignored the distinctions between political systems. The following quotations—from the director of a small company, from Paulo Ayres Filho, and from an executive of a very large metalworking corporation—illustrate their view of the military regime:

The Goulart government was a government on the left. It was revolutionary. The population is not revolutionary. It is democratic. The military regime was not authoritarian, it was an authoritative democracy. [23 Sep. 1987]

Brazil cannot have a democratic government like in the United States. We need a tough government. The best government ever in Brazil was the Castello Branco government because it brought discipline and democracy. The subsequent governments were also good. No one talks about the growth rates in Brazil [during the military governments], but they complain about censorship. There was no censorship. The *Folha* [*de São Paulo*] wanted to be censored, so they would publish the newspaper with white spots. They were never forced to do that. The only time there had to be infringement on liberties was when national security was threatened. [22 Oct. 1987]

Under all of the military presidents there was liberty, not authoritarianism. The only thing you couldn't do was call the president an ugly name. I know that there were political prisoners, but they wanted it; they were asking for it. They wanted to be martyrs. Nothing changed in Brazil after the military regime; there was always liberty. I always could do what I wanted. If the minister of labor called me up and said, "I don't like it that you dismissed those workers," I'd say, "Okay, I'll rehire them." But others refused. They were asking for it. The only difference was that there was more discipline. People were afraid. [15 Sept. 1987]

While these statements indicate a general preference for democracy over authoritarianism, they also indicate that these industrialists considered the type of political system irrelevant as long as the government provided stability. Indeed, they valued stability, particularly with regard to investments, more highly than the democratic values of "opposition, public contestation, or political competition."[25] In order to reconcile their contradictory preferences, they redefined democracy to include governments that not only protected political order and promoted economic growth but also repressed democratic rights and freedoms. Thus, they accepted both democratic and authoritarian governments that provided investment stability, but tended to label them all democratic. More accurately, they generally accepted the status quo, whether authoritarian or democratic, unless their interests were severely threatened. Thus, when the military regime began the transition to democracy, these business leaders also accepted that political system.

Industrialists' loyalty to the military regime resulted from the investment stability that the regime provided. The military regime proved competent in managing the economy and eliminating threats to the economic and political order. It was also legitimate, in most industrialists' opinion. It derived its legitimacy in large part from its ability to convince industrialists and the public at large that the threat of communism and internal subversion required drastic measures. As a result, it commanded authority and obedience from the population. At least during its first decade, the regime's efforts worked. Most industrialists valued political control and the suppression of subversion far more than democratic rights and freedoms. Thus, most industrialists accepted the regime's draconian efforts to restore political stability by eliminating the left and denying Brazilians political liberties. Indeed, they applauded the regime's efforts when these directly benefited them.

However, the obvious short-term benefits of the military regime's economic program and social order did not cause the business community to accept the regime uncritically. As early as 1964, industrialists criticized the government for excluding them from economic decisions. This concern manifested itself in the frequent appearance of writings and speeches by industrialists praising "collaboration" and asking to be consulted on economic issues. As one industrialist stated, "It is not only a democratic right or tradition and a law but also a duty, that the State, in order to fulfill its democratic responsibilities, must listen to the thoughts of industry."[26] Another example of industrialists' concern was their reaction to wage controls. While they obviously benefited from lower wages, they reacted against what they perceived as the regime's attempt to take away their control over labor relations.

Industrialists' sense of a loss of influence resulted from the institutional changes that transpired during the course of the military regime. During the early years of the military regime, Brazilian business leaders could influence the regime via four mechanisms: official business associations; extracorporatist, or parallel, associations representing the interests of specific industrial sectors; bureaucratic rings (informal networks between state agencies and specific industrial sectors); and personal contacts with public officials.[27] However, after Castello Branco's administration, the regime greatly reduced the decision-making power of Congress, centralized decisions in the ministries, and excluded business leaders from government councils. Thus, scholars of Brazilian business associations contend that the business community's lobbying efforts via official and parallel business associations had little effect. Instead, industrialists primarily used bureaucratic rings and personal contacts to gain influence. However, even these efforts proved generally ineffective because the government operated in a vacuum and had its own set of economic priorities. Thus, one of the problems industrialists had faced during the Goulart government—the loss of influence over government decisions—reappeared under the military regime. As one scholar writes:

> In its attempt to contain the "pressure from below," the bourgeoisie supported measures that essentially destroyed its own direct political expression. It is true that the bourgeoisie never had effective political organization and pressure instruments. Now, however, not only the political party system but all other forms of political action open to the bour-

geoisie became dependent on contacts and alliances with the military and technocratic groups that alone controlled the state apparatus . . . The bourgeoisie lost all leverage to shape its more immediate political interests.[28]

Although industrialists were critical of their loss of influence, they retained the protection of private property. As long as the military regime could convince them that property rights would be threatened by political liberalization, most industrialists continued to accept the regime and even their own loss of direct political influence. They were willing to sacrifice direct political participation for protection of the private sector generally.

In short, the uncommitted business leaders neither endorsed nor rejected authoritarian rule; they merely adapted to it. They adapted, in part, because they derived benefits from the regime's effective economic management and enforcement of social order, and its protections for the private sector. Yet, despite the regime's significant advantages, most of these industrialists neither actively endorsed it nor passively acquiesced to it. Instead, they criticized it for not allowing business groups to have direct influence over policies affecting them. As long as the regime's policies reflected industrialists' interests, the conflict over business influence did not develop into open confrontation. As discussed in the next chapter, however, during the second phase of the military regime business leaders sensed that even their indirect influence began to erode, intensifying the latent conflict in business-state relations.

Adaptive Industrialists and the Military Regime

Two incontrovertible facts emerge from this study on business leaders' political attitudes toward the military regime. First, industrialists widely supported the overthrow of the Goulart government. Second, they benefited greatly from the policies enacted during the first decade of the military regime. Political stability and protection of private property were restored. The military regime also provided high growth rates, restricted wage increases and labor activity, and excluded the left from national politics.

The theory of the bureaucratic-authoritarian state assumes on the basis of these two facts that business leaders supported the military coup *in order to* install a military regime capable of bringing social order and economic growth. However, there is little evidence to support that claim.

Despite industrialists' active support for the 1964 coup, there is no reason to conclude that they knew that a military regime would be installed after the coup. The historical pattern of military intervention in Brazil would have led them to assume that the regime would intervene only long enough to restore order and call democratic elections. There is also no evidence to confirm that industrialists played a role in designing or shaping the policies of the military regime. Indeed, their frustration over their exclusion from the regime's policy decisions suggests the opposite. In other words, business leaders did not support the coup as a means to stimulate economic growth; the dramatic economic growth that followed the coup was a favorable but unanticipated outcome.

There is also no evidence to support the view that business leaders collectively endorsed the regime. Evidence suggests the contrary. As the adaptive actor approach asserts, the business community's diversity prevented such a consensus from emerging. The only strong endorsement of the military regime came from a small minority of reactionary industrialists who were motivated by their fear of subversion and were unconcerned about democratic rights and liberties. They defended and bolstered the regime's repressive policies. In contrast, another small minority within the business community, including some who had supported the 1964 coup, opposed the authoritarian regime and its repressive policies. They had endorsed the coup owing to their perception that Goulart threatened their firms, the private sector, and the democratic system. They believed that the military, as in the past, would restore order and call new democratic elections. When the military failed to do so, and instead imposed a military-authoritarian regime, these business leaders withdrew their support.

The majority of business leaders were uncommitted either to democratic or to authoritarian rule. As the data presented in the chapter demonstrates, some of them endorsed both democratic and military presidents. Others endorsed the first military president, Castello Branco, but disapproved of his successors and expressed a preference for democracy. They thus demonstrated the adaptable nature of business elites. Rather than rigidly adhering to a specific type of regime, they evaluated governments on the basis of the extent to which those governments protected investment stability. If a government, whether democratic or authoritarian, provided investment stability, business elites accepted it and used their significant political resources to influence it from within the system. While representing very different forms of government, both the Castello Branco and Kubitschek regimes provided that stability. Castello Branco and Kubitschek were not the presidents who produced the highest levels of economic growth or social order. Indeed, consistent with the adaptive actor approach, business leaders were critical of other military presidents, even those who provided the highest levels of economic growth and social order, because of those presidents' exclusion of business influence and (as discussed in the following chapter) their questionable legitimacy.

The data presented in this chapter also suggest that those who most strongly preferred authoritarian governments to democratic ones were also those who were most threatened by the Goulart government—specifically, executives in multinational corporations and domestic entrepreneurs who had conducted business during the Goulart administration. These industrialists' political preferences were no doubt shaped by their past experiences and perceptions of threat. Thus, as suggested by the adaptive actor approach, a change in their perceptions during the transition from authoritarian rule should produce a concurrent change in their attitudes toward democratic governments.

Chapter Four

Industrialists and Political Liberalization

The 1964 Revolution was the best thing for the country, when it happened. A Revolution doesn't last forever, and it should have already ended. Once it was institutionalized it created serious problems. Everything that the Revolution was supposed to correct over time became worse than it was before.[1]

This quotation from a leading industrialist in Brazil exemplifies the dissatisfaction within the business community during the second decade of military rule. It was during that decade that, under the leadership of General Ernesto Geisel (1974–79) and General João Batista Figueiredo (1979–85), the military regime guided and controlled the first phase of the transition from authoritarian rule. During this phase, industrialists generally agreed that the nation faced serious problems. Specifically, they feared the regime's eroded legitimacy, the regime's incompetent economic management and threats to private property, renewed labor conflict, and loss of business influence.

Despite these serious problems, and their resemblance to those experienced during the Goulart years, business leaders did not oppose the democratic transition. Indeed, they defied predictions in the literature on the transitions from authoritarian rule, which asserted that in the face of serious threats they would opt for an authoritarian reversal. The first phase of the transition to democracy thus provides insights into the constraints on business elites' collective action (e.g., their relationship with the state; diversity and individualism within the business community; and lack of social support) that are overlooked in the transitions literature.

Threats to Industrialists during the Early Transition

The Government's Loss of Legitimacy

During the second decade of military rule, the regime faced internal pressures for change, as well as broad societal and international ones. Consensus within the ruling coalition had broken down as the hard-line and soft-line officers within the military vied for political control. The hard-liners wanted greater authoritarian controls, while the soft-liners advocated a gradual and controlled transition to democracy. This polarization within the ruling coalition made consensus on the direction of the government impossible. It also led to presidential succession crises, which were resolved by compromises that resulted in the selection of inefficacious presidents (Geisel and Figueiredo) who lacked strong support from either faction within the military, and from the general population. Industrialists also rejected these leaders. Many of those I interviewed used the terms *bad, stupid,* or *corrupt,* to describe the leadership abilities of the military rulers who succeeded Castello Branco. The president of a medium-sized metalworking firm stated, "The military is a middle-class group. They brought a middle-class revolution. They wanted order. Castello Branco was excellent—an excellent, energetic leader. But with Costa e Silva things went down the drain. This began the second, inferior, class of military leaders . . . The military didn't turn out to be what people expected them to be" [25 Sept. 1987].

The regime also lacked support within society. ARENA, the political party representing the military, was soundly defeated in the 1974 congressional elections.[2] Domestic opposition to the regime grew in numbers, organizational strength, and visibility. Antiregime protests erupted. Moreover, the opposition movement included both popular and elite sectors of society: lawyers, clergy, politicians, human rights activists, students, slum dwellers, workers, and others. It demanded a greater political opening, including an end to human rights abuses and censorship; legalization of political parties; amnesty for exiles and political prisoners; and direct elections.[3]

International forces, including human rights groups such as Americas Watch, Amnesty International, and various religious organizations, exposed and condemned the regime's practices (particularly its violation of human rights) and advocated political change. In addition, the United States government (i.e., the Carter administration) attached tangible costs to the regime's practices by making foreign aid contingent on human rights improvements.

Industrialists doubted that the regime could sustain its policies and practices given its loss of control and legitimacy. This political instability threatened their investments, because they were not sure what kind of government would replace the existing regime. Although they universally recognized the political problems in the country, they did not agree on what changes should be made to overcome instability and threats to their investments. A 1980 survey of business leaders depicted these diverse views: 23 percent (the democrats) thought that the pace of the transition was too slow; 29 percent (the reactionaries) believed that it was too fast; and nearly half, 48 percent (the uncommitted), believed that it was adequate.[4]

The Democrats.   The democrats, although still a minority within the business community, became increasingly visible during the first phase of the democratic transition. They publicly criticized the military regime and endorsed the transition to democracy. They rejected the gradual and restricted democracy initiated by the regime, and called for a "democracy without adjectives."[5]

The group included individuals who had opposed both the military coup and the regime but had remained silent until the political liberalization. Because of the progressive political views of many of these industrialists, the Brazilian press often referred to the democratic industrialists as "liberals."[6] One such industrialist, the director of a medium-sized metalworking company, explained [26 Oct. 1987] that he had been active in a leftist student organization while he was in college in the 1960s, but that after the military seized power he abandoned his political activities for fear of government reprisals. Ten years later, after General Geisel announced a transition to democracy, he felt that he could again become active in support of social change. By that time he was the director of his family's prestigious industrial firm.

However, the prodemocracy group also included conservative industrialists who had supported the coup because they believed that it was the only way to restore democratic rule in the country.[7] Once they realized that the regime planned to remain in power, they turned against it. They rejected its circumvention of the legal system, particularly its violation of human rights. Most industrialists could no longer ignore the regime's human rights abuses, since they personally knew, or knew of, people who had been the victims of these abuses. Some of these industrialists were religious. For example, the *empresários cristãos* (Christian entrepreneurs) formed groups that opposed human rights violations. These organizations, which included the International Union of Christian Entrepreneurs (UNIAPAC) and the Association of Christian Entrepreneurs (ADCE), claimed seven hundred members in São Paulo, Porto Alegre, and Belo Horizonte.[8]

The prodemocracy industrialists believed that they could publicly state their position because their social status, as well as the regime's announcement of a political opening, would protect them from government reprisals. As the president of a very large Brazilian firm stated: "I was a part of a group of Paulista business leaders who were right-wing, informed, [and] strong because of wealth, information, status. We were the only ones who could challenge the state. We could criticize the economy and the social situation . . . We wanted to keep our profits up" [14 Oct. 1987].

Indeed, it was the more prominent industrialists who first publicly advocated democracy. For example, in 1977 Einar Kok and Cláudio Bardella, directors of large capital-goods firms and heads of industrial associations in São Paulo, publicly demanded a transition to democracy. In 1978, eight prominent industrialists signed the Documento dos Oito (Document of the Eight), a manifesto outlining democratic industrialists' blueprint for political change.[9] Its signatories were among the "top ten business leaders" in the country chosen by members of the business community in polls conducted by the business newspaper *Gazeta Mercantil*.[10] They were primarily from large, well-established capital-goods firms in São Paulo. (The Documento dos Oito is discussed in more detail below.)

Despite their social status and the political opening, however, not all of the outspoken democratic industrialists were protected from intimidation by the military during the early transition period. In June 1976 João Batista Figueiredo, the head of the SNI, the government's intelligence agency, informed President Geisel that opposition within the business community, especially in the industrial sector, had reached a dangerous level.[11] The military responded to this danger by "visiting" the outspoken industrialists. The director of a paper company recalled, "In 1977, I came out for a transition to democracy. All I said was that democracy would not hurt economic development. I was visited by a military officer who said I was now a *persona non grata*. I kept my mouth shut after that" [5 Nov. 1987]. And the director of a large Brazilian firm reported [26 Oct. 1987] that he had gone into self-imposed exile after a "visit" from a military official, fearing more serious retribution if he remained in the country. While I did not find any evidence that business leaders had been arrested or tortured in retaliation for their statements in favor of democracy, many industrialists suspected that they were not exempt from repression, because the security forces did not necessarily discriminate by class.[12] Thus, while symbolically important, the outspoken prodemocracy group remained a small minority of elite business leaders during the first phase of the transition.

The Reactionaries.   The reactionary industrialists opposed a transition to democracy and demanded a return to authoritarian rule. This is not because they were necessarily satisfied with the military regime under Geisel and Figueiredo. On the contrary, they acknowledged that the regime had brought political instability, economic crisis, social unrest, and reduced influence for the business community. However, their solution to these problems was a military crackdown rather than a political opening. Indeed, they believed that the political opening had created these problems in the first place. They argued that political debate had weakened the regime and its policies by creating internal dissension and weak leadership. They further argued that the liberalization had increased the appeal and the activities of subversive elements. Thus, these industrialists called on the regime to reverse the process of liberalization and restore authoritarian rule.

The reactionary industrialists engaged in few public activities or protests. No evidence exists to suggest that any business leaders were financing the repressive apparatus as they had during the first decade of military rule, and contributions to OBAN from business leaders had apparently ended after Boilesen was assassinated.[13] The reactionary faction's most significant action was a public letter sent to president-designate Figueiredo in May and June of 1978 warning of the dangers of the political liberalization and asking him to resurrect the goals of the 1964 "revolution": national security and economic development. The letter criticized the signers of the Documento dos Oito and denounced business leaders who had publicly proclaimed their support for democracy. It stated that the press gave "excessive" attention to business leaders favoring political opening, and asserted that this was not an opinion representative of the majority of the nation's industrialists. The letter also accused the prodemocracy business leaders of "demagogic agitation." It added, "The true business person, 100-percent business person, does not need publicity or have political ambitions." It concluded by asking rhetorically how Brazil could consider revoking the prudent measures taken in 1964 when Europe was beset with difficulties in its efforts to resist communism.[14]

The letter sent in May 1978 was signed by 32 business leaders, but when it was sent to president-designate Figueiredo again in June 1978 it had 102 signatures. Notable among those who signed the letter were two of the founders of IPES, Paulo Ayres Filho and João Batista Leopoldo Figueiredo (a relative of SNI director and president-designate João Batista Figueredo); as well as Adolpho Lindenberg, the director of the right-wing Catholic organization the TFP, alleged financier of OBAN, and owner of a civil construction company; Jorge Duprat Figueiredo, a conservative former director of FIESP and of the CNI; and Paulo D'Arrigo Vellinho, a self-made entrepreneur whose popularity in the industrial community won him seventh place in the *Gazeta Mercantil*'s ranking of the "top ten business leaders" of 1977. Analysis of the signers of the letter reveals that most of them (52%) were industrialists, while 19 percent were in commerce, 15 percent were in agriculture, and 8 percent were in the construction industry. Many of the signers were leaders in the business community. For example, 25 percent were directors in state federations of industries or in the CNI. They were also geographically diverse: 17 percent were from São Paulo, 25 percent from Rio de Janeiro, and 60 percent from other states.

The Uncommitted.   Most industrialists neither endorsed nor opposed democracy as a solution to the nation's problems. One industrialist summarized this view when he commented that the business community lacked a clear consensus on the issue of a political opening.[15] They recognized that change was inevitable, and perhaps even desirable, given the regime's loss of legitimacy under Geisel and Figueiredo. Their tolerance for the transition, however, must not be equated with rejection of authoritarianism. The uncommitted industrialists were unconcerned about the regime's repressive apparatus, except, perhaps, insofar as it would provoke an international reaction (e.g., loss of international aid) that might affect business. Some industrialists even continued to deny that the military regime employed authoritarian and repressive tactics, despite incontrovertible evidence to the contrary. For example, the director of a small Brazilian firm stated, "People say there was a lot of torture under Médici, but you can't prove this" [23 Nov. 1987]. The president of a multinational corporation's very large Brazilian operation stated, "No real repression existed in Brazil" [20 May 1988]. Indeed, most industrialists would only accept the transition to democracy if it retained those aspects of the authoritarian system which protected them—especially the repression of labor conflict. As one industrialist candidly observed, business leaders supported a political opening as long as it occurred without strikes or other forms of social tension.[16]

In short, while industrialists agreed that during its second decade the military regime encountered legitimacy problems that increased political instability, they disagreed on how the regime might overcome those problems. Three strong currents of opinion emerged within the business community. The democrats rejected military control over the transition and advocated a more rapid and extensive transition to democracy. The reactionaries called for increased authoritarian controls and restoration of the dictatorship. The uncommitted adapted to the gradual transition underway and used their extensive political resources to influence its course.

Economic Incompetence and Threats to Property Rights

By 1974 the "economic miracle" had ended, and the Brazilian economy was on a downward course. Because of the 1973 and 1979 oil price shocks, Brazil, which depended on foreign countries for 80 percent of its oil, was forced to substantially increase its spending on imports. Although the regime enacted export expansion programs, the world recession had reduced the demand for Brazilian goods, resulting in a trade deficit. The rising cost of imports also fueled inflation. International borrowing skyrocketed.

Despite this bleak economic situation, however, industrial production and profits remained relatively high. The situation took a more severe turn for the worse in the period 1981–83, when Brazil faced its most serious recession since the 1930s.[17] As table 4.1 demonstrates, industrial production and profits plummeted. Meanwhile, unemployment and idle-capacity levels soared. Many companies went bankrupt. The severity of the crisis has led some to refer to this period as the "deindustrialization" of Brazil.[18] Industrialists uniformly agreed that the regime's ineffective management of the economy eroded their confidence in its decisions and policies.[19] As the president of FIESP, Theobaldo deNigris, stated:

> The difficulties encountered over the last two years by those in charge of economic policies in achieving objectives announced at the beginning of each year have done nothing to reduce the degree of uncertainty that dominates the Brazilian economy today. The facts have shown that those who hold the instruments of economic policy and the control of the economy in their hands have not always managed to achieve the goals planned *a priori*.[20]

Table 4.1.   Brazil's Economic Indicators, 1974–84

Year	Inflation (%)	Change in GDP (%)	Current Accounts ($ millions)	Change in Industrial GDP (%)
1974	27.6	9.7	− 7.562	8.3
1975	29.0	5.6	− 7.008	4.7
1976	42.0	9.7	− 6.554	11.7
1977	43.7	2.9	− 5.112	3.1
1978	38.7	4.9	− 7.036	6.3
1979	52.7	6.8	−10.478	6.6
1980	82.8	9.3	−12.806	9.1
1981	105.6	−4.4	−11.751	−9.1
1982	97.8	0.6	−16.312	0.0
1983	142.1	−3.5	− 6.837	−6.3
1984	197.0	5.1	0.420	6.2

Sources: International Financial Statistics, 1974–84 (Washington, D.C.: International Monetary Fund, 1975–85); and *Anuario estadístico de América Latina y el Caribe* (Santiago, Chile: United Nations Economic Commission for Latin America and the Caribbean, 1975–76, 1978–81, 1983–84, 1985–89).

Industrialists even turned against Antônio Delfim Neto, whom they had once idolized as the "wizard" behind the economic miracle. They believed that after he became planning minister in 1979 Delfim Neto failed to eliminate distortions in economic policy, to lower interest rates, to build national industry, and to increase credit lines to the private sector.

However, industrialists' concern with the regime's economic management was not solely due to the regime's incapacity to check economic decline. They were also reacting against the orientation of the regime's economic policies. Indeed, although business leaders had privately and individually criticized the regime since its inception, it was not until 1974 that they launched their first broad public protest against it: the *desestatização* (antistate) campaign. The campaign received widespread attention from the media. It also won broad support among industrialists. Its goals were sufficiently broad, and its organizational structure sufficiently amorphous, to appeal to the diverse groups within the business community.

The primary goal of the campaign was to reduce the military regime's excessive control over the economy. The regime had monopolized credit, import licensing, price and wage setting, tax assessments, and markets for goods, all of which severely impaired the private sector's ability to produce and invest.[21] As two industrialists, the director of a small Brazilian company and the president of a medium-sized Brazilian company, stated:

Businessmen reacted to the immediate situation. They distrusted the military. They wanted new order, fewer rules. The military had begun restricting their freedom of action. [5 Oct. 1987]

Businessmen supported the authoritarian regime, but they created a monster. It was authoritarian even in economics! Only a few benefited. [24 Sept. 1987]

Industrialists also believed that the expansion of state investment in productive enterprises preempted expansion by the domestic private sector, and indeed threatened its very survival. This view was expressed by the director of a medium-sized company, who said, "I expected the military to step down after Castello Branco; after the goals of order and hierarchy were restored in Brazil. Instead the military stayed and carried out highly interventionist measures—60 percent of Brazil's industry is state owned" [5 Oct. 1987]. The manager of a multinational corporation's very large Brazilian operation called the military regime's involvement in the economy "socialist" because the regime controlled the "ownership of the means of production" [30 July 1987].

The second thrust of the campaign, supported exclusively by domestic private industrialists, accused the regime of granting excessive concessions and influence to foreign investors, while ignoring national private initiative. Domestic industrialists argued that the regime had granted government contracts to, and had purchased products and equipment from, foreign companies (e.g., Bayer, of West Germany) even when equivalent equipment and services were available in Brazil from national firms. They also claimed that the government allowed excessive foreign input into decisions that affected the national economy. They viewed Geisel's February 1977 dismissal of Severo Gomes, the minister of industry and commerce, as one example. Gomes, a textile manufacturer from the state of São Paulo, frequently attacked Delfim Neto's policies of granting a privileged position to multinational investments at the expense of domestic private enterprise. Although not all industrialists agreed with Gomes's extreme nationalism, they generally perceived his dismissal as an indication that the regime had shifted its economic strategy away from stimulating the domestic private sector, and toward the encouragement of direct foreign investment.

Despite business leaders' widespread support for the desestatização campaign, the campaign failed to achieve its objectives because they conflicted with those identified by the regime. The regime's technocrats considered expansion by multinational corporations and the state in specific sectors to be the best and most efficient means of achieving economic expansion, and were not particularly concerned about the impact on private domestic entrepreneurship.[22] The campaign also lacked strong leadership. And, apart from the demand that the domestic private sector be given more influence over economic decisions, there was little consensus among industrialists as to the specific policy objectives of the campaign. In addition, while industrialists from various factions agreed that the economic situation was threatening, they could not agree on solutions. For example, a 1984 poll of members of the business community conducted by *Exame* revealed that 60 percent were pessimistic about the country's economic future. The *Exame* poll also reported that 84 percent of Brazil's business leaders thought that the country's economic problems would be unsolvable until the political crisis was resolved.[23] However, although the democratic, reactionary, and uncommitted factions within the business community concurred that business confidence depended on political change, they did not agree on the direction change should take.

The Democrats.   The democratic industrialists made a direct link between democratic political change and economic growth. These views were embodied in the Documento dos Oito:

> We believe that social and economic development, as we conceive it, will only be possible within a political context that encourages participation by all. And there is only one political system capable of promoting the expression of interests and opinions, with sufficient flexibility to resolve tensions without turning them into undesirable class conflict: the democratic system. Moreover, we are convinced that the free enterprise system in Brazil and the market economy are viable and will be long lasting as long as we build institutions that protect the rights of citizens and guarantee their liberty. Above all, we defend democracy because it is a superior social system. It provides opportunities for the development of the human potential.[24]

Specifically, the Documento dos Oito argued for a two-pronged approach to developing an industrial policy. On the one hand, it outlined what industrialists believed the government should do to fortify the fragile private domestic industrial structure: encourage import-substitution industrialization; diversify production; expand consumer-goods and capital-goods industries; develop rural areas and agroindustries; and assist small and medium-sized enterprises. The government could implement these measures by eliminating distortions in finance, increasing long-term lending for industrial expansion, modernizing the industrial infrastructure, and developing certain high-risk or complex industries. The document also advocated increasing the availability of appropriate technology and alternative energy, without damaging the environment. It recommended that funds for these programs be generated by limiting public spending on state enterprises (which, the document stated, should play a subordinate role to national private industry), controlling foreign investment, and reducing the external debt.

On the other hand, the Documento dos Oito advocated the reduction of social inequalities as a means of developing the economy. It argued that such inequalities create social instability, which, in turn, threatens economic development. The document suggested several remedies to this problem. It argued for a just wage to increase consumer demand and purchasing power, which would also stimulate the consumer products industry. It also called for direct negotiations between employers and workers, which would increase the working class's rights and freedoms and modernize the union structure. Moreover, it advocated increased spending on health, sanitation, housing, education, public transportation, and environmental protection. These increased public expenditures would have a dynamic effect on the producer-goods industry; they would increase investments, which would, in turn, increase employment. The document further argued that the funds needed for these public expenditures could be generated with a progressive taxation program and a revision of the current public expenditure policy.

Individual democrats within the business community echoed parts of the Documento dos Oito: specifically, its thinly veiled charges against the regime's wage repression. As table 4.2 illustrates, real wages continued to fall during the second decade of military rule. Some industrialists began to view wage repression as a principal cause of economic decline in the country. As the president of a very large Brazilian firm stated: "One of the old guard talking at a FIESP meeting said that wages had gone up in real terms. I said, 'I'd like to see your figures, because the ones I've seen, the ones produced by DIEESE, show the opposite, and in my firm, I think that DIEESE is right. A minimum wage used to buy a bag of beans and rice. Now it doesn't even buy a tiny roll.' Government policies were hurting workers and employers" [23 Sept. 1987].

Associating the regime's wage repression with economic decline, some industrialists began to endorse income redistribution to stimulate consumption and expand industrial production, investment, and profits. According to the director of a small metalworking company, "We realized that workers are also consumers, and increased wages would be good for business" [11 May 1988].[25] And the director of a very large chemical company confessed, "My own perception of and attention to problems improved due to changes in the union movement. I realized that Brazil's growth will occur only with an increase in the income of the population" [23 Nov. 1987].

These industrialists further believed that with higher wages, firms' productivity would increase: workers would be satisfied, reducing turnover rates and improving production levels. The following statements, made by the president of a large Brazilian company and the manager of a multinational corporation's large Brazilian operation, illustrate this view:

Twenty years ago I wasn't so dependent on the workers. [Now] I don't want to lose them. There is competition out there. I don't want to lose the investment I made in my workers

Table 4.2.   Real Minimum Wage in Brazil, 1974–84

Year	Real Minimum Wage in Cruzados (October 1987 Value)	Real Minimum Wage Index (July 1940 = 100)
1974	4,828.77	54.48
1975	5,043.70	56.91
1976	5,011.05	56.54
1977	5,221.95	58.92
1978	5,379.55	60.70
1979	5,431.91	61.29
1980	5,475.48	61.78
1981	5,614.17	63.34
1982	5,851.57	66.02
1983	4,972.40	56.10
1984	4,612.01	52.04

Source: Departamento Intersindical de Estatística e Estudos Sócio-Econômicos (DIEESE), 1987.

just because the other firm is willing to pay them one cruzado more than I am. [12 Nov. 1987]

Paternalism was authoritarian. The directors went from being the "good papa" to being the "good boss." They began to think in terms of productivity and the important role labor played in improving production. [3 Aug. 1987]

In short, the prodemocracy industrialists endorsed democracy as a means of increasing their influence in government and reducing social inequalities. They believed that business influence would create an industrial policy capable of stimulating industrial investment, production, and profits. Economic growth also depended on expanding consumption and improving productivity, which could be achieved through a fair wage policy.

The Uncommitted.   The uncommitted industrialists endorsed, at least in their rhetoric, many of the democratic industrialists' views about democracy and economic growth. They agreed that higher wages would improve the economic health of the nation. In 1977, for example, the chairman of the National Federation of Banks, who was not associated with the prodemocracy faction within the business community, described the need for greater redistribution of wealth in this way: "The continuity of our economic success is ever more dependent upon the improvement of our political system and the establishment of just solutions to the social question. It would frustrate the nation if the community were not allowed to share the benefits of the wealth being created."[26]

These uncommitted industrialists also anticipated that their participation in economic decision making would be increased owing to the political liberalization underway during the second decade of military rule; this, they believed, would ineluctably lead to an improved economic climate. For example, in November 1977 the fourth CONCLAP convention included the following statement in its manifesto: "Decentralization of the economy is needed, to achieve not only greater efficiency, but also political pluralism, which is the best way to accommodate the natural divisions in society."[27]

Indeed, scholars contend that the desestatização campaign was an attempt by the majority of (uncommitted) industrialists to use the political liberalization to their advantage and influence economic outcomes from within the political system. A prominent Brazilian economist and businessman, Luiz Carlos Bresser Pereira, claims that the state and multinational investment strategies of the 1970s generally stimulated, rather than threatened, domestic production, since multinational and public enterprises purchased raw materials and industrial inputs from domestic firms. He therefore argues that industrialists participated in the desestatização campaign not because of immediate threats due to state and multinational control but rather, for the sake of long-term survival.[28] They launched the campaign as a threat, giving notice to the regime that unless it returned to promoting private domestic investment and allowing business to influence policies affecting the private sector, they would withdraw their support. Thus, it appears that uncommitted business leaders were generally satisfied with the pace of the transition from authoritarian rule and used the new opportunities available to them through the political liberalization to defend their investments.

The Reactionaries.   The reactionary industrialists recognized that the second decade of the military regime had brought serious economic problems for business. However, they believed that only firm, authoritarian control could guide the nation out of the economic crisis. A military crackdown that returned the hard-line faction to power would eliminate the increasing demands on the state which constrained its ability to be flexible in resolving the economic crisis. Moreover, firm control over the government would reduce the conflicts within the ruling military elite which impeded effective decision making and industrial expansion. In further contrast to the democratic and uncommitted industrialists, the reactionaries opposed income redistribution. Indeed, they blamed labor activism and other social protests for draining state resources, diverting those resources from economic growth and thereby threatening economic interests.

Labor Conflict

Overlapping business leaders' concerns about government legitimacy and economic health was the rise in social conflict, particularly labor activism. The rising number of protests against the regime, involving massive numbers of workers, undermined the regime's claim of a popular mandate. Workers acted in direct defiance of the military regime, challenging its legitimacy. Labor conflict, moreover, had a direct impact on the economy, because striking workers slowed production and demanded just wages. Business leaders were concerned about labor conflict because of its impact on political and economic stability, as well as its impact on their individual firms. Strikes threatened their ability to produce, invest, and make profits.

In 1978 labor relations in Brazil began to change. For the first time since the 1968 strikes, workers in the industrial suburbs of São Paulo seriously challenged the authoritarian regime's control over labor. They circumvented the rigid constraints the military regime had imposed on their organization, activity, and leadership, and they proved that they were willing to risk repression in order to press their demands. They led massive and illegal strikes—the first in ten years. They demanded wage increases above the government-mandated level, and called for direct negotiations with employers.

Although the labor courts declared the strikes illegal, the military regime, perhaps acting in the spirit of the political opening, did not intervene. The government's lack of response forced employers to negotiate directly with striking workers. Although employers had debated the merits of direct negotiations, this was their first opportunity to practice this new form of wage setting. Some negotiated directly with the workers in their firms, while others negotiated with representatives of the appropriate trade unions. Still others relied on employers' associations to represent their interests.[29]

Industrialists were shocked by the strikes and their aftermath. As one industrialist remarked: "At the time of the 1964 coup, I was still in college. I have only voted once for a president, and that president resigned. A strike had never occurred in my firm. Many other industrialists have had the same experiences as I. This [labor conflict] was a new situation that caught us unprepared, without experience."[30]

The outbreak of strikes, and the government's reticence to intervene, fundamentally altered capital-labor relations. It increased the power and visibility of representatives of both employers and labor.

The employers' federation, FIESP, tried to assume a leadership role in labor negotiations in the 1970s. It argued that employers' strength and skill in negotiating sessions depended on their unity. It encouraged employers to "maintain solidarity during negotiations with strikers"[31] rather than participating in independent bargaining sessions with workers in their firms. It established guidelines to assist industrialists in resisting pressure from strikers, and set up a telephone communication network to gather and disseminate information on strikes. FIESP also established permanent negotiating teams, led by labor relations experts (rather than employers), to centralize bargaining sessions. The most powerful negotiating team was the "Group of Fourteen," which negotiated on behalf of the metalworking, mechanical, and electrical firms in São Paulo.

The new labor relations also led industrialists to question the regime's control over labor representation. They realized that the regime-appointed "pelego" trade union leaders no longer led the labor movement[32] and that successful bargaining would require labor representatives who could make binding agreements on behalf of workers. Thus, by 1981 some industrialists advocated a liberalization of government controls over union leadership, including the removal of the government appointees who had replaced authentic trade union leaders because of the involvement of the latter in illegal strikes. FIESP adopted this position. It stated that it would only negotiate with the government-imposed leaders if the union membership accepted them. The president of FIESP said, "We do not want to negotiate with the government, but with workers."[33] FIESP argued that those who negotiated on behalf of employers were not only the heads of business associations but also representatives of the business community's positions, and that workers also needed their own elected representatives in negotiations. As one FIESP director stated, "Both sides have the right to choose who will speak in their name at the negotiating table."[34] One industrialist added that he would have no problem negotiating with Luís Inácio ("Lula") da Silva, the leader of the 1978 strikes in São Bernardo, not as a deposed union leader but as a representative of workers.[35]

Despite industrialists' increasing willingness to negotiate with authentic trade union leaders, most opposed worker, or shop-floor, representation within individual firms. Debate on this issue began after the 1978 strikes, when a few industrialists allowed *comissões de fábrica* (plant committees) in their factories.[36] These industrialists believed that plant committees could communicate workers' demands to the employers and thus avert future strikes. However, most employers were adamantly opposed to this reform.[37] In 1979 the Group of Fourteen refused to negotiate the issue of plant committees, which it deemed "inappropriate for the moment." When additional firms adopted plant committees in 1980 to reduce conflict, they were criticized by the heads of other firms. The president of FIESP said that plant committees would open the way to "undesirable" union delegates.[38] When the São Paulo, Osasco, and Guarulhos metalworkers' unions demanded plant committees, FIESP rejected the idea, stating that such a system required more investigation before being implemented.[39] Many industrialists were not opposed in principle to such an arrangement but felt that Brazilian workers and employers were not experienced enough to adopt it.[40] By 1981 FIESP appeared more conciliatory on this issue: it stated that it would begin suggesting to employers that they allow plant committees.[41] However, there is no evidence that FIESP actually made that suggestion. Indeed, remarkably few firms permitted shop-floor representation.

Industrialists' intransigence toward the demands of labor was also revealed by their reliance on government intervention. Despite their success in direct negotiations with labor and their rhetoric in favor of those negotiations,[42] they repeatedly relied on the military regime to protect them from labor disputes. They frequently argued that they could not negotiate wage increases as long as the government controlled prices and wages, because the regime generally forbade businesspeople to pass the cost of higher wages on to consumers via higher prices.[43] Indeed, some industrialists blamed the 1979 strikes on pressure that Minister of Planning Simonsen exerted on industrialists to harden their positions vis-à-vis the wage demands.[44] Not everyone believed this excuse, however. Trade union leader Lula charged that industrialists preferred to blame the government for difficulties in negotiations even though they had the capacity to make independent decisions.

Industrialists also refused to negotiate with striking workers once the labor courts had outlawed a strike. They argued that workers and employers alike must respect the law. For example, FIESP issued a public letter stating that the continuation of the 1978 strikes despite a labor court's declaration of illegality caused "unforeseeable consequences to national security."[45] That same year, one industrialist argued that to protect democracy the regime must uphold the law: "In the democratic regime in which we live, the first thing to be respected is the law. Once the Labor Court determined that the strike was illegal, the Executive should have enforced this decision."[46] However, no objective observer would have called the Brazilian political system of 1978 democratic. In a 1982 strike, Roberto Della Manna, the head of FIESP's industrial relations department, refused to negotiate with the striking workers. He said, "We can't set ourselves up against the Labor Court's decision" (which had declared the strike illegal).[47] By honoring the labor courts' decisions, industrialists unquestioningly accepted the legitimacy of the legislation governing—or severely limiting—strikes.

Moreover, when workers engaged in illegal strikes, industrialists generally sought protection from the military regime rather than independently negotiating a solution with workers. The National Association of Automobile Manufacturers (ANFAVEA), for example, demanded that the Ministry of Labor intervene to end the 1978 strikes because the labor courts had declared them illegal. And in 1979 the president of FIESP and individual industrialists called on the government to intervene to end the strikes declared illegal by the labor courts. In contrast to its inaction in 1978, the military regime responded with brutal force.[48] Again in 1980 the regime intervened in strikes, virtually declaring a state of siege in São Paulo and its nearby industrial suburbs.[49] Industrialists justified the regime's actions by stating that if workers disobey the law in any democracy they must suffer the consequences.[50]

Most employers also took a hard-line approach to the 1983 general strike. FIESP's president told employers that if "industries want to restore normal levels of production, they should simply call the police. In five minutes the police will have reestablished order."[51] And in response to police brutality, arrests of striking workers, the regime's intervention in unions, and the invasion and bombing of a church in São Bernardo where workers had sought refuge,[52] the president of FIESP remarked, "Government authorities showed firmness in quickly responding to our requests and in guaranteeing the right to work and protect our firms during the strike."[53]

Industrialists did not always resort to calls for government intervention, however. At times they devised their own intimidation tactics to resist direct negotiations with labor. For example, the FIESP guidelines mentioned above suggested several measures that could be used to resist employees' demands. The most widely used of these measures were layoffs and lockouts of striking workers.[54] As one industrialist threatened with the possibility of a strike stated: "We will react within our means. They, the employees, have the strike. We have our methods, such as suspension, dismissal, and . . . the lockout."[55] In 1980 FIESP took out full-page advertisements in newspapers, threatening to layoff striking workers if they did not return to work.[56] In 1984 the industrialist Antônio Ermírio de Morães told the 350 workers on strike in his firm that if the labor courts judged the strike illegal he would dismiss all of them. He said, "I accept dialogue, but I will not permit the inversion of power. After having attended to workers' demands, I can only interpret this strike as a cowardly act and a treasonous gesture. Making demands is one thing. But wanting to sit in my chair is another, and I will not accept this idea."[57] He subsequently dismissed fifty labor leaders.

Industrialists similarly retaliated against members of plant committees by dismissing them when they engaged in illegal strikes.[58] The FIESP guidelines also advocated forcing workers engaged in *braço cruzado* (folded-arm) strikes out of the firm and into public areas to facilitate security apparatus control over labor conflict.[59] There were also isolated cases of violence by reactionary employers in 1978. In one incident, an employer began to hit the striking workers in his plant with the butt of a rifle he carried with him and yelled, "Work or get out." The next day he locked the factory doors, prohibiting workers from returning to work.[60]

Despite this evidence of intransigence, the vast majority (86%) of the industrialists I interviewed stated that the strikes and negotiations that began in 1978 had brought changes in industrialists' attitudes toward labor relations (although only 42% said that their own attitudes had changed).[61] These industrialists characterized the change in attitudes as bringing a greater willingness to negotiate with workers and recognize workers' rights, communicate with workers, improve working conditions, and raise wages.

When asked to explain the change in industrialists' attitudes, most of those I spoke to stated that the business community could no longer rely on the military regime to protect them from labor conflict, and had to become more directly involved in capital-labor issues. Two presidents of medium-sized Brazilian firms described this form of change:

> From 1964 to 1978 the regime was strong. No change took place in those fourteen years. It was a dictatorship. Before 1964 also there weren't really any changes because the union was not organized. During the dictatorship, the employers just said no to every demand labor made. After the 1978 strike there was, at first, some resistance on the part of the industrialists to change, and to giving in to [labor] demands. It would be better to keep things the way they were during the fourteen years, being able to deny requests from labor. But we had no choice, we had to change. [14 Sept. 1987]

> Under the military regime, industrialists didn't have to change. The law protected them. The government repressed workers in a violent way. With the political change, the laws didn't change, but there was no longer unilateral action on the part of the government and employers. Repression was more difficult. And employers had to adapt. [24 Sept. 1987]

Not all industrialists, however, concurred that the liberalization of labor relations, the cessation of state intervention in negotiations, and authentic labor representation were changes in positive directions.

The Reactionaries. A small group of industrialists (3.9% of those I interviewed) indicated that their experience with labor conflict had made them more intransigent. As the president of a small Brazilian firm, the director of a multinational corporation's large Brazilian operation, and the director of a medium-sized Brazilian firm explained:

> In general, businessmen became more liberal. Not I: I became more conservative. As unions got more radical, so did I. [28 Apr. 1988]

> I couldn't trust workers anymore. It made me tougher. I wasn't so understanding anymore. I began to think of the worker as an enemy. [16 June 1988]

> Industrialists' attitudes changed, but for the worse. Fifteen years ago the political crisis began. There hadn't been any political mobilization before then. Relations in the firm were intimate and personal. [22 Oct. 1987]

This group of industrialists believed that their colleagues in the business community had surrendered too much to labor. As the president of a medium-sized Brazilian firm stated: "The change was that workers started winning and employers started losing. Employers became more tolerant and lost their ground" [28 Oct. 1987]. The reactionary industrialists believed that FIESP had given up too much to labor. Some believed that the labor relations specialists in charge of negotiations were more willing than owners of firms to accede to labor demands. As two industrialists, a manager of a medium-sized Brazilian company and the director of another such company, commented:

> The labor relations experts give away too much because they have learned so much about labor and labor conditions—they're too sympathetic. Industrialists want to go back to the old days, when they negotiated with labor, because the experts give up too much. [1 Oct. 1987]

> It is better to get in front to discuss things with workers instead of using intermediaries, which weaken the position of employers. [24 Sept. 1987]

Some reactionary industrialists were opposed, in principle, to unions. For example, Henry Maksoud, a self-made entrepreneur and the founder of the São Paulo planning firm Hidroservice, argued in his magazine *Visão* that unionism was intrinsically violent, threatened liberty, and would lead to totalitarianism and antidemocratic ends, just as it had brought the Communist Party to Italy, chaos to Argentina, and the threat of totalitarianism to Sweden.[62] Maksoud apparently saw no contradiction in his opposition to both totalitarianism and workers' democratic right to representation.

Other industrialists also feared the emerging labor movement. The president of a medium-sized Brazilian firm and the director of another such firm warned against negotiating with activist labor leaders, who they believed were unrepresentative subversives who were attempting to seize the labor movement and undermine the country:

> My philosophy has always been to avoid paternalism, pay well, and give workers the freedom to make their own decisions. But then, a few years ago, workers decided they didn't want to work overtime. This was crazy. Most of them did want to work overtime, but a few leaders didn't want this. So they went out on strike. I fired four hundred workers that I had spent time and money training. The church had organized the strike. The workers didn't want to join. I'm Catholic, but there are some elements in the church that are agitators. They think they are looking out for the best interest of the workers and that's why they thought the workers were working too many hours. But most of my workers are young, single men looking for a future and some money to spend. They want these extra hours. But sometimes it means working on Saturday and Sunday. The church didn't like that. [28 Oct. 1987]

> The unions were being trained by the Germans. They were trained there. Germany didn't want us to undermine German production—to compete with Germany. So they wanted a

more radical labor force here. Lula was illiterate, but the Germans trained him. Lula had more of an American attitude. He was saying, "I want what is mine." But then the Germans turned him into a socialist. [6 Oct. 1987]

The reactionary industrialists were particularly concerned about labor unrest because they believed that it threatened their economic interests and Brazil's national security. One industrialist reflected this concern when he stated, "The biggest problem with the political opening is the labor issue."[63] Thus, the reactionaries opposed changes in labor legislation (unless, of course, those changes increased controls over labor) and called for government intervention to end strikes.[64] In short, the reactionaries believed that labor conflict increased political instability, obstructed coherent economic policies, and harmed national growth. They argued in favor of hard-liners within the military taking control of the government and ending labor conflict by force.

The Democrats.   As expressed in the Documento dos Oito, democratic industrialists viewed social tensions—particularly labor-management tensions—as inextricably tied to the regime's overarching policy of political and economic exclusion. Accordingly, they believed that social and economic redistribution would ameliorate the increasing rate of poverty and social conflict in Brazil. They further contended that political opening would provide channels for the peaceful articulation of demands, thereby creating domestic stability. Thus, these industrialists blamed the military regime, and especially its wage repression and political exclusion, for heightening tensions. They believed that the outbreak of strikes in 1978 had resulted from poor wages and the unavailability of political institutions through which workers could peacefully channel their demands.

Democratic industrialists also accepted the likelihood that labor conflict would erupt under democratic leadership. As the vice-president of a very large Brazilian firm stated: "Unions and union problems are part of a democracy. We had to accept those problems" [15 Sept. 1987]. Democratic industrialists believed that demanding democracy while simultaneously restricting workers' rights and freedoms was hypocritical:

> Brazilian entrepreneurs need to stop being afraid. They are scared to death that the unions will grow strong . . . but there is no other solution. How do you expect to be heard if you don't listen?[65]

> If you speak of a government where entrepreneurs participate, you presuppose that workers also participate, and that everyone in society participates.[66]

Indeed, three democratic industrialists—the president of a medium-sized Brazilian company, the director of a very large Brazilian company, and the director of a multinational firm's very large Brazilian operation—expressed some embarrassment for having resisted changes in labor relations:

> There were new businessmen who wanted to pay decent wages, who believed in the dignity of the worker, who believed in strong unions. We knew that we had to give up a few rings to save our fingers. We wanted stability in relations, but with justice. We had convictions. [25 Nov. 1987]

> There was a strike in my firm . . . It came as a complete surprise . . . It was obvious the workers were not happy, and that surprised us. We took them to court and won. But then I began to realize that the workers were right, and the court was wrong. Things had to change in the company. I had always been a liberal, but—it pains me to admit it, even today—I hadn't put my beliefs into practice in the firm. The strike forced me to think about it. [2 Oct. 1987]

> We knew that we shouldn't be using legislation designed for fascist Italy in the 1920s. [16 Nov. 1987]

As part of their commitment to political change, democratic industrialists opposed government intervention in labor relations and supported direct negotiations with workers. However, they often viewed FIESP as intransigent in these negotiations and believed that such intransigence both impeded collective bargaining and intensified labor conflicts. They also criticized FIESP for relying on the regime to end illegal strikes. For example, while most industrialists clamored for government intervention in the 1979 strikes, some democratic industrialists issued public statements against it: "If there is an intervention [by the government] it would be profoundly lamentable for all: the government, workers, industrialists, and the future of the country."[67]

In short, the prodemocracy industrialists blamed the military regime, and its exclusionary policies, repression, and wage squeeze, for the eruption of labor conflict in the late 1970s. They also viewed democracy, increased wages, authentic representation of workers, and improved communication and negotiations with labor as the only means by which social order and stability could be restored. Thus, they advocated more democratic labor relations and opposed government intervention in labor disputes.

The Uncommitted.   The uncommitted industrialists generally applauded FIESP's efforts at uniting disparate firms and protecting them from what they considered excessive wage demands.[68] Two industrialists I interviewed, the director of a multinational corporation's very large Brazilian operation and a vice-president at a very large Brazilian company, exemplified the attitude of this faction:

Employers started negotiating in their firms. These firms started to give up a lot—make a lot of concessions to labor—too many. FIESP realized that this situation of negotiations was going to continue, and industrialists couldn't keep giving away so much. So FIESP got tough. It tried to centralize negotiations, to end firm-by-firm negotiations and put a brake on concessions. [27 July 1987]

Without the Group of Fourteen, industry would be faced with a domino effect. Unions would get something from one industry and then go on to another, and eventually win all of their demands from all of the industries, and industries would have to give in to avoid a strike. [11 Oct. 1987]

However, not all uncommitted industrialists endorsed FIESP's labor policies. Like the democrats, some in this faction negotiated independently with workers and set wages above those stipulated by FIESP. While not necessarily linking wages to democratic change, these industrialists believed that FIESP's intransigence increased labor conflict, disrupted production, and damaged industry.

FIESP reacted negatively to industrialists' efforts to independently resolve labor conflict in their firms. As the manager of a multinational corporation's large Brazilian operation stated: "We're under pressure from the FIESP Mafia to keep from paying higher wages. We do pay better wages and provide better benefits, but we don't want that to get out, because the FIESP Mafia will be after us" [15 July 1987]. When several firms (particularly those associated with ANFAVEA and the Syndicate of Automobile Manufacturers [SINFAVEA]) negotiated separate labor agreements in 1979 and 1980, FIESP attacked them for breaking the law by negotiating with illegally striking workers, and for hurting small and medium-sized companies by accepting high wage demands. Roberto Della Manna, the head of FIESP's labor relations department, labeled the companies that negotiated separate agreements "traitors," and suggested that they withdraw from the Group of Fourteen and from FIESP instead of undermining the position taken by those organizations. SINFAVEA defended its actions by arguing that the automobile companies needed to end a strike that would have continued indefinitely, seriously damaging the companies. It also argued that wealthier companies should pay higher wages than poorer companies.[69] FIESP's defense on behalf of small firms was undermined when in 1980 numerous small firms affiliated themselves with the National Association of Small and Medium-Sized Industries (ANAPEMEI) and made separate agreements with workers to avoid the prolonged strikes that they believed resulted from negotiating via the Group of Fourteen.

Despite these disagreements within FIESP, uncommitted industrialists were generally satisfied with labor relations. Partly because of their experience negotiating with workers, they did not fear that the political opening would increase labor unrest. The president of a very large metalworking company stated, "I changed in the 1970s. I was a lot more conservative in the early 70s. I changed because I was forced to look at things differently after working more closely with the working class" [1 Dec. 1987]. Industrialists whom I interviewed also mentioned that their fear of labor conflict subsided after they observed capital-labor relations in Europe, Japan, and the United States. One such industrialist, the director of a small Brazilian firm, remarked, "My own personal views changed. I used to be more on the right. But after I studied what was going on in the rest of the world—when I toured Europe, the United States, and Japan and saw that negotiations worked—I began to accept new ideas. Sitting at the negotiating table was a good experience. I learned a lot, gradually" [21 Sept. 1987].

Moreover, few industrialists blamed the transition to democracy for the outbreak of strikes. Instead, most expressed the view that strikes were an undesirable, but natural, consequence of industrial development which Brazilians, like their counterparts in older capitalist countries, had no choice but to endure. As the director of a medium-sized company and the director of a very large Brazilian firm stated:

> You can't have a modern capitalist system without having unions or social demands. You have to have conflict. It is natural. [26 Oct. 1987]

> I wasn't surprised by the labor activity [of the 1970s] because it was normal. It was following in the footsteps of labor relations in other countries that developed decades before ours. [27 Oct. 1987]

Indeed, the 1978 strikes occurred mainly in the modern industrial sectors—for instance, the multinational automobile factories and the large domestic capital-goods firms. The frequency of strikes in their firms, the size of their operations, their dependence on the scarce skilled-labor force, and their ability to absorb increased labor costs all contributed to the uncommitted industrialists' willingness to negotiate labor demands.[70] As the director of a multinational corporation's very large Brazilian operation stated: "Big changes occurred in businessmen's attitudes, but it depends on who you're talking about. The big firms went through big changes. The small and medium-sized firms went through little or no change. São Paulo experienced more change than the northeast" [1 Dec. 1987].

Finally, industrialists were often protected from the threat of labor conflict. At times, the government intervened to repress strikes. Industrialists also proved capable of adapting to changes in labor relations by using new tactics to end strike activity. While they did not necessarily advocate change, they were versatile enough to live with those changes that did occur.

Loss of Political Influence

Industrialists universally felt that they had lost political influence during the second decade of the military regime. Regardless of their opinion of Minister of the Economy Severo Gomes, his dismissal meant that they had lost a spokesperson in government. Their perception that the regime increasingly controlled the economy and favored state expansion rather than private industry further eroded their feeling of influence over government policies. Most industrialists also believed that they had lost certain specific channels of influence. For example, they felt that most of the regime's important economic decisions were made in the executive branch rather than in the ministries, and that this limited the business community's influence over, and access to, information about those decisions.[71] Business leaders retained contacts and communication with the regime, but they believed that their interests were no longer reflected in its final decisions. One businessman described this view: "I do not know of any members of the business community who, if they wished, have not had the opportunity to converse with a government authority. But at the moment a decision is made, they have not had even a small amount of influence."[72]

Industrialists generally criticized the regime for excluding them from important decisions. However, they did not react by collectively mobilizing in order to win more influence. As set forth in more detail below, business leaders' relationship to the state, and their traditional individualism and diversity, often prevented them from becoming an autonomous and unified force.

The obstacle posed by business leaders' relationship to the state is best illustrated by the desestatização campaign and by labor conflict. While the campaign sought to defend the domestic private sector against state and multinational expansion, it failed because its goals conflicted with the regime's strategies. Thus, business leaders' subordinate role in relation to the state limited their ability to influence political outcomes. In addition, their reliance on the state to intervene to end labor conflict indicates that they continued to depend on a strong authoritarian state to protect them from threats, even though they had proved capable of independently defending their own interests. In other words, many industrialists were reluctant to forego state protection.

Individualism and diversity within the business community further eroded business leaders' political influence. Their independent actions in labor relations, for example, partially undermined FIESP's effort to build a strong, unified bargaining position for employers in negotiations. The three factions within the business community—the democrats, the reactionaries, and the uncommitted—could not agree on which kind of political system would best protect their interests. Moreover, none of these three groups could win the overall support of the business community or of society. Each faction was therefore unable to effectively promote its goals for the transition.

The Democrats.   The democratic industrialists spearheaded the opposition to the military regime from within the business community and demanded a faster and more extensive political liberalization. They lent their support to a strong manifesto (the Documento dos Oito) outlining their demands for political change, economic growth and redistribution, and labor rights. The group, which included highly influential business leaders, received significant media coverage and symbolized the erosion of the regime's legitimacy. After all, industrialists were the key civilian supporters and beneficiaries of the military regime. Their mounting disaffection eliminated one of the only remaining pillars of support for the military regime within civil society.[73]

Despite their promise and their public exposure, the democratic industrialists' success was highly limited. They remained important in symbolic terms only, never becoming the foundation for a wider prodemocracy movement within the business community. Not surprisingly, they had little direct impact on the regime's policies and practices.

The prodemocracy movement within the business class was limited for a number of reasons. It was largely a media creation: according to the signers I interviewed, a journalist drafted the Documento dos Oito and secured industrialists' signatures, and the media then sponsored round-table discussions and extensively covered the attitudes, statements, and actions of these prodemocracy business leaders. In other words, the media transformed a group of important but isolated individuals into a prodemocracy "movement." These individuals did not reject their assigned role, but neither did they independently initiate it or seek to use it to build a movement. They were cautious about embarking on an aggressive opposition movement and were easily intimidated by the regime. Moreover, they lacked support from the business community at large to pursue their demands any further, and hesitated to join the broad social movements for political change.

The democratic industrialists' limited success within the business community is illustrated by their lack of influence over the FIESP presidential elections in 1980. Theobaldo deNigris had been the uncontested president of FIESP for thirteen years. He was a traditional industrialist from a small graphics company who was extremely cautious about opposing the military regime. His attitude toward democracy was contradictory. For example, in February 1977 he stated that he was in favor of a transition to democracy. In August 1977, however, he recanted and stated, "Democracy would bring too many problems"; but about ten days later he returned to his original view and said, "It would be absurd not to applaud the eventual arrival of democracy and of human rights."[74] In his 1979 Christmas speech, however, deNigris warned that industrialists should be vigilant against the subversion and chaos that would accompany democratic opening.[75] This speech was applauded by members of the business community who worried about the number of "antipatriotic" individuals in Brazil and the threat that Brazil might follow Portugal's path of transition.[76] The "prodemocracy candidate" was Luis Eulálio Bueno Vidigal Filho, the owner of a large capital-goods firm. Vidigal eventually defeated deNigris, with 56 percent of the 108 votes cast.[77]

Once in office, Vidigal played a cautious role vis-à-vis the military regime. He advocated a Geisel-style "relative democracy" and warned against "pure union freedom," stating that it was still too soon for unions to participate in politics.[78] He endorsed indirect elections, even for the governor of São Paulo in 1982. Vidigal's views of democracy contrasted sharply with the following statement, made by one of the democratic industrialists who had supported him: "We must be clear that we favor our political opening . . . the people's political opening. We are not working for the political opening thought up in Brasília behind closed doors."[79] Thus, while the democrats helped to defeat the incumbent, Vidigal represented the uncommitted industrialists more than the democratic ones, thereby limiting the influence of the latter within the business community.

Moreover, the military regime was impervious to democratic industrialists' pressure. It maintained a gradual and restricted transition despite their efforts to quicken the pace and broaden the scope of the liberalization. The specific policy changes that these industrialists advocated did not occur. There was no marked increase in real wages during the period 1974–84. As table 4.2 shows, the minimum wage, upon which official wages were based, remained well below its 1940 level throughout this period and was actually lower in 1984 than in 1974. In addition, although some industrialists directly negotiated higher wages for their workers, most negotiated via employers' associations, which limited wage increases owing to the government's controls over prices and its desire to protect those firms that could not afford such increases. Their rhetoric notwithstanding, many industrialists resisted workers' demands for higher wages, either by calling on the military regime to intervene or by using their own newly acquired skills in direct negotiations with labor.

In other words, although the democratic industrialists played an important symbolic role in the transition to democracy, they never formed an opposition movement that had any impact on government policies. Moreover, they had little influence within the business community. Indeed, most of the support for democracy within the business community developed as a result of the regime's liberalization rather than the actions and attitudes of prodemocracy industrialists. As democratic values became increasingly accepted by mainstream society (as well as among international groups and in the soft-line faction within the military), previously uncommitted industrialists began to sound like democrats. As the director of a very large metalworking firm stated, "Suddenly, after the announcement of a political opening, there were many more liberals [among the industrialists]" [29 Oct.1987]. However, rather than being transformed into democrats, most of these industrialists merely accepted the political change already under way.

The Reactionaries.   This group had the potential to form a strong business movement against the transition to democracy. It included important business leaders and received numerous signatures in its open letter against the transition, but never engaged in any subsequent activities. Indeed, the timing of the letter suggests that it was prompted by both the publication of the Documento dos Oito and the massive strikes that had erupted in São Paulo. Therefore, it is likely that these business leaders simply hoped to undermine their prodemocracy colleagues and remind the business community of what reactionary industrialists perceived as the most significant danger of political opening: labor unrest. Most industrialists, however, were not threatened by labor unrest or by the military's control over the transition from authoritarian rule.

Not only did the reactionary industrialists lack support within the business community, but there were few other social sectors that shared their goals. They could only count on the hard-line faction of the military, which had lost power within the Geisel and Figueiredo governments and had also lost the Brazilian public's respect. In contrast, the more moderate factions in the regime had initiated the gradual and restricted political opening. Moreover, a broad cross-section of domestic and international groups endorsed democratic change. The reactionaries thus lacked sufficient strength to mount a movement against the democratic transition. They became increasingly isolated within the business community and the broader civil society.

Thus, like the democratic industrialists, the reactionaries failed to promote their political demands. Instead, they, too, represented a symbolic force within the business community, becoming vocal only to defend their interests against potential changes and threats to their investments. In short, despite the appeal that a return to authoritarian rule held for many business leaders, a movement to derail the transition to democracy never evolved. Instead, the slow and gradual transition initiated by the military continued, and the reactionary industrialists became marginalized within the business community.

The Uncommitted.   The uncommitted industrialists did not advocate change; they merely accepted and adapted to the transition already under way. They used the political liberalization to their own advantage and proved quite skillful in some of their endeavors. For example, they adapted to the reduced role of the state in labor relations by increasing their bargaining and intimidation skills, while also relying on authoritarian controls and legislation. In general, however, their influence over government policies was constrained. The diversity within the group prevented them from developing a specific set of policy positions. As the desestatização campaign illustrated, the regime easily ignored their demands. They were also reluctant to abandon their reliance on the state for protections from labor. That dependence prevented them from forming an autonomous pressure group. However, because they found the means to protect their interests within the political system, they did not need to mobilize collectively against the regime.

Adaptive Industrialists in the Early Transition Period

Scholars of transitions from authoritarian rule recognize that business elites might play a delegitimizing function during the final stages of a military regime.[80] The Brazilian case may partially confirm that view. To the extent that the democratic business leaders played any role in the transition, it was a symbolic one. They were a group of industrialists who had (in some cases) supported the regime and had benefited from its policies, but who withdrew their support and began demanding democratic change. Therefore, although they lacked any direct influence over the transition, they may have helped influence public opinion against the regime.

The transitions literature also argues, however, that business elites will turn their back on the transition once they face serious problems.[81] The Brazilian case refines that assumption. During the second decade of military rule in Brazil, business leaders faced serious threats to their investments not only because of the regime's loss of legitimacy, its incompetence in managing the economy, and its threats to private sector investments, but because of labor conflict and the business community's loss of influence over policies affecting business. Despite these problems, industrialists did not universally support an authoritarian reversal. Only a small group of business leaders, the reactionaries, sought to end the transition and restore authoritarian rule. And this group lacked sufficient support within the business community and the rest of society to build such a movement.

Consistent with assumptions in the adaptive actor approach, most industrialists—the uncommitted—learned to adapt to the changes under way. They did not have the ideological convictions that defined and motivated the prodemocracy and antidemocracy factions within the business community. They also lacked the motivation to defend a continuation of authoritarian rule. After all, the military governments, like their democratic predecessors, had lost their legitimacy and stability, had failed to produce effective and predictable economic policies, were facing widespread social protests, and denied industrialists channels of influence within the government. In addition, international opinion had shifted against military rule.

Yet, despite their withdrawal of support for the regime, the uncommitted industrialists also hesitated to endorse a faster or more extensive liberalization owing to their fears of the instability and threats to their interests that such a change might engender. Instead, they favored a gradual and restricted transition controlled by the military regime. The slow pace of this transition enabled industrialists to adapt to changes by, among other things, developing their own negotiating skills and those of the employers' associations that represented them. And although the liberalization forced industrialists to face new challenges, such as renewed strike activity, the restrictions on that liberalization allowed them to retain some of the protections they had enjoyed under the military regime, such as government intervention in strikes, and the right to dismiss workers. In other words, rather than wholeheartedly endorsing or attempting to derail the transition to democracy, most industrialists merely learned to accept it and make the most of it.

Industrialists' ability to influence the scope of the transition was, however, limited. On the one hand, control over the transition remained firmly in the hands of the military regime, which often proved unresponsive to business leaders' demands. On the other hand, industrialists' efforts to promote political change (e.g., the desestatização campaign, the prodemocracy and antidemocracy movements, and the transformation of FIESP into an employers' association involved in direct labor negotiations) were hindered by a lack of internal consensus over objectives, as well as by indifference and diversity within the business community. Business leaders also had few allies in civil society or within the military upon whom they could rely for collective action against the existing political situation.

Moreover, the adaptive actor approach suggests that there was little motivation for industrialists to organize collectively. Although business leaders experienced some threats to their investments, these threats were not felt uniformly throughout the business community. Diverging political attitudes toward change, coupled with the existence of individual means to offset perceived threats to their interests, prevented the business community from mobilizing. However, industrialists' attempts to shape the evolving democracy intensified, and met with greater success, during the New Republic, the second phase of the transition.

Chapter Five

Industrialists and the New Republic

The transition from authoritarian rule moved into its second phase when the military ceded power to a civilian president, José Sarney, in 1985. Business leaders, as in the earlier democratic period, recognized that their interests were threatened by the economic crisis, political instability, radicalism on the part of labor and the left, labor conflict, and a loss of business influence. Despite these similarities, however, industrialists did not mobilize against the transitional government. They made no public pronouncements against the transition, and only two of the industrialists I interviewed claimed that the only solution to the problems they faced during the New Republic was a military coup and authoritarian control. Although anti-democratic views prevailed within the business community, especially regarding labor relations, industrialists nonetheless adapted to, attempted to influence, and even benefited from the political transition.

In this chapter, I compare industrialists' political attitudes and behavior during the New Republic with their attitudes and behavior during 1964 in order to identify the factors that shape industrialists' political attitudes. Specifically, the altered domestic and international context and the new opportunities to influence change which were available to industrialists in the 1980s reduced their fears during the New Republic government and enabled them to cooperate with, rather than undermine, the transitional government.

Threats to Industrialists during the New Republic

The level of perceived threat during the New Republic was significantly lower than under Goulart. Less than half (46%) of the industrialists I interviewed felt threatened during the New Republic, compared to 64 percent during the Goulart period. The perception of threat during the New Republic depended on industrialists' experiences, ideology, and economic opportunities. Table 5.1 illustrates that industrialists who had not supported the 1964 coup or who considered themselves centrists or leftists were less likely to feel threatened during the New Republic. In addition, a large percentage of industrialists from multinational corporations and from Brazilian firms with significant export production had no fear of the New Republic.

Table 5.1. Percentage Distribution of the Industrialists Interviewed, by Attitudes toward the New Republic, and Several Statistically Significant Variables

Characteristics of Interviewees and Their Firms	N	Attitude toward New Republic	
		Threatened (%)	Not Threatened (%)
Attitude toward 1964 coup			
Supported	82	56	44
Did not support	44	34	66
Industrialist's ideology			
Rightist	71	55	45
Centrist	36	28	72
Leftist	24	46	54
Nationality of firm			
Brazilian	95	52	48
United States	20	25	75
Other non-Brazilian	23	39	61
Extent of firm's export production			
None	35	60	40
Some	99	40	60

Note: The totals vary for each category because not all interviewees answered the entire questionnaire.

These industrialists enjoyed various production, marketing, or financing options that provided them with ample opportunities to offset the government's deleterious economic policies. In addition, their experience abroad had exposed them to labor conflict and the left, undoubtedly making them less fearful than their counterparts who had no international experience.

Nevertheless, a significant proportion of the industrialists I interviewed did feel threatened during the New Republic. While lacking a consensus as to the cause of their fears, these industrialists drew strong parallels to the Goulart period. As the director of a large textile firm stated: "I supported the '64 revolution. Why? Because the situation was exactly as it is today: corruption, demagoguery. I wish the military would come in again and end this embarrassing government. This is the worst Brazil has ever been. Workers were threatening the country with leftist ideology then, and they are now, too" [14 Dec. 1987]. Indeed, as table 5.2 illustrates, the industrialists I interviewed mentioned the same kinds of threats under President Sarney that they had mentioned under President Goulart.

Economic Crisis

As table 5.3 indicates, the Sarney government proved incompetent at resolving the economic crisis it had inherited from the military regime. Although the first two years of the New Republic brought economic growth, inflation and debt remained

Table 5. 2.   Types of Threat Perceived during the New Republic and 1964 by the Industrialists
Interviewed

Type of Threat	New Republic		1964	
	No.	%	No.	%
All types[a]	63	100	85	100
Political instability	31	49	54	64
Economic problems	16	25	18	21
Leftist subversion	15	24	51	60
Labor unrest, radicalism	13	21	20	23
Other	7	11	4	5
Do not know	1	2	0	0

Note: The totals add up to more than 63 and 85, and the percentages add up to more than 100%, because
interviewees provided multiple responses.
[a]Fifty-four percent of the 137 respondents to the question of threat in the New Republic, and 36% of the
133 respondents to the question of threat in 1964, reported that they perceived no threat.

Table 5. 3.   Brazil's Economic Indicators, 1985–89

Year	Inflation (%)	Change in GDP (%)	Current Accounts ($ millions)	Change in Industrial GDP (%)
1985	226.9	8.3	−0.273	8.9
1986	145.2	7.6	−4.477	11.2
1987	229.7	3.6	−1.275	0.6
1988	682.3	−0.3	—	—
1989	1287.0	—	—	—

Sources: International Financial Statistics, 1985–89 (Washington, D.C.: International Monetary
Fund, 1986–90); and *Anuario estadístico de América Latina y el Caribe* (Santiago, Chile: United
Nations Economic Commission for Latin America and the Caribbean, 1985–89).

high. Moreover, after the initial years the economy began to decline. Industry was
hit particularly hard, and reacted by blaming the government. One FIESP director
stated that Sarney had failed to guarantee the minimum needs of industry: a little
profit, a market, affordable credit, stable rules, and solid institutions.[1] In particular,
industrialists attacked the government for its unpredictable economic policies, its
price and wage controls, and its unsuccessful efforts at social pact negotiations.

Unpredictable Economic Policies.   Economic policy was highly volatile during
the New Republic. In his five years in office, Sarney appointed four different

finance ministers (Francisco Dornelles in 1985, Dilson Funaro in 1985, Luiz Carlos Bresser Pereira in 1987, and Mailson Ferreira da Nóbrega in 1987), who issued five different economic programs (the first Cruzado Plan in 1986, the second Cruzado Plan in 1986, the Bresser Plan in 1987, the Social Pact in 1988, and the Summer Plan in 1989) as well as numerous modifications of those programs. These ever-changing economic programs not only failed to resolve the economic crisis but made it more unpredictable. For example, the Brazilian currency was changed twice (from the cruzeiro to the cruzado in 1986, and from the cruzado to the novo cruzado in 1989), and price and wage controls were periodically implemented and repealed. Moreover, the government did not warn industrialists of anticipated policy changes in advance, and even when it made assurances to business, it ignored those assurances when they proved inconvenient.[2] In short, industrialists could not predict with any certainty the short-term or long-term economic future of the country. The following statements from industrialists illustrate this point:

> Private initiative needs a clear signal from the government regarding the paths that it will take, so that it knows where to put risk capital . . . If we're going to run the risk of making long-term investments, we need the certainty that the rules are not going to change in the middle of the game.[3]

> The most terrible thing in the world for businesspeople is uncertainty. We businesspeople live with risk, and we know how to manage it. But this history of freezing prices for nine months, unfreezing, refreezing, now regulating, deregulating tomorrow, indexes, disindexation . . . This constitutes an intolerable level of uncertainty, which prevents us from investing and planning our future. I repeat: any rule is better than no rule at all.[4]

Mario Amato, the president of FIESP, exaggerated industrialists' desperate need for economic predictability (as well as the ideological indifference in the business community) when he claimed that, as far as the business community was concerned, the government "could be socialist, or even communist. The important thing is that there are rules that the business community can count on."[5]

In response to the unpredictability of economic policies, industrialists demanded participation in, influence over, and information about economic decisions. They sought an end to the government's practice of developing policies in the isolated national capital, or, as one industrialist called it, the "Brasília laboratory."[6] Nevertheless, industrialists had more influence over these economic policies than other social groups did. For example, two of the four finance ministers (Funaro and Bresser Pereira) were Paulista business leaders. In addition, Sarney personally attended meetings with industrialists and even occasionally solicited their opinions with regard to economic policies.[7] Furthermore, the government modified its economic policies in order to prevent a collapse of the Brazilian private enterprise system.[8] In sum, Sarney, unlike Goulart, proved responsive to business leaders' economic demands and defended private property rights, thus reducing the threats that the economic decline might otherwise have posed to industrialists.

Price and Wage Controls.   Industrialists argued that the price and wage controls implemented by the New Republic government in order to contain inflation hindered their ability to produce, invest, and make profits. For example, when the government froze retail prices, it did not always control the prices for industrial inputs. Thus the cost of producing a given item sometimes exceeded its government-mandated retail price.

Businesses used various strategies to protect themselves from profit losses due to price controls. Some reduced the contents of their packages without reducing prices, thus defrauding consumers.[9] Others simply ignored the price controls and charged exorbitant black market prices.[10] Still others withheld their products from the market, thus causing product shortages (primarily in meat, dairy, and soybean products), until the government allowed them to raise their prices.

Not only did individual firms adopt diverse strategies but business associations repeatedly demanded that the government withdraw the price controls. For example, on two separate occasions FIESP president Mario Amato threatened to organize business groups to carry out civil disobedience unless the government realigned prices.[11] This threat was never carried out, even though the government did not repeal the price controls.

Business leaders also opposed the recessionary effects of wage controls, which suggests a victory for the democratic forces within the business community. After an initial consumer boom under the first Cruzado Plan, workers suffered serious wage losses that industrialists believed reduced consumer demand and, therefore, industrial sales and profits. At that point, the real minimum wage had reached a level comparable to that seen during the 1950s. Nearly all (81%) of the industrialists I interviewed considered the minimum wage in 1987–88 to be insufficient. The following quotations, the first two from published sources, and the last from my interview with the director of a medium-sized metalworking company, illustrate this concern:

> We cannot live in a country of 130 million people, 82 percent of whom do not consume. This might seem like a PMDB or PT discourse, but I am a businessman, concerned with the internal market.[12]

> If we want to produce cheaply via low wages, we are eliminating any possibility of forming a more powerful internal market . . . We have to pay adequate wages for self-interested motives, to bring about a strong internal market.[13]

In 1987, wage increases were below inflation. There were no jobs. There was a drop in consumer power. And a fall in the internal market. The president forgot the internal market. He squeezed wages to pay the international debt. Workers are starving to death. [8 Oct. 1987]

Industrialists responded to the wage controls in various ways. For example, most paid wages that were above the minimum level:[14] only 3 percent of the industrialists I interviewed paid their lowest-paid skilled workers the minimum wage, 70 percent paid 2 to 4 times the minimum wage, and 8 percent paid 5 to 7 times the minimum wage.[15] Yet, even though most paid their employees above the minimum wage, 47 percent still considered their base wages too low,[16] although they did not necessarily plan on raising them.

Although most of the industrialists I interviewed endorsed a national minimum wage,[17] they questioned the government's exclusive control over the setting of that wage: only 38 percent believed that the government should set the wage, while 24 percent believed that representatives of labor and business should work together with the government to set the minimum wage, and 27 percent believed that business and labor should set the minimum wage without the government's interference.[18] In other words, 51 percent wanted business to participate in wage setting and did not feel that the government should set wages unilaterally.[19]

Industrialists also opposed government involvement in setting wages above the minimum level. Of the industrialists I interviewed, 82 percent believed that the market should determine such wages, while 17 percent supported the government's role in setting wages.[20] Moreover, industrialists often rejected government limitations on wage increases and granted increases above the stipulated level. For example, when Finance Minister Bresser Pereira recommended in 1987 that employers offer no more than a 10-percent increase in wages, at first individual firms, and then FIESP as a whole, rejected his proposal and granted 46-percent increases.[21] Some petitioned the government for more flexibility in wage setting. After the Bresser Plan was implemented, for example, FIESP predicted that average real wages would fall by about 10 percent, and recommended that the government allow a wage bonus to reduce the impact of wage losses on industrial production.[22] Some called on the government to allow the market to determine wages and prices. Finally, some industrialists threatened to join workers in their general strike against the wage controls of the Bresser Plan.[23]

Social Pact.   Throughout the New Republic period a social pact, in which business, labor, and the government would accept certain sacrifices for economic recovery, was identified as a solution to the nation's economic problems. Industrialists' views of such a pact were ambiguous. In 1985 one analyst reported that members of the business community were "clearly against the pact, mainly because it would impose restrictions on them (benefits for workers) currently not in force."[24] Yet, by 1986 several business leaders favored a pact as the only way to resolve Brazil's problems. As one industrialist noted, "members of the business community have a clear idea that renewed economic growth cannot occur alongside social regression."[25] By 1987 business, labor, and government seemed to have established enough common interests to allow for their involment in democratic decision making. However, the discussions on the establishment of a social pact broke down long before their projected completion in March 1987. Both labor and business groups blamed the government for the pact's failure. The socialist labor federation, the Central Workers' Organization (CUT), asserted that the government had failed to make concrete proposals on debt repayment and economic policy, or to address the demands of labor. Business groups withdrew from the pact when the government raised the prices of electrical goods and services without a corresponding wage increase.

Again, in November 1988, government, business, and labor failed to carry to completion a sixty-day economic pact. Both employers and workers accepted sacrifices: the pact limited wage increases to 21 percent during the first thirty days and 26 percent during the second thirty days; and price increases were limited to 27 percent and 25 percent, respectively. Yet, despite these sacrifices, inflation continued to increase. When inflation eventually climbed to 40 percent, the pact broke down. Labor and business groups again blamed the government. They attributed the excessive inflation to the government's failure to reduce public expenditures.

A majority (85%) of the industrialists I interviewed believed that it was impossible to form a social pact in Brazil. Only a minority (15%) believed that it was both possible and necessary.[26] Industrialists were divided on what they believed prevented a pact from evolving. Some (38%) of those I interviewed blamed all three parties (business, labor, and the government), claiming that the interests they represented were too diverse to create a consensus. In addition, these industrialists argued that Brazil lacked a "culture" of trust and compromise, and that this lack prevented a negotiated pact from evolving. According to this argument, pact formation was undermined because none of the social groups involved trusted the others to abide by their promises. These industrialists also contended that the various groups made unrealistic demands. Finally, they attributed the failure to form a pact to problems of representation and leadership in the groups: that is, because the constituents of these groups did not trust any leader to fairly represent their interests, the leadership could not guarantee compliance from the rank and file.

However, a significant proportion (32%) of the industrialists I interviewed believed that the government alone was responsible for the failure to form a pact. They argued that the regime had no interest in carrying out a pact, lacked the requisite competence, and failed to formulate any proposals or alternatives. Others maintained that, rather than acting as an equal partner, the government tried to dominate the pact discussions. The government's role as arbiter was compromised by its status as one of the largest employers in the country, as well as by disagreements among the ministers of finance, planning, and labor over key issues in the social pact discussions.

In sum, it appears that, as in 1964, nearly all industrialists were dissatisfied with the "democratic" government's ability to resolve the economic crisis. However, the vast majority (79%) of those I interviewed did not consider the crisis, or the government's inability to resolve it, a threat.[27] Their reduced fears no doubt resulted from their perception that the government was responsive to business leaders' needs and guaranteed the right to private property.

That perception also led business associations to endorse the government's economic policies, often in defiance of their members' opinions. In October 1987, for example, during the height of industrialists' vehement protests against the Bresser Plan, FIESP publicly declared support for President Sarney. A FIESP director defended this position, stating, "The president of the Republic needs respect to begin to take charge of the political structure in the country and to establish economic rules that restore confidence and stimulate investment."[28] FIESP thus proved inconsistent in its response to the government's economic program. By vacillating, it failed to mount a strong opposition to that program. Many of FIESP's members accused the association of taking an accommodationist position toward the government (perhaps to encourage personal favors) rather than defending industrialists' interests and articulating their demands.

Thus, Brazilian industrialists' dissatisfaction with the economy, like that of their counterparts in advanced industrial and democratic countries, does not normally lead them to endorse a regime change. Instead, industrialists use their considerable political resources to influence economic policy from within the existing political framework. Industrialists' significant economic power in society and their social ties to key economic decision makers enabled them to exert influence over the Sarney government. Yet, while the government modified some of its policies to protect businesses from failure, it failed to make its policies any more predictable or to repeal price and wage controls, and it did not grant business groups any formal access to, information about, or participation in policy making.

Industrialists' efforts to influence economic policy were constrained by the individuality and diversity within the business community, and by that community's dependence on the government. Because not all business leaders agreed that Sarney's economic policies threatened the private sector, the business community did not collectively protest those policies. Instead, industrialists used individual strategies (e.g., defrauding customers or ignoring price controls) to overcome the adverse impacts of the policies on their own firms. In addition, business associations—more specifically, FIESP—hesitated to confront the government, because they believed that they would gain as much from cooperation as from confrontation. FIESP's inconsistent response to the government's economic policies undermined individual industrialists' efforts to change those policies. Finally, the Sarney government only granted business leaders' demands when it considered them to be consistent with its perception of the national interest.

Because of their limited influence over the Sarney government, and because of that government's deleterious economic policies, most industrialists looked forward to presidential elections to remove Sarney from office. For example, according to an article in a FIESP publication of 1988, "The dark clouds accumulating on the horizon at the turn of the year will only be dissipated with an authentic and democratic government. A weak government without credibility . . . will not be able to do anything to change the economic picture for this year, i.e., recession, inflation, unemployment."[29]

Political Instability

By 1987, industrialists generally viewed the Sarney government as lacking legitimacy, and therefore inherently unstable. Nevertheless, the number of industrialists who felt threatened by political instability at this time did not reach the 1964 level: 49 percent of those I interviewed feared political instability during the New Republic, compared to 64 percent in 1964.[30]

Several industrialists, however, drew parallels between the Goulart and Sarney governments with respect to political instability. According to one of them, the president of a very large Brazilian company: "the same kind of [political] vacuum that existed with the death of Tancredo occurred in the 1960s when Jânio resigned. It left a feeling of emptiness and brought in an incompetent government" [2 Oct. 1987]. Industrialists described the two governments as having three main characteristics in common: a lack of popular support for the president; corruption and favoritism; and uncertain political rules and procedures.

Most industrialists believed that Goulart and Sarney both lacked strong popular support. Both were former vice-presidents who had alienated those sectors of the population which had supported the presidents they replaced: the right distrusted Goulart's leftist tendencies, and the movement that opposed the military regime distrusted Sarney's former alliance with the military party. Moreover, because of their ineffective policies, both presidents had failed to build their own base of support within the population.

Industrialists identified another weakness in the Sarney government which eroded Sarney's legitimacy: his incapacity to deal with the economy had heightened social unrest and prevented him from maintaining authority and political stability in the country. The following excerpts from interviews with industrialists, two presidents of medium-sized Brazilian firms and the director of a small Brazilian firm, illustrate these concerns:

> I am afraid of radicalization due to the miserable conditions Brazilians live in. It is a pressure cooker. [5 Nov. 1987]

> The biggest threat in Brazil is hunger and unemployment. [27 Apr. 1988]

> There is no threat from the left today. There is the threat of social injustice. Brazil does not provide the basic conditions for survival, and this threatens stability. [16 May 1988]

One industrialist whom I interviewed stated that poverty in Brazil had engendered a period of cyclical crises, marked by protests and coups, which would destroy long-term political stability. Another, the president of a medium-sized Brazilian company, agreed that increased poverty would create social unrest, which would inevitably lead to a military coup. He said, "Today I don't think that a leftist threat to stability is inevitable, but I think there will be a social convulsion. I think that injustice and poor distribution will lead to total social upheaval and then to a military coup" [25 Nov. 1987].

Industrialists further accused both the Goulart and Sarney governments of corruption, of using rewards to buy political support from powerful individuals or groups so as to extend their own terms in office.[31] Sarney had originally agreed to a four-year term. However, when the Constituent Assembly, the legislative body assigned the task of writing a new constitution, debated the length of the presidential term (1986–88), Sarney lobbied hard and allegedly used bribes to extend his term to five years. Many industrialists were highly critical of Sarney's lobbying efforts. They considered these acts corrupt, indicative of Sarney's lust for power, and unbefitting a president. Most industrialists (and people in other social sectors) were so dissatisfied with Sarney that they opposed an extension of his term. In a 1988 poll of 103 business leaders, an overwhelming majority (86%) called for elections in 1988, at the end of Sarney's four-year term. A majority of FIESP's directors also advocated a four-year term. One, who labeled the Sarney administration "a weak government—a president who doesn't govern," even demanded Sarney's immediate resignation in 1987.[32] Even within the conservative CNI, 75 percent of the federations endorsed the holding of presidential elections in 1988.[33]

Finally, most industrialists believed that both the Goulart and Sarney governments consistently changed political rules and procedures, thereby increasing industrialists' sense of insecurity. However, the contexts were very different: whereas Goulart had independently challenged the existing rules and procedures, during the New Republic a Congress cum Constituent Assembly was elected (in November 1986) to redefine them. However, the constitution which that body formulated was not ratified until October 1988. Thus, while the authoritarian rules lacked legitimacy owing to the transition to democracy, they remained in place for most of the New Republic. In other words, for well over half of its five-year term the Sarney government had few legitimate and clearly defined rules or procedures. This increased industrialists' sense of political instability. The head of a state-owned enterprise succinctly summarized this fear of undefined political rules and procedures: "Currently there is political anarchy. There is a dispute over leadership. Congress is filled with out-of-date politicians who profess populism and think social programs don't cost anything. Subversion exists. It will always exist. But institutions have to exist so that majority rule is always respected. That way there can't be subversion by a minority" [9 Dec. 1987].

Despite parallels with 1964, however, few industrialists advocated a change of regime as a solution to the government's incompetence, corruption, unpredictable rules and policies, and lack of support. The significant difference between the two periods is industrialists' perception of options within the political system. During the New Republic, industrialists generally believed that they would be able to replace Sarney in elections, even if a year later than anticipated. They did not think that Sarney would attempt to remain in political office indefinitely, as they had believed that Goulart would do.

Radicalism on the Part of the Left and Labor

Brazilian industrialists' fear of the left seems to have been greatly exaggerated. Only 24 percent of the industrialists I interviewed felt threatened by leftist subversion during the New Republic. Moreover, 55 percent of the industrialists I interviewed did not feel threatened by the left either in 1964 or during the New Republic. Most industrialists argued that the left had never appealed to Brazilians. According to the director of a large metalworking firm and the director of a small metalworking firm:

> Brazilians don't have a revolutionary spirit. They are peaceful. They like fun, happiness, peace, and they don't like political agitation. [25 Nov. 1987]

> The Latin people are not conflict-oriented. They like to have fun. Communism would be really hard to implant here because it is not happy, it is tough. [29 Sept. 1987]

In addition, whereas considerable fear of the left had existed in 1964, it had greatly diminished by the time of the New Republic. Of the industrialists I interviewed who had supported the 1964 coup, 60 percent stated that they had done so because of fear of the left. However, 36 percent who had feared the left in 1964 no longer feared it during the New Republic.[34]

Domestic and international factors explain the reduced fear of the left. Cold War rhetoric and ideology, rampant in the 1960s, waned with détente. In addition, leftist governments were elected to office in Western Europe without undermining the capitalist order. Perestroika, glasnost, and the Solidarity movement further indicated that the left did not necessarily threaten capitalist development. Several industrialists mentioned that their perceptions of the left had changed along with these international trends.

On the domestic front, Brazilian industrialists pointed to two important lessons that industrialists had learned from the military coup and the military regime. The first lesson was that the military would intervene if the left threatened national security. This was a comfort to industrialists. As the director of a small metalworking company stated: "There is still leftist subversion, but I believe that this won't bring about destabilization because the armed forces will move in before that happens. I trust the armed forces. They are not corrupt. They act at the right moment. There is no other way out" [11 May 1988]. The second lesson was that the left, because of its experience under the military regime, had learned that its survival depended on modifying its radical positions. Therefore, these industrialists argued, the left had abandoned its revolutionary ideals and adopted moderate positions, and was working for change within the existing political framework. As a result, most of the industrialists I interviewed did not fear the left in Brazil during the New Republic, because they considered it moderately progressive, rather than radical.

Indeed, some industrialists had even supported the left in elections. This is not entirely surprising, given that a significant minority (18%) of the industrialists I interviewed considered themselves to be on the left.[35] Fernando Henrique Cardoso of the center-left political party PMDB—whom many business leaders considered a dangerous leftist—received votes from some industrialists in the 1985 São Paulo mayoral elections.[36] Some industrialists also voted for the socialist Workers' Party (PT), formed in 1979, in various elections.[37]

Indeed, evidence suggests that industrialists did not view Brazilian society as ideologically polarized. They tended to view political groups and leaders as moderates rather than placing them on the extreme right or the extreme left. On average, when asked to rate key Brazilian political actors who represented the political left and right according to a 10-point ideological scale, the industrialists I interviewed identified those actors as moderates rather than extremists.[38] The only exception was the PT and its allied labor federation, CUT, which industrialists considered to be on the extreme left.

The minority of the industrialists I interviewed who feared the left during the New Republic stated that the left was capable of subverting political stability.[39] Yet, when asked to provide examples of such subversion, they cited situations in which the left had actually attempted to become institutionalized in Brazil and work within the political system rather than destabilize it. For example, they condemned the political amnesty that had allowed many of the 1960s politicians and parties of the left—in particular, the two communist parties (the PCB and the PCdoB), and Leonel Brizola (who had formed the Democratic Labor Party [PDT])—to return to Brazil, reorganize, and win important elections on both the local and the national level. They also feared the new left, and in particular the PT and CUT. In addition, these industrialists were concerned about the growing power of leftist intellectuals and the Catholic church, both of which they believed were radicalizing society. The following excerpts from my interviews—with the director of a medium-sized Brazilian firm and with Paulo Ayres Filho—illustrate these fears:

> Today there is a threat from the Moscow-led politicians such as Brizola and the CUT leaders. They are trying to destabilize Brazil. [6 Oct. 1987]

> Today is just like 1963. Brizola and Goulart were only different in that they had the courage to stand up and say what they thought. Today the communists have learned. They hide. It makes it hard to fight against them. But they're all from the same class. They are rich kids fighting to get votes from the left. The Constituent Assembly is filled with leftists who know nothing about the economy and are threatening the nation. [22 Oct. 1987]

One might expect even those industrialists who are tolerant of the left in general to be highly sensitive to labor radicalism, since it might affect their day-to-day operations. However, of those who felt threatened during the New Republic, only 21 percent mentioned labor as a source of their fears, and this group comprised only 9 percent of the industrialists I interviewed. The differences of opinion among industrialists with regard to the threat from labor broke down according to the sectors they represented. Those industrialists from family-owned or individually owned firms in traditional areas of manufacturing (e.g., wood products, paper, leather, furs, textiles, clothing, food, beverages, glass, and ceramics) tended to fear labor, while those from modern enterprises did not. The former were undoubtedly more sensitive to labor threats owing to their lack of domestic or international experience with labor conflict; their relative dependence on labor; and their greater emotional sensitivity, resulting from their perception of their workers as family (although they do not often treat them as family) and from their sense of betrayal when those workers confront management. In general, however, Brazilian industrialists during the New Republic categorized workers either as radical and threatening; as moderate, with radical and threatening leaders; or as radical and nonthreatening.

Radical, Threatening Workers.   The manager of a Brazilian company described Brazilian workers as "anarchists who rob stores" [18 Aug. 1987]. He went on to add that their strikes destroy the national economy, the firms at which they work, and the labor movement itself (the latter because disruptions in production reduce investments and jobs). Another industrialist, the director of a large textile firm, stated, "Workers were threatening the country with leftist ideology [in 1964], and they are now, too" [14 Dec. 1987]. These industrialists viewed the increased capital-labor conflict, the legalization of left-wing political parties and labor unions, and the relaxation of controls over the selection of labor leaders as exposing the nation to leftist subversion, which would undermine political, economic, and social stability.

Judging from industrialists' evaluation of the ideology of the workers in their firms, only a minority of industrialists shared the view that workers are radicals. As table 5.4 indicates, most of the industrialists whom I interviewed classified the workers in their firm as moderately left-wing or as centrist; and a significant number even put workers on the right. Only three placed the workers in their firms on the extreme left.[40]

Although most did not place workers on the extreme left, they generally considered them to be further to the left than they themselves were. On average, the industrialists I interviewed placed themselves at position 6 (just right of center) and workers at 5 (center); and 58 percent placed the workers in their firms to the left of where they placed themselves on the ideological scale. The latter group were primarily characterized by their heightened sensitivity to the left: they identified themselves with the right and had been in business in 1964.[41] Nonetheless, industrialists' perceptions of workers' ideology was not statistically significant in determining whether or not they feared labor during the New Republic.

Moderate Workers with Radical, Threatening Leadership.   While most of the industrialists I interviewed agreed that the rank and file were not radical, some believed that political parties (particularly the PT), the church, labor federations (particularly CUT), and trade union leaders incited workers, often through intimidation, to engage in radical activities. The following excerpts, the first from a published interview, and the second from my interview with the director of a very large Brazilian metalworking firm, illustrate this sentiment:

> Some strikes in the industrial sector are being provoked by the Workers' Party (PT) with the assistance of the church. . . . The PT's action is becoming more effective given the lethargy that has overcome the other parties with respect to their activities in the union area.[42]

> CUT and the PT are trying to destabilize the economic situation. They want a country run by workers . . . [They want] to be owners of production and politics. [20 Nov. 1987]

The industrialists who considered workers as moderate, but working-class leaders as radical and threatening called the union leadership "artificial." They stated

Table 5.4. Ideological Ratings Chosen by the
Industrialists Interviewed for Workers in Their Firms

Rating	Interviewees Choosing Rating	
	No.	%
Extreme left	4	3
Moderate left	37	29
Center	59	46
Moderate right	25	20
Extreme right	3	2
Total	128	100

Note: The average rating selected by the interviewees
was 5.

that union leaders only used the workers for their own personal or ideological gain and did not represent the workers' interests.[43] The director of a multinational corporation's large Brazilian operation stated [11 Aug. 1987] that labor leaders use the trade union as a "trampoline" to political office. And the president of a very large Brazilian firm said, "Union leaders are demagogues. They do not care about the workers; they only care about getting reelected . . . [The labor federations] are immature, and they lack interest in their workers. They are playing politics for their own power. And they play on the workers' fatalism" [23 Sept. 1987].

Indeed, industrialists generally viewed labor confederations as being on the extreme left. While only 3 percent of those I interviewed placed workers in their firms on the extreme left, 77 percent placed CUT and the PT on the extreme left, and 23 percent placed the more conservative CGT in that position.[44]

In addition, industrialists generally considered labor confederations to be to the left of the workers in their firms. As noted above, on average the industrialists I interviewed placed the workers in their firms at position 5 (center) on the ideological scale. However, they placed CUT and the PT at position 2 (extreme left) and the CGT at 3.5 (moderate left). In addition, 92 percent placed CUT and the PT to the left of the workers in their firms, 7 percent placed them at the same position on the ideological scale, and 1 percent put them to the right. Fifty-five percent put the CGT further to the left than they put the workers in their firms, compared to 35 percent who put workers and the CGT at the same position, and 10 percent who put the CGT to the right of workers in their firm.

Industrialists' fear of partisanship in the trade union movement also fed their fears of radicalism. While most of the industrialists I interviewed accepted the concept of multisector trade unions, more than half (54%) stated that partisanship prevented these federations from fulfilling their potential.[45] Moreover, 39 percent said that they could not accept ties between political parties and trade unions, while 41 percent said that they preferred that such ties not exist but believed they were inevitable, and 20 percent said that they accepted those ties. Industrialists' concern over partisanship reflects the strongly corporatist ideology, present in Brazil since the 1930s, that denies class struggle and champions the notion of common national interests.

Despite industrialists' perception of partisanship and extremism in CUT and the CGT, there was no statistically significant relationship between industrialists' fear of labor during the New Republic and their perceptions of labor confederations' ideology. In other words, industrialists were not, in general, threatened by the leftist tendencies in the trade union federations.

Nonthreatening Workers and Trade Union Leaders.   Most (91%) of the industrialists I interviewed did not fear workers or the labor movement during the New Republic. Table 5.4 demonstrates that only 32 percent considered workers in their firms to be on the left, while 68 percent saw them as being in the center or on the right. In addition, a comparison of industrialists' evaluation of their own ideology to their evaluation of the ideology of the workers in their firms illustrates that many industrialists—including the self-proclaimed right wing of the business community—classified the ideology of the workers in their firms in the same way that they classified their own: 21 percent of those who considered themselves to be on the right also placed workers on the right; 41 percent of those who placed themselves in the center also placed the workers in their firms in the center; and 42 percent of those who classified themselves as being on the left also placed workers on the left. In all, 31 percent of the industrialists I interviewed placed the workers in their firms at the same position on the ideological scale that they had put themselves. Some (11%) even viewed workers as more politically conservative than themselves. These industrialists obviously included those who identified with the left: 38 percent of those who placed themselves on the left considered workers to be to their right, compared to 13 percent of those who put themselves in the center, and 2 percent of those who put themselves on the right. They also tended to be individuals who had become industrialists after the 1964 coup; they comprised 18 percent of that group, whereas they comprised only 7 percent of those who had become industrialists before 1964.[46]

In short, the data suggest that most industrialists did not view labor as either radical or threatening. This perception was based on their interpretation of Brazilian workers' character, needs, and desires. For example, some industrialists believed that workers shared their capitalist goals and aspirations. The director of a very large chemical company stated, "I don't think that workers are revolutionary; I think they are conservative and capitalist" [23 Nov. 1987]. The following excerpts from my interviews—with the director of a small Brazilian firm, the president of a very large Brazilian firm, and the director of a multinational corporation's very large Brazilian operation—further illustrate this perspective:

> A threat from workers is unlikely because they admire people with money. They dream of someday having it, even though it wouldn't be easy for them to get it—so many barriers exist. They think things will change, not because they are working toward it but because they might land something someday. They are not fatalistic; they are dreamers. [29 Sept. 1987]

> Brazilian workers are courteous, not conflictual. They avoid conflict. They don't have any ideology. They all have petty bourgeois aspirations to have a little house, security. They do not think of class struggle. They think of someday being in a better situation. [14 Oct. 1987]

> The Brazilian people are calm, not reactionary. They adore the [political] center. They have free enterprise ideas in their blood. Everyone from the workers to the students (once they've graduated) wants to own their own little firm. [20 Nov. 1987]

Some industrialists also argued that labor's leadership was not as radical as conservative industrialists claimed. For instance, the manager of a multinational corporation's very large Brazilian operation asserted, "Workers are not radical today. There are no extremes, no exaggerated behavior. Even CUT is trying to find a way to dialogue. There is no threat" [2 June 1988].

A second perspective among industrialists was that Brazilian workers were pragmatic—too concerned with their immediate needs to become involved in radical political movements. As the director of a very large metalworking company stated: "When things get bad, the workers will only demand their basic survival needs . . . There is no risk of revolution" [1 Oct. 1987].

A third perspective among industrialists was that Brazilian workers were passive, and therefore unlikely to engage in revolutionary activities. According to the president of a multinational corporation's large Brazilian operation, "There is no threat from the workers. Thank God, since the wage differential could make things difficult in Brazil. I'm surprised that it doesn't happen and it is only due to the peaceful nature of the workers" [6 Oct. 1987].

On the other hand, there are some industrialists who considered both the labor movement and individual workers radical but still did not feel threatened by them. These industrialists viewed the Brazilian labor movement as fragmented, marginalized, and disorganized, and therefore incapable of posing a threat to industrialists. As the director of a small metalworking firm stated: "Workers are not a threat because they have no force. They are not supported by the people. They have no way of mobilizing" [27 Oct. 1987]. Another industrialist, the director of a large rubber company, stated [11 Aug. 1987] that workers could threaten the country if they were united and supported the PT, but that the opposite situation existed. The following quotations, from the director of a very large metalworking company and the director of a rubber firm, also reflect this view:

> Workers today are conservative. They don't think about revolution. They rarely try to destroy property. They are the first to defend property. The PT and CUT are radical. They are profoundly radical. But the PT doesn't represent the workers. It represents the intellectuals. CUT is interested in radical change, but it lacks support among workers. [1 Dec. 1987]

> The PT, the PCdoB, and the progressive church accelerated the radicalization of the unions . . . But the PT and the PCdoB did not win votes from the workers. They won just a minority of votes from them. They are supported by a left minority. [5, 24 Nov. 1987]

In addition, some industrialists felt that the labor movement, whether radical or not, contributed to political stability because it represented the interests of an important social sector. They also believed that it ensured a degree of economic stability, because its demands for greater income redistribution would increase the buying power of consumers.

These different perspectives within the industrial community were influenced by several changes in labor relations during the New Republic. For example, the perception of workers as capitalist or pragmatic was probably influenced by a new strain of unionism that evolved during the New Republic: *sindicato de resultados* (goal-oriented unionism). Luiz Antonio Medeiros (president of the São Paulo Metalworkers' Union) and A. Rogério Magri (president of the São Paulo Union of Electrical Energy Workers) had adopted this new approach. They discouraged the involvement of trade unions and union leaders in national lobbies, campaigns, strikes, and protests, and instead advocated negotiation and bargaining as the most effective ways to achieve workers' goals. Many industrialists, such as the director of a small metalworking company and the president of a multinational corporation's very large Brazilian operation whom I interviewed [29 Sept. 1987; 16 Nov. 1987], believed that Medeiros and Magri represented the true conservative interests of the Brazilian working class. They demonstrated this viewpoint in their placement of Medeiros and the workers in their firms on the ideological scale. Most considered both Medeiros and the workers in their firm to be centrists. Moreover, a large percentage (48%) placed the workers and Medeiros at the same position, while 29 percent placed Medeiros to the left of the workers in their firms, and 22 percent placed him to the right of the workers. The industrialists who considered Medeiros to be on the left no doubt distrusted his past association with the PCB and his experience working in factories in the Soviet Union and Eastern Europe during the military regime. They believed that Medeiros was using pragmatic rhetoric to win power but would radicalize the labor movement once he achieved that power.[47]

The belief that workers were passive, or that the labor movement was too weak to threaten industrialists, was probably influenced by workers' tepid support for the general strikes the leadership called during the New Republic. On 20 August 1987 the labor federations called a general strike to demand real wage increases, agrarian reform, the inclusion of workers' rights in the 1988 Constitution, and a debt moratorium. A poll conducted by the *Folha de São Paulo* showed that although 87 percent of the population considered the workers' demands just, only 39 percent would honor the strike. Indeed, rank-and-file support was low. Even in the "militant" industrial suburbs of São Paulo, participation only reached about 20 percent. FIESP reported that workers' rate of absenteism, normally 3 percent, reached only 5 percent on the day of the strike. The strike was only "general" in five small capitals and a few small cities.[48]

Finally, the perspective that the labor movement contributed to, rather than threatened, political stability was probably influenced by the participation of the labor movement and various leftist political parties in the Constituent Assembly process. The changes in the national labor relations system which the left and the labor movement proposed including in the 1988 Constitution had already been won in individual collective bargaining sessions by the most powerful trade unions. Thus, the left and labor demonstrated moderation in their demands and a willingness to work through democratic channels to attain them.

Labor Conflict

Direct labor negotiations without intervention from the state, which had begun during the first phase of the transition to democracy, became more prevalent during the New Republic. With the transfer of power from the military to civilians, industrialists engaged more often in collective bargaining sessions. The challenges that labor had posed to the existing system of capital-labor relations in Brazil during the first phase of the transition to democracy continued and intensified during the New Republic. Trade unions increased their demands, both in collective bargaining sessions with employers, and in national arenas such as the Constituent Assembly. And labor movement activities contributed to a growing number of changes in labor relations.

Most industrialists accepted, and attempted to influence, the liberalization in labor relations that occurred during the New Republic. A majority (73%) of those I interviewed claimed that they had altered labor relations in their firms during the New Republic, while only 27 percent said that they had not. The changes that were mentioned included improvements in working conditions, new communication networks between management and workers, increased worker participation in firms' decisions, higher wages, direct negotiations with workers, and the granting of workers' demands.[49] Despite these significant changes, most (64%) of the industrialists I interviewed expressed satisfaction with labor relations in their firms during the New Republic. They stated that they had experienced few strikes and that their negotiations with workers had gone smoothly.[50] Nonetheless, a significant proportion (36%) stated that labor relations were worse than ever before. The key sources of tension were strikes and conflicts over job security, worker representation, and reduction of the work week.

Strikes.   As table 5.5 demonstrates, the number of strikes increased significantly during the New Republic. Moreover, industrialists suspected that strikes would continue to occur often because the 1988 Constitution included an unrestricted right to strike, and extended that right to public employees and to workers in "essential" sectors.

The insertion into the 1988 Constitution of provisions granting workers the unrestricted right to strike was a serious blow to employers. Only 9 percent of those I interviewed accepted the unrestricted right to strike. These industrialists were primarily from multinational corporations or Brazilian firms with some foreign capital. In contrast, 11 percent opposed any right to strike. Those who had this attitude tended to resemble the stereotype of the traditional paternalistic Brazilian industrialist—founder of a small firm, relatively uneducated, and having little experience and few contacts abroad.[51] The vast majority (80%) of the industrialists I interviewed accepted neither the unrestricted right to strike nor the prohibition of all strikes. Yet, although they agreed that there should be some restrictions on strike activity, they did not agree on what these restrictions should be. While 9 percent advocated total freedom in declaring strikes, 35 percent demanded all of the regulations debated in the business community, and 56 percent accepted some, but not all, of the proposed rules.[52]

While industrialists generally opposed government intervention in labor relations, they clearly favored it—even in its most violent form—with regard to strikes. The director of a paper company explained this apparent contradiction. He stated, "I am against government intervention, unless it is used to protect the firm from labor" [5 Oct. 1987]. Indeed, although employers continued to successfully negotiate labor demands without the intervention of the state, FIESP and individual industrialists repeatedly called on the Ministry of Labor to intervene to end strikes declared illegal by the labor courts. For example, FIESP advocated military intervention during the 1985 strikes in the metalworking sector in São Paulo and during the 1986 general strikes against the first and second Cruzado Plans. Employers also accused workers who engaged in illegal strikes of undermining the nation.[53]

Table 5.5.   Strikes in Brazil, 1985–89

Year	Total Number of Strikes	Total Number of Strikers
1985	712	5,916,905
1986	1,148	4,871,400
1987	1,201	7,797,649
1988	656	7,275,422
1989	1,702	16,597,585
Total	5,419	42,458,961

Source: Departamento Intersindical de Estatística e Estudos Sócio-Econômicos (DIEESE), *Boletim,* 1985–90.
Note: When DIEESE lacked information on the number of workers who participated in a strike, that strike was not included in the total number of strikes, causing an underestimation of strikes (often by as much as 30%).

This alarmingly prointerventionist sentiment was reflected in interviews. Most (69%) of the industrialists to whom I spoke believed that the use of the armed forces was necessary to control labor conflict. Only 31 percent opposed it. Those who favored intervention by the armed forces tended to be from small firms or large firms (79% of the former group and 73% of the latter group favored intervention), as well as relatively old (72% of those born before 1944 favored intervention). Industrialists from small firms no doubt felt powerless in the face of labor conflict. Those from large firms, on the other hand, probably hoped to win protection from the increasingly frequent strikes in their firms. Older industrialists, finally, may have come to depend on this form of protection and did not want to lose it.

As table 5.6 indicates, those industrialists I interviewed who favored intervention by the armed forces provided a wide range of reasons for their opinion. Some believed that military intervention was necessary to protect private property and individuals' lives, or to assist the police in controlling massive strikes. Others advocated the use of the armed forces to protect firms from picketing and illegal strikes. By endorsing the use of the armed forces, especially in the case of minor labor conflicts, these industrialists demonstrated their continued reliance on authoritarian controls to protect them from labor when necessary.

These overwhelmingly prointerventionist sentiments among industrialists were frustrated, however, since the New Republic's labor minister, Almir Pazzianotto, was committed to legalizing the right to strike and limiting the role of the Ministry of Labor and the armed forces in the resolution of strikes.[54] He encouraged direct negotiations between workers and employers, stating, "Interventions prolong conflicts because they neither resolve the problem of the strike, weaken the demands of

Table 5.6.   Reasons Cited by the Industrialists
Interviewed as Justification for Armed Forces
Intervention in Strikes

	Interviewees Citing Reason	
Reason	No.	%
To protect property	45	31
To preserve order	42	29
To protect individuals	33	22
To disband pickets	20	14
To assist police	16	11
To end illegal strikes	14	9
To end occupations by strikers	12	8
None (intervention never justified)	45	31
Do not know	1	1

Note: N = 147. The total adds up to more than 147, and
the percentage adds up to more than 100%, because
interviewees provided multiple responses.

workers, nor resolve the owners' problems."[55] Pazzianotto's attitude angered industrialists. "His behavior is not good for the country. One must never ignore the law," one remarked.[56] Pazzianotto's rebuttal was that he would not apply the authoritarian law against strikers because "the Ministry of Labor is no longer the praetorian guard of savage capitalism."[57]

Aware that they could no longer depend on the government to end strikes, industrialists engaged in their own forms of self-protection against them: they dismissed workers involved in strikes, they honed their bargaining skills in courses on collective bargaining, and they added labor relations experts to their management teams.[58] To assist employers in strike negotiations, FIESP also circulated a revised manual that included suggestions on how to avoid and cope with strikes. In addition, industrialists mobilized to defeat the job security measure in the Constituent Assembly. The defeat of the measure would guarantee employers the right to hire and fire at will, thereby providing some protection against strikes.

Conflicts over Job Security.   Concerned about the growing rate of unemployment during the New Republic, the labor movement, both in collective bargaining negotiations and in the Constituent Assembly, demanded job security measures. These measures would provide workers with guarantees against arbitrary dismissal. However, due in no small part to industrialists' widespread opposition, this measure never passed in the Constituent Assembly and was only rarely adopted in collective bargaining contracts.

None of the industrialists I interviewed was in favor of the job security measure. They articulated several reasons for their opposition. They asserted that they needed maximum flexibility in hiring and firing in order to produce goods profitably; they argued that because good workers are so scarce in Brazil, workers who did their jobs well would have job security; and they further maintained that employers have no interest in firing workers because they have invested time and money in training them. As the president of a small Brazilian firm stated: "The best security is a good worker. Job security only protects the incompetent" [28 Apr. 1988]. Industrialists also noted that the government could not provide similar security for employers. The manager of a multinational corporation's large Brazilian operation asked rhetorically, "And where is the security for companies, for employers?" [15 July 1987], and another industrialist asked, "Will the government also protect the level of sales?"[59] Similarly, the president of a medium-sized Brazilian firm remarked, "If there is no security in one of the oldest institutions in the world—marriage—how can we be expected to give security to workers?" [28 Oct. 1987].[60]

This strongly felt, and nearly unanimous, opposition to job security allowed industrialists to mobilize their resources. The CNI and FIESP collected the signatures of nearly 1.5 million voters who opposed including the proposed job security and hour-reduction measures (discussed below) in the 1988 Constitution.[61] Business groups also helped form within the Constituent Assembly a conservative block called the *Centrão* (broad center). This block, although not formed only to protect industrialists' interests, included an estimated 291 of the 559 members of the Constituent Assembly and was committed to defending the free enterprise system.

The business lobby's efforts were successful in opposing the job security proposal. The national lobbying organizations pooled their resources. One business representative in the Constituent Assembly claimed that business groups had developed a fund of $35 million to defeat the measure. The Union of Brazilian Businesses (UBE) ran a fifteen-day television campaign against it.[62] The National Front for Free Enterprise (FNLI) distributed posters listing those members of the assembly who supported employers' unrestricted right to discharge workers. The posters, which implicitly guaranteed the listed members of the assembly generous financial support from businesses in future elections, encouraged other members to follow their example. Most importantly, the Centrão adopted an acceptable alternative to the job security measure: an indemnity clause that would allow employers to fire employees at will as long as they compensated them. The amount of compensation, or severance pay, would depend on the number of years the employee had worked in the firm. Although this kind of indemnity was already part of Brazilian law and had not provided any protection for workers,[63] the Centrão contended that the new level of compensation was four times what employers had previously paid, and would therefore make arbitrary dismissals too costly.

In my interviews, industrialists expressed a variety of opinions on alternatives to job security. A sizable percentage (37%) endorsed indemnity as a means of protecting workers from arbitrary dismissal. Some (35%) defended just-cause legislation.[64] They mentioned fairly typical criteria for "cause," including insubordination (mentioned by 28% of the industrialists interviewed); errors, absenteeism, or low productivity (mentioned by 27%); economic problems in the firm (mentioned by 25%); and technological changes in the firm (mentioned by 17%). However, 17 percent also mentioned union activity or leftist activity as just cause for firing workers.[65] This intolerance of workers' involvement in union or leftist activity indicates that a sizable minority within the industrial community has strongly antidemocratic values. Another indication of industrialists' intolerance is the fact that 65 percent of those I interviewed rejected just-cause legislation and demanded the freedom to fire and hire at will.[66]

Most (79%) of the industrialists I interviewed advocated unemployment insurance as an alternative to job security. Those who opposed it argued either that the Brazilian government was too indebted to be able to afford such insurance or that unemployment insurance would encourage unemployment by paying workers not to work. Indeed, a significant proportion (33%) opposed providing any unemployment compensation, or giving workers any protection against arbitrary dismissal.[67]

This discussion of the job security measure indicates some conditions whereby industrialists can become a formidable political power. When they are united behind a particular issue they can mobilize the necessary resources to defend their interests. However, because diversity within the industrial community makes the formulation of consensus alternatives difficult, that community's most successful form of political action is often the veto. Industrialists agreed that constitutional provisions mandating job security had to be defeated, and they successfully mobilized their resources behind that effort. They had more difficulty, however, designing and implementing an alternative to that legislation, because of the diversity of their views regarding the circumstances under which employees can be dismissed, and the type, if any, of postdischarge compensation workers should receive. Instead, they relied on the Centrão to propose and defend alternative legislation in the Constituent Assembly. Thus, this example of successful collective action by the business community was defensive (e.g., the veto of a legislative proposal) and depended on external support.

The defeat of the job security measure also indicates that a strongly antidemocratic sentiment existed within the business community. The antidemocratic industrialists not only hoped to deny workers any protection against employers' arbitrary and antilabor actions but also hoped to undermine unions and political parties (which were workers' sole form of autonomous protection from employers and the government) by listing leftist and union activity as legal grounds for discharge.[68] This antidemocratic tendency was also revealed in many of my interviewees' attitudes toward worker representation.

Conflicts over Worker Representation.   Industrialists' debates over the representation of workers' interests in negotiations intensified during the New Republic. The Constituent Assembly debated the possibility of replacing the existing system mandated by the CLT, which established a monopoly of representation and state control over labor representation, with a system providing union freedom and autonomy, consistent with the International Labor Organization charter. In contrast to what one would expect, the majority (61%) of the industrialists I interviewed opposed the CLT's restrictions on labor representation and advocated union autonomy and freedom, while a significant minority (38%) opposed changes in the CLT's system of representation.[69] Although the strongest opposition to union autonomy came from industrialists who identified with the extreme right, and the strongest support came from industrialists who identified themselves as being on the left and in the center, ideological consistency also broke down over this issue.[70]

Industrialists justified their support for union autonomy on several grounds. Democratic industrialists endorsed union autonomy because it was consistent with the democratic values of representation and freedom. Moreover, for pragmatic reasons, both democratic industrialists and some uncommitted ones believed that union autonomy would ensure authentic labor representation and effective negotiations. Reactionary industrialists and some other uncommitted ones, however, saw union autonomy and freedom as something that could strengthen industrialists' power vis-à-vis unions, since plurality and competition would fragment the union movement. As the president of a Brazilian company candidly stated, "the more they [the trade unions] fight between themselves, the weaker they are, and that benefits us" [1 June 1988]. Another industrialist, the vice-president of a large Brazilian company, stated that union plurality was the only way to weaken the force of the union movement and end the "república sindicalista" (republic of unionists) [6 May 1988]. Reactionary and uncommitted industrialists also thought that union freedom and autonomy would eliminate compulsory union dues and enable employers to create and finance trade unions favorable to business interests. Indeed, several of the industrialists I interviewed confirmed rumors that members of the business community had already engaged in this kind of action by financing the election of conservative trade union leader Luiz Antonio Medeiros to the presidency of the São Paulo Metalworkers' Union.

The democratic and uncommitted industrialists who opposed union autonomy argued that union monopoly strengthened an otherwise weak and ineffective union

movement. A monopoly on representation ensured workers a centralized and powerful leadership organization, funded by mandatory dues, which would act as an
official representative of labor, both in collective bargaining sessions and on national issues. One industrialist who held this view, the director of a large textile
company, stated that union freedom "sounds great; but in practice it creates polarization within the union, and that creates disorder and makes it impossible to negotiate" [12 May 1988]. These industrialists further argued that union autonomy would
allow employers to finance their own trade unions and thereby undermine authentic
representation of workers' interests. Reactionary industrialists, on the other hand,
believed that only a state-controlled and monopolistic system of labor representation would protect them from radical labor activity. These industrialists seemed
particularly concerned about controlling, and even outlawing, labor federations.

No evidence suggests that industrialists attempted to have, or actually had, an
impact on the final decision made by the Constituent Assembly with respect to
union autonomy and freedom. The decision was highly ambiguous. It granted
workers the freedom to form unions, but allowed only one union to represent workers in each industrial sector in a given region. In other words, it struck a compromise
between workers' freedom, on the one hand, and competition and fragmentation,
on the other. Industrialists, who obviously lacked consensus on this issue, did not
object to the compromise.

The question of whether to allow for the representation of workers' interests in
firms resurfaced during the New Republic. In contrast to industrialists' published
views during the earlier transition period, the vast majority (85%) of the industrialists I interviewed believed that some form of worker representation in firms was
desirable, although a significant minority (15%) opposed this basic demand. The
strongest support came from non-Brazilian executives and from industrialists at
medium-sized and large firms. These individuals probably had experience with, or
exposure to, shop-floor representation, and were both less likely to fear it and more
likely to derive some benefits from it.[71]

Despite this broad support for worker representation, however, industrialists
were reluctant to allow workers to organize and to control their own representatives
in the workplace. Instead, they tended to endorse representative groups that per-
formed functions such as reducing accidents (accident prevention committees
[CIPAs] were required by law for every factory with more than ten employees) or
improving production methods (quality control circles [CCQs]). When it came to
representing workers' demands or grievances, industrialists advocated manage-
ment-controlled systems such as opinion polls, round-table discussions between labor and management, and open-door policies. Several industrialists referred to
these channels of communication as methods by which workers could participate
without union "interference." The manager of a multinational corporation's very

large Brazilian operation bluntly stated, "We try to resolve our problems without the union" [6 Aug. 1987]. And the director of another multinational corporation's very large Brazilian operation remarked, "Anything that keeps the union out is fine. The union destroys things" [20 May 1988]. Still another industrialist, the director of a small metalworking firm, remarked that he would allow any kind of worker participation in the firm "as long as it doesn't mean allowing the union in. I am allergic to the union" [1 June 1988].

Only 30 percent of the industrialists interviewed stated that they believed that worker representation without management control (e.g., codetermination [worker representation in companies' policy decisions], union delegates, or plant committees) could be effective, and only 15 percent permitted these forms of shop-floor representation. This latter group tended to be with firms from the modern industrial sector—for instance, large multinational firms and metalworking firms.[72] However, few of these executives were happy with such forms of representation. During the New Republic, many of them attempted to undermine their plant committees by, among other things, systematically firing committee members who engaged in illegal strikes. As mentioned above, 17 percent of those interviewed defended their right to do so, arguing that it was essential for employers to be permitted to discharge workers who were involved in leftist or union politics in the firm. As long as industrialists enjoyed the freedom to fire employees for these reasons, they continued to possess a weapon against the unwanted plant committees; and thus, few industrialists protested the measure in the 1988 Constitution which recognized workers' right to form plant committees.

Conflicts over Reduction of the Work Week.   The labor movement endorsed reduction of the work week as a form of protection against unemployment. The movement believed that if the maximum limit on the number of hours individuals could be required to work was reduced, firms would hire more employees. As with the job security proposal, the labor movement made this demand both in collective bargaining sessions and in the Constituent Assembly. In the Constituent Assembly, labor originally demanded that the maximum work week be reduced from forty-eight hours to forty.[73]

A great majority of the industrialists I interviewed strongly opposed the original proposal for a forty-hour week: 79 percent opposed it, and 21 percent accepted it.[74] In the end, the Constituent Assembly adopted a forty-four-hour week, a compromise between forty-eight and forty hours. Industrialists also opposed this compromise. In interviews, 81 percent stated that the maximum work week should be longer than forty-four hours, and only 19 percent favored setting the maximum at forty-four hours or less. On average, the industrialists I interviewed believed that forty-seven hours was an acceptable maximum. Several argued that in order for the nation to resolve its economic crisis and achieve economic growth, workers needed to produce more by working longer, not shorter, hours.[75]

However, industrialists could not mount a credible protest against the reduced work week for three key reasons. The first was that many industrialists (including 60% of those interviewed) accepted the idea of a statutory maximum work week.[76] The second, and more important, reason was that many industrialists (also including 60% of those interviewed) had already accepted a work week of forty-four hours or less in collective bargaining agreements. As one would expect, this latter group tended to run firms in the most dynamic sectors: namely, metalworking firms, nontraditional firms, foreign firms, and firms engaged to some extent in the production of goods for export.[77] Having accepted the forty-four-hour week, these industrialists proved that firms could tolerate a reduction without being undermined. Indeed, key business leaders publicly expressed this view. Albano Franco, head of the CNI, stated that the forty-four-hour week might cause difficulties, but that "in truth, firms are not going to close because of these changes."[78] In addition, the most progressive members of the business community announced that they could accept the forty-four-hour week but not the job security measure.[79]

The third reason for industrialists' inability to effectively protest the reduction of the work week was that the Centrão disbanded shortly after the job security measure was defeated but before the work-week proposal was debated. One analysis described the reasons for this dissolution as follows: some members left owing to ideological differences; others owing to the widespread corruption used by the Centrão to win votes; and others because the bribes used to win loyalty to the group were not high enough.[80] Whatever the exact reasons, the defections from the Centrão meant that industrialists lost an organized bloc that had defended their interests in the Constituent Assembly and insight therefore have done so in the debate on the work-week reduction proposal.

In sum, during the New Republic industrialists changed their manner of dealing with labor conflict in limited, but not insignificant, ways. They engaged in collective bargaining sessions more frequently, and honed their skills. They compromised with labor on a number of issues, thereby causing significant changes in capital-labor relations. And, for the most part, they accepted those changes. However, they opposed most of the labor legislation changes proposed for inclusion in the 1988 Constitution. In addition to the unrestricted right to strike, job security, and the reduced work week, they opposed social legislation mandating such things as maternity leave and protection for minors. Before the ratification of the 1988 Constitution, the head of a state-owned enterprise remarked, "The Constitution will not be passed. It is ridiculous" [3 June 1988]. FIESP claimed that the constitutional provisions would increase industrialists' labor costs by 30 percent. Industrialists warned that workers would suffer, because employers would compensate for the legislative changes by reducing their work force or simply by not registering workers. Thus, these industrialists predicted that under the 1988 Constitution workers would actually enjoy fewer, rather than more, jobs and rights. Despite these dire warnings, most of the provisions that industrialists opposed became part of the 1988 Constitution. Nevertheless, it appears that industrialists are protected from any great threats that the Constitution poses to their interests. They can promote trade union leaders favorable to their interests; and, because they defeated the job security law, they can still dismiss those leaders who challenge them. In other words, simply because industrialists accept liberalization of capital-labor relations does not mean that they lose control over workers and unions.

Industrialists' Influence during the New Republic

During the New Republic, business leaders engaged in forms of individual and collective political action—specifically, election campaigns, lobbying, and collective bargaining—which they had virtually abandoned during the two decades of military rule. As a result of these activities, business associations began to play a more critical role in national politics. However, these associations often did not succeed at their new role. The diversity within the business community, and that community's dependence on the state and allies in civil society, constrained their efforts.

Elections

Industrialists generally perceived elections during the New Republic as crucial to political stability, and as the solution to national problems. This view contrasts starkly with their perceptions in 1964. As the president of a small Brazilian firm stated: "Today there is much more corruption. The government is as incompetent as the Goulart government. There is even some radicalism. But there are alternatives short of a coup: elections" [20 June 1988]. Industrialists were concerned both with the future presidential election and with the immediate elections to the Constituent Assembly, because both would influence long-term political stability.

Most industrialists wanted presidential elections to be held in 1988 rather than 1989. Their demand was not satisfied, however. The influence of the military, and Sarney's independent lobbying efforts, proved a more formidable influence over the Constituent Assembly than pressure from industrialists (and the popular sector). The military backed Sarney's demand for a five-year term, since it would guarantee a more controlled transition to democracy. When the military took this position, opinion within the industrial community fragmented. Mario Amato, president of FIESP, soon succumbed to political pressure and endorsed a five-year term. Amato believed that this was the most circumspect position to take, given the military's influence in society. His position was backed by the more cautious members of the FIESP directorate. As the following excerpt from an interview with the president of a medium-sized Brazilian firm suggests, during the New Republic many industrialists were still concerned about government reprisals against business leaders' disloyalty:

> Things are still happening underground. People are still afraid to say certain things . . . There are a lot of right-wing people out there . . . Industry is so dependent on the state and the oligopolies for credit, price levels, industrial inputs, fiscal legislation, authorization to open a factory . . . that they are afraid to rock the boat. The state will send auditors into your firm, just to threaten you. [24 Sept. 1987]

Most business leaders, however, viewed Amato's endorsement of the five-year term as a cowardly act, indicative of FIESP's accommodationist position toward the government. New business groups, such as the National Grassroots Business Association (PNBE), emerged partly in response to FIESP's acquiescence. One PNBE leader, the director of a small Brazilian company, stated [10 Sept. 1987] that FIESP was "completely tied to the state" and therefore incapable of adequately defending the interests of business. Some industrialists accused FIESP directors of taking this position in order to win personal favors from the government, while ignoring their obligation to represent the interests of the business community.

Industrialists' concern with elections to the Constituent Assembly resulted from the critical role this body would play in determining the legislation affecting the business community. To influence the outcome of these elections, industrialists allegedly created a "war chest" of $600 million to elect approximately 300 representatives to the 559-member Constituent Assembly.[81] Confirming the existence of such a fund, one leader of the business community remarked, "The economic power of the business community, and its ability to influence, will be used to a great extent to ensure the election of candidates committed to private enterprise."[82] Industrialists succeeded in winning a significant number of seats: while manual workers comprised only 1 percent of the assembly (6 seats), members of the business class comprised 38 percent (211 seats).[83] In addition, the proportion of industrialists who were elected to the assembly remained about the same as in past congressional elections: 5 percent (30 seats).[84] Moreover, the ideological composition of the assembly did not appear to jeopardize industrialists' interests. The center won a solid victory—70.5 percent of the seats, compared to 19 percent won by the right and 10.5 percent won by the left.[85]

Industrialists, however, did not achieve all of their goals. They elected eighty-eight fewer representatives than they had hoped. Moreover, they suffered a major defeat when their nemesis, Luís Inácio "Lula" da Silva, the former head of the São Bernardo Metalworkers' Union and president of the PT, won more votes in these elections than any other candidate in the history of Brazil. In short, industrialists neither won a clear victory nor suffered total defeat in their effort to elect representatives to the Constituent Assembly.

Lobbying

Industrialists also formed a business lobby during the New Republic. Like their electoral efforts, it achieved limited results. FIESP had the potential to become a strong pressure group. It represented a powerful constituency: seventy thousand firms, which employed 1.8 million workers. In addition, its president was in a position to coalesce the different factions within the business community. Mario Amato, who became president in an uncontested election in 1986,[86] appealed to both the conservative "old guard" and to the liberals, such as Cláudio Bardella and José Mindlin.[87] Mindlin described Amato as "a conservative who accepts change."[88] Moreover, FIESP adopted a political platform that appealed to the entire business community. It defined its role in the Constituent Assembly as "making members of the Congress sensitive to business concerns," working for private enterprise, defining the role of government in economic activities, and building "an open, free, and just society with greater distribution of wealth, but within the capitalist system."[89]

Furthermore, FIESP's prestige and its interest in promoting private sector interests enabled it to coordinate its activities with those of national business associations. For example, it joined various national business pressure groups, including the UBE, the Informal Business Forum, and the FNLI. The UBE had been formed in 1986, and by February 1987 it had more than five hundred members, including sixty business federations and two hundred private firms. Its executive council included the presidents of the CNI, the National Confederation of Commerce, the National Confederation of Agriculture, the National Confederation of Transportation, and the National Federation of Banking. The UBE primarily concentrated on economic policy. Specifically, it hoped to limit the government's role in the economy, defend the laws of the marketplace, restore respect for free enterprise, and end restrictions on the development of new technology. The UBE also advocated certain broad social reforms: an increased role for private firms in the distribution of social services; an end to abuses of economic power; workers' rights; and income redistribution.[90] The Informal Business Forum was composed of nearly the same business leaders as the UBE and advocated the same principles. However, it focused its lobbying efforts on the executive branch rather than on Congress. The FNLI was formed in November 1987 to combat the proposed job security provision in the Constitution. It was made up of many of the same groups that belonged to the UBE and the Informal Business Forum, but it also included a far-right rural landholders' organization, the Rural Democratic Union (UDR).

Despite this network of organizations, FIESP, like the business lobby in general, did not fulfill its potential. As the president of a very large metalworking company stated, "FIESP has extraordinary force but doesn't know how to use it" [12 Nov. 1987]. Indeed, only 31 percent of the industrialists I interviewed believed that FIESP played an important role in defending industrialists' interests; 31 percent considered it only somewhat important, and 37 percent considered it unimportant. This view of FIESP tended to break down along ideological lines: the majority (69%) of those who considered FIESP important were on the right, and the majority (54%) of those who considered FIESP unimportant were on the left. Centrists were divided. In addition, industrialists from firms with some foreign capital had a more favorable view of FIESP's role than did those from firms with no foreign capital: 68 percent of the former group, but only 56 percent of the latter, considered FIESP important. These findings suggest that FIESP primarily represented and defended the interests of right-wing industrialists and foreign firms.

Indeed, industrialists were critical of FIESP's undemocratic representation in lobbying. They charged the organization with excluding certain kinds of industrialists from its decisions. One industrialist whom I interviewed, the director of a very large Brazilian company, sarcastically described FIESP as an organization that represented only highly conservative traditional firms—firms that produced hats, ribbons, soap, candles, canes, and umbrellas—since FIESP had created a syndicate for each one of those sectors, and each had a vote in the organization [23 Nov. 1987].[91] Other industrialists accused FIESP of representing only large domestic or foreign conglomerates. Analysis of the 1986–89 FIESP directorate indicates that this accusation may have been valid. Of the sixty-seven directors, 18 percent were from small businesses (with less than 500 employees), 28 percent were from medium-sized firms (with 500–1,999 employees), and 33 percent were from large firms (with more than 2,000 employees). As far as I could discern, not one of the directors came from a firm with less than 10 employees.[92]

The industrialists who felt marginalized in FIESP belonged to firms that were small, new, or innovative. In particular, they demanded an organization that would actively lobby for increased low-cost credit to support high-risk ventures and to sustain small firms during economic crises. Although these marginalized industrialists never withdrew from FIESP, they thought their interests might be better served by alternative organizations, such as the PNBE and small-business associations.[93]

FIESP's actions indicate that it felt threatened by these autonomous organizations. For example, it attempted to regain the support of small businesses by setting up CIESPs in locations where small businesses had begun to organize their own associations. Because being a director of a CIESP was more prestigious than heading up a small-business organization, many owners of small businesses accepted these positions rather than working for autonomous organizations. FIESP also organized a Department for Assistance to Small and Medium-Sized Industries (DAP) at its headquarters in São Paulo. Designed to centralize and coordinate the affairs of small and medium-sized manufacturing firms, DAP conducted studies and developed projects to defend the interests of such firms. None of the heads of small-business associations whom I interviewed, however, believed that DAP provided any direct support for business or that it changed FIESP's overall bias in favor of large enterprises. They felt it was only a token gesture on the part of FIESP.

FIESP leaders also took measures—often unsophisticated ones—to reduce competition from the PNBE. They allegedly turned off PNBE leaders' microphones when they spoke out at FIESP meetings. They urged FIESP directors not to attend PNBE meetings, and labeled the members of the PNBE "PTistas" (members of the Workers' Party) in an effort to undermine their credibility in the business community. One PNBE founder, the director of a small metalworking company, who greatly exaggerated the PNBE's power within the industrial community, noted, "FIESP is jealous of the PNBE. It began to lose power and reacted. It is a normal reaction when you feel your power slipping away" [29 Sept. 1987]. FIESP also attempted to reduce the PNBE's appeal by adopting some of the PNBE's own initiatives—in particular, by broadening its contacts with trade union leaders.

When FIESP attempted to establish consensus positions within the business community, it only weakened its lobbying efforts. For example, FIESP promoted the idea that the new Constitution should protect the free enterprise system. This principle was both important to and agreed upon by all members of the business community. But because the Constituent Assembly was drafting very specific legislation rather than broad principles, FIESP was forced to abandon its lobbying strategy. Because of fragmentation within the business community, it lacked the consensus to formulate alternatives to the specific legislation debated by the Constituent Assembly.

Another criticism directed at the FIESP lobby was the charge that it was reluctant to challenge the state in order to actively defend industrialists' interests. Industrialists from firms of various sizes which depended on diverse sources of capital shared this view. As the head of a state-owned enterprise observed, "FIESP wants to win too easily. It doesn't want to get into the fray and fight" [3 June 1988]. Some of these industrialists blamed Amato for this posture. The director of a small metalworking company remarked about FIESP, "We have the right institutions, but the quality of leadership is poor" [11 May 1988]. Others believed that Amato altered his opinions according to the prevailing political attitudes, as exemplified by his change of mind regarding the presidential term.[94] Some believed that his style of leadership was patterned after traditional FIESP presidents who sought rewards through accommodation. Indeed, Amato had been a FIESP director since at least 1964, when he had served as treasurer, and he therefore might have had more of an "old school" approach than a new business leader would have.[95]

These criticisms of FIESP by its own members reflect two phenomena. The first is the great diversity of the industrial community. Whatever strategy or positions FIESP adopted would inevitably have alienated some sectors within the community. Industrialists themselves recognized that their views were highly fragmented. When asked whether they felt that their political views were typical of those held in the Brazilian industrial community as a whole, the vast majority (69%) of the industrialists I interviewed said they were not.[96] As the director of a very large Brazilian metalworking firm stated:

> There is no typical [businessperson]. There are those who support *capitalismo selvagem* [savage capitalism], who only want to make a profit. There are the cheaters who want to send their money abroad. There are the enterprising entrepreneurs who make social investments. There are the honest and the dishonest. There are the socially conscious and the unconscious. There are those who go for the left because they think it's trendy. There are the extreme rightists. [20 Nov. 1987]

The second phenomenon contributing to members' criticism of FIESP is that the transition to democracy caused the industrial community to make new demands concerning FIESP's strategy of representing its interests. Industrialists now wanted broad representation within the organization; they opposed leadership by a closed group of like-minded individuals. They also demanded that FIESP abandon its traditional role of acquiescence toward government and begin to challenge the regime's policies and practices. These demands generally required internal tinkering rather than a complete restructuring of the network of traditional business organizations.

Indeed, despite their criticisms, most industrialists maintained their membership in existing business associations. For example, only 14 percent of those I interviewed had no affiliation with a business association, while 64 percent were members of at least one powerful industrial association, as well as other business groups.[97] In addition, despite the flaws of the business association lobby, most industrialists considered it the best vehicle for representing their interests. As table 5.7 indicates, the association lobby received endorsement from 70 percent of the industrialists interviewed.

Finally, table 5.7 also shows that industrialists appeared to trust the business lobby more than other forms of representation, especially political parties. Among the industrialists I interviewed, 85 percent had never belonged to a political party, and only 8 percent had belonged to a political party during the New Republic. A new party, the Popular Party (PP), had been formed in 1979–80 to represent business interests; it had strong support among financial leaders, for which it received the nickname "the bankers' party." However, the PP was short-lived; by 1982 it had

Table 5.7.   Types of Representation Cited by
the Industrialists Interviewed as Serving Business
Interests Well

Type of Representation	Interviewees Endorsing Representation	
	No.	%
Association lobby	108	70
Representatives in congress	45	29
Representation on government councils	34	22
Political parties	19	12
Lobbying by individual firms	18	12
All of the above	12	8
Other	2	1
None	5	3
No response	5	3

Note: N = 155. Total adds up to more than 155, and the
percentages add up to more than 100%, because
industrialists provided multiple responses.

been absorbed into the PMDB.[98] Despite a reluctance to join parties, a significant minority (16%) of the industrialists I interviewed had held positions in government, and three had held government posts during the New Republic.[99]

Collective Bargaining

Although most industrialists opposed the CLT system of labor representation, the majority endorsed the corporatist system of employer representation. Of the industrialists I interviewed, 61 percent believed that conducting centralized negotiations with labor through FIESP was the best system. Those who held this view most strongly were from the oldest, most traditional firms with memberships in the corporatist business associations.[100] These industrialists had not changed their view since the earlier transition period. They still believed that FIESP centralized, organized, and simplified labor relations. Moreover, they thought that by providing a united front, centralization strengthened employers' power in negotiations and better enabled them to resist the demands of labor. This explains why some industrialists held seemingly contradictory attitudes toward the corporatist system of representation: they wanted to eliminate it where it strengthened labor, but endorsed it where it strengthened employers.

However, a significant minority (39%) of the industrialists I interviewed advocated conducting negotiations without the participation of business associations.

Some (26%) endorsed direct negotiations with workers in individual firms but opposed the participation of trade unions, employers' associations, or the government. Others (13%) endorsed negotiations with unions but opposed the participation of employers' associations or the government. Indeed, many industrialists continued a process begun during the earlier transition period: they bypassed FIESP and made separate agreements with workers.[101] These industrialists continued to feel that FIESP's intransigence in negotiations intensified rather than reduced labor conflict, since it ignored workers' needs and forced unions to take a more militant stance.[102] In contrast with those who favored the existing system of representation, these industrialists might be considered "modern" business leaders, since they were generally from newer firms in nontraditional sectors of industry.

Small firms also felt constrained by FIESP's intransigence. As the director of a small company stated:

> They [the leaders of FIESP] are traditional, right-wing, against direct negotiations in small firms. They support their own monopoly over labor relations. They inhibit the process of change. They are against modernity. They are retrograde. They do not work on behalf of the small firm. They put a wall up. They force negotiations through the Group of Fourteen. And the smaller firms have just ignored the Group of Fourteen and done things their own way. [16 May 1988]

These small firms argued that prolonged strikes provoked by FIESP's intransigence on wage increases were often more costly than granting workers' initial demands.[103]

This discussion of industrialists' attitudes toward the participation of employers' associations in collective bargaining negotiations suggests that two factions existed within the business community. A status-quo group, made up of industrialists from older firms that were in traditional sectors of industry and were members of the prominent business associations, hoped to maintain the forty-year-old corporatist system of employer associations and adapt it so as to defend employers' interests within the new context of direct negotiations. In contrast, the modern group, which consisted of industrialists from nontraditional and newer firms that did not belong to the prominent business associations, advocated a change in the existing structure, whereby the business associations would exert less control over individual firms' actions. Rather than adapt the business associations to the new demands of direct negotiations, these industrialists hoped to eliminate them from those negotiations altogether.

Adaptive Industrialists in the New Republic

Industrialists experienced many of the same fears during the New Republic that they had faced under Goulart (e.g., political instability, economic decline, leftist subversion, and labor unrest). Moreover, during the New Republic antidemocratic attitudes prevailed in the industrial community. However, in contrast to the events of 1964, and the predictions in the literature on transitions from authoritarian rule, industrialists did not once again endorse authoritarian rule. Instead, they adapted to the political situation. As the director of a small Brazilian company explained: "They [businesspeople] have a flexible attitude toward the political situation. When the authoritarian regime began to promote democracy . . . businessmen learned to adapt. This is not an essential change; this is an adaptation to government-initiated change" [10 Sept. 1987].

Two crucial differences between the New Republic and the 1964 period allowed industrialists to adapt rather than rebel: the political context and the business community's diversity. One element of the political context was that industrialists no longer viewed authoritarianism as the solution to national problems. After two decades of military rule, they recognized that authoritarianism did not guarantee political or economic stability. Moreover, international and domestic pressure for democratic change during the 1970s and 1980s contrasted sharply with the widespread support for the coups of the 1960s and 1970s. As leftist governments took office in various countries around the world without undermining the capitalist order, and as the Cold War ideology flagged, industrialists' perceptions of threat from the left diminished. Furthermore, industrialists' experience with labor negotiations and their increased confidence in their ability to succeed in these negotiations reduced their fear of labor conflict. In addition, the fact that labor and the left had moderated their demands and adopted a strategy of working within political institutions to achieve those demands further reduced industrialists' fears of political instability under democratic rule.

Another element of the political context was that the new opportunities available to industrialists to influence political outcomes and protect their investments also increased their willingness and capacity to adapt during the New Republic. Indeed, despite the number of problems they faced, the majority of business leaders did not feel threatened by the New Republic. Industrialists proved capable of mobilizing their extensive financial, organizational, and social resources in their lobbying efforts, election campaigning, and informal relations with decision makers. They also used their considerable power over labor to offset disadvantageous changes in labor relations and legislation.

Industrialists proved somewhat successful in their endeavors to influence political outcomes. Owing to their key positions within the economy and their social ties to decision makers, they successfully pressured the government to modify some of its deleterious economic policies. And as a result of financing various political campaigns, they won many seats for their representatives in the Constituent Assembly. They also organized a business lobby to defeat key labor legislation on job security which had been proposed in the Constituent Assembly.

However, business leaders' influence over political outcomes was limited owing to their diversity and their dependence on government and on other social sectors. The business community's successful defeat of the job-security measure resulted from the fact that the community reached a consensus to oppose the measure and relied on the Centrão to defend an alternative. Such consensus and support were rare. For example, business leaders' divergent ideological perspectives on labor and labor relations prevented them from presenting a united front in negotiations, or defeating the right-to-strike initiative. Industrialists' varying capacities to absorb labor demands prevented them from uniting to defeat the reduced work week. Moreover, business leaders' lack of social support prevented them from achieving their goals in the Constituent Assembly elections: winning three hundred seats and preventing the left from gaining ground.

Business leaders' dependence (whether perceived or real) on the state also prevented them from working together to defend their collective interests. Fear of government retribution led some industrialists to pursue a quiescent strategy, while others advocated more confrontational approaches to defend business interests. This conflict over strategy eroded business unity and prevented effective collective action. The business community's diverse needs also produced conflicting demands on the state. While some industrialists demanded government protection in labor conflicts, others adamantly opposed government intervention of any kind in capital-labor relations.

In addition, business leaders' influence was constrained by the government's attention to other, often conflicting, national goals and social interests. For example, the military proved more influential than business (and other social sectors) in deciding the question of the length of the president's term. Thus, industrialists had to suffer an additional year under President Sarney, against their wishes. And although the labor movement possessed fewer resources than the business community, the former proved more effective in winning support from the legislature on certain key issues such as the right to strike and the reduced work week. Indeed, the government's own national agenda conflicted with business interests. Its goal of reducing inflation and restoring economic stability prompted it to pursue strategies that clashed with industrialists' desire for market-determined wages and prices. Thus, while the government did not threaten the capitalist system, it also refused to surrender to the demands of the private sector.

The New Republic thus demonstrates that business elites can adapt to democratic change, even when that change conflicts with their interests. Moreover, it confirms that although business elites have potential power within democratic societies, the business community's diversity and its dependence on the state and on other social sectors generally prevent it from holding the government hostage to the interests of the private sector.

Chapter Six

Brazilian Industrialists and Democratic Stability in Theoretical and Comparative Perspective

In his essay on the Latin American bourgeoisie and the consolidation of democracy, Guillermo O'Donnell suggests that conditions seem propitious for bourgeois support for democracy. Business elites, as a result of their historical experience under military regimes, have learned that such regimes are unreliable protectors of the private sector owing to their unpredictable policies, strong nationalism, and prostatist strategies. Business elites have also recognized that the left is no longer a threat to capitalism. Moreover, the new democratic governments are promoting more orthodox policies, which are consistent with industrialists' desires. These conditions have convinced Latin American business elites that democratic governments may safeguard their interests better than authoritarian regimes would. O'Donnell is skeptical, however, that these conditions will endure. He argues that if the current conditions change, and especially if radical populist movements assert themselves, the "bourgeoisie, as well as a good part of the middle sectors, will again look for its unreliable, but indispensable, military guardians."[1] Although he states that it is not too late to offset the threat to democracy from the private sector, he does not specify the measures necessary to do so.

In this study I dispute O'Donnell's interpretations of the Latin American bourgeoisie and the conditions needed for democratic stability. I argue that business elites do not choose between democratic and authoritarian rule, but rather react to existing governments and the extent to which those governments protect investment stability. Thus, radical popular uprisings alone would not provoke business elites to reject democratic governments.

In this chapter, I draw on my research regarding changes in Brazilian business leaders' political attitudes and behavior over twenty-five years, and analyze its implications for democratic change in Brazil. By comparing the Brazilian case to similar research on Argentina, Chile, and Spain, I demonstrate that the Brazilian case is not unique. This comparison fortifies an assumption integral to the adaptive actor approach: the view that business elites generally will not rebel against democratic governments.

Brazilian Industrialists and Democratic Change

This study has suggested two reasons why industrialists do not necessarily threaten transitions to democracy. First, industrialists' political demands and preferences are not necessarily inconsistent with democracy. Second, democratic (and authoritarian) political systems can generally protect themselves from industrialists' pressure.

The Political Preferences of Brazilian Industrialists

Most Brazilian industrialists supported the 1964 coup and initially accepted the military regime it implanted, but this support does not necessarily imply that industrialists are inherently authoritarian. Instead, their political views are diverse, usually ill-defined, and changeable. Moreover, because their specific needs can be accommodated—or threatened—by either a democratic or an authoritarian system, they are not generally predisposed in favor of either system.

The diversity of Brazilian industrialists' political attitudes is apparent throughout this study. A small minority of industrialists strongly defended democracy. While some of them had supported the coup and the initial stage of the military regime, they had done so only because they believed that the Goulart government threatened constitutional order and democratic representation. They expected the military not to remain in power indefinitely but to rule only until democratic elections could be called. Therefore, when the military regime failed to restore democratic order in the country and instead institutionalized an authoritarian government that excluded political participation and representation, these industrialists withdrew their support.

This is not to deny, of course, that a strongly authoritarian strain also exists within the business community. It is this minority of industrialists that the theory of the bureaucratic-authoritarian state best describes. These industrialists believe that social order, political stability, and economic security are more important than political liberties. They often openly advocate authoritarian rule, arguing that Brazilians are incapable of accepting the responsibilities that accompany democratic liberties. Reactionary industrialists do not always openly defend authoritarian rule. For example, during the military regime they expressed a preference for democracy, but equated democracy with the procedural facades and social order installed by the military, and denied or ignored the regime's repression.

These two strong political preferences within the business community belie any facile interpretation of Brazilian business leaders as either democratic or authoritarian. Any interpretation of this group is further complicated by the business community's general indifference to political systems. Most industrialists are unconcerned about political systems but extremely sensitive to specific governments and their policies. Business elites will accept either democratic or authoritarian political systems if they believe that their essential interests are protected.

Those essential interests have often been misconstrued in the literature on political change. Specifically, the theory of the bureaucratic-authoritarian state exaggerates business elites' demands for economic expansion and social order. If those demands had been paramount, industrialists would have endorsed General Médici's government over all others, because it brought about unprecedented levels of growth during the "economic miracle" and controlled popular unrest by means of its brutally effective repressive apparatus. However, at least in hindsight, Médici was endorsed by only four of the industrialists I interviewed. In contrast, the industrialists I interviewed most strongly endorsed the government of Kubitschek (which was democratic) and that of Castello Branco (which was military-authoritarian).

Industrialists' presidential preferences affirm that they are more concerned about investment stability than about economic growth, social order, and the nature of the political system. In particular, industrialists accept governments they perceive as legitimate; competent in managing the economy; capable of protecting, and willing to protect, private property; and open to business influence. In their view, both Kubitschek and Castello Branco satisfied the business community's need for investment stability. Both were legitimate. Kubitschek had a constitutional mandate, and Castello Branco had a "popular mandate" to restore order. They both received widespread respect and support from the population. They were both successful at formulating and implementing effective policies and resolving national problems. They both guaranteed private property rights. And they both responded to business leaders' desire for inclusion in the formulation of economic policies.

Aside from the Kubitschek and Castello Branco governments, most Brazilian governments in the past three decades did not satisfy industrialists' demands for investment stability. It was only during the period leading up to the 1964 coup, however, that concerns over investment stability prompted industrialists to mobilize against the government. Thus, investment instability alone, although it is a crucial concern, is not sufficient to mobilize industrialists against the political regime. Two other factors proved critical in this regard: context and opportunity. Industrialists' perceptions are influenced by international trends and opinions. Moreover, industrialists' political preferences are strongly influenced by the availability of opportunities to counter threats to their investments. If business elites have either individual or collective options for protecting their interests within the political system, they are not likely to reach consensus, or mobilize collectively, against that system. In other words, although industrialists' demands for investment stability remain constant, their attitudes toward governments vary according to domestic and international trends and opinions, and the availability of individual and collec-

tive opportunities to influence political outcomes. A summary of industrialists' re-
actions to political regimes in Brazil from 1964 to 1985 illustrates these arguments.

The 1964 Coup.   Industrialists generally believed that Goulart threatened their investments. They considered his government highly unstable as a result of his leadership and management style. In the view of most industrialists, Goulart lacked a
constituency. His base of popular support, never strong to begin with, waned over
time. He alienated his primary constituents on the left by trying to control them, or
by failing to implement progressive policies. They further questioned his legal
mandate, especially in light of the widespread perception that his government
would disband Congress, rewrite the Constitution, and postpone presidential elections. In short, industrialists largely believed that Goulart lacked respect for the
laws of the country and the wishes of its citizens. They believed that he was leading
the country toward anarchy or totalitarian rule.

Many industrialists felt that their investment and production decisions were further threatened by Goulart's incompetent management of the economy and
disregard for private property. He proved incapable of securing support for his proposals from a hostile Congress, and one key adviser reacted by suggesting the
dismissal of Congress. He rejected existing property rights by threatening to expropriate and nationalize private firms. Although Goulart's proposed changes would
have affected only a minority of firms, industrialists believed that these actions
symbolized his anticapitalist tendencies, which would eventually undermine all
private property.

Industrialists' perceptions of revolutionary threats were undoubtedly influenced
by the prevailing anticommunist ideology of the 1960s, which was fueled by the
Cuban Revolution and by Cold War propaganda. Goulart unwittingly fanned the
domestic and international anticommunist fires with his antibusiness rhetoric; his
strong alliance with the leftist leader Leonel Brizola; and his proposals to expropriate and nationalize private firms and legalize the Communist Party. In truth, during
the 1960s the Brazilian leftist and popular movements were relatively weak, moderate, and demobilized. Thus industrialists' perception that labor movements and
the radical left were increasing their power under Goulart and threatening the
capitalist order was a reaction more to prevailing international fears than to any objective threat.

Industrialists' perception of Goulart as a threat to their interests was further
heightened because of their loss of influence over his government. When they perceived threats to Congress, the Constitution, presidential elections, and checks on
executive-branch power, industrialists sensed a loss of their traditional means of
influencing political outcomes. Moreover, Goulart appeared oblivious to their po-

tential economic reprisals against the government, such as capital flight and decreased investments.

In short, industrialists' perception that the Goulart government threatened their investments was so widespread that they mobilized against the government. Because nearly all business leaders felt threatened by some aspect of the Goulart government, differences between the democratic, reactionary, and uncommitted industrialists became less of an obstacle to collective action. Moreover, business leaders' perception that Goulart had eliminated all of the business community's traditional individual and collective means of self-protection meant that they saw no opportunities for individuals, or the community as a whole, to work for change within the political system. Finally, the prevalent domestic and international fears of revolution heightened their sense that Goulart was likely to undermine the capitalist order. They acted defensively against the Goulart government to protect their investments.

The Military Regime.   Initially most industrialists considered the military regime legitimate. They felt that, given the threat to constitutional order and national security under Goulart, Castello Branco had the right to govern. They also believed that the widespread popular support for the coup and Castello Branco's government gave Castello Branco de facto, if not legal, authority to govern. However, with the successive military governments, industrialists increasingly came to view the military regime as illegitimate and unstable. Hard-line and soft-line factions within the ruling coalition competed for power, creating decisional paralysis that undermined the government's stability. Moreover, the regime's reliance on repression, and the widespread popular demand for democracy, indicated to industrialists that the regime no longer commanded obedience or respect from the population. International condemnation of human rights violations, and pressure for democratic change, further eroded the regime's legitimacy. Indeed, its own controlled and gradual transition to democracy suggests that the regime itself recognized that democracy, and not authoritarian rule, was legitimate. After its initial success with the "economic miracle," the regime also demonstrated its incompetence in managing the economy and producing predictable economic policies. The economy moved into a recession. And, despite strong evidence to the contrary, industrialists sensed that private enterprise was threatened. They considered the regime's excessive control over the economy, and its encouragement of the expansion of state and multinational corporations, detrimental to the future of private domestic businesses.

Industrialists reacted to investment instability during the military regime by openly criticizing the regime and its policies, especially through the desestatização campaign. However, their opposition never gained much momentum. It proved both unnecessary and untenable. It was unnecessary because the regime itself announced a political transformation that promised industrialists more influence over the policies affecting them, and it was untenable because not all industrialists agreed that the military should step down. Only a minority of industrialists demanded the end of the military regime and endorsed democratic rule. Another minority within the business community believed that the military should remain in power and increase authoritarian controls to end social and economic chaos. The majority of industrialists believed that the military should remain in power but did not demand an end to the liberalization process. On the contrary, they accepted the military's gradual and controlled transition process. This process guaranteed protections for industrialists, granted them more opportunities for influencing political outcomes, and was consistent with international and domestic pressure for political liberalization.

The New Republic.   The New Republic government under President Sarney did not restore investment stability, but neither did it mobilize industrialists against the political transition. In most industrialists' view, Sarney had not been popularly elected, was a weak president without popular support, and had improperly used his political power to convince politicians to extend his term in office. He also proved incapable of managing the economy and producing competent and predictable economic policies.

However, by the 1980s anticommunist sentiment had dissipated. At the same time, democracy, and particularly the protection of human and civil rights, became an important political value, and Latin American governments responded by gradually permitting the transition from authoritarian rule. Indeed, in contrast to the 1960s, the transition from authoritarian rule was the dominant form of political change under way throughout the world. There were few alternative political models on which regimes could pattern their political developments.

As Brazil, like the rest of the world, became less anticommunist and increasingly democratic, Brazilian industrialists followed suit. During the New Republic government, the authoritarian elements within the business community remained silent. That is not to say that industrialists became democratic. Indeed, there is ample evidence to suggest that a strongly authoritarian segment of the business community continued to endorse authoritarian views, especially with regard to labor relations. These industrialists, for example, felt that employers should have the right to fire workers involved in labor or leftist activity; that workers should not have representatives within firms; that trade unions should not have links with political parties; that all strikes should be illegal; and that the armed forces should intervene to end illegal strikes. Although business groups did not propose these authoritarian controls for inclusion in the Constitution, they had significant success

in defending private sector interests. They employed their substantial financial, organizational, and social resources to help elect candidates of their choice, lobby the
legislature, shape popular opinion on key events via the mass media, and influence
the appointment, as well as the views, of decision makers within the government.
They also used sanctions to protest unfavorable economic policies: they withdrew
investment, lowered production rates, discharged workers (which increased turnover and unemployment rates), defied government regulations by charging illegally high prices or defrauding customers, and threatened to engage in civil
disobedience. In addition, they used their substantial power over labor to defend
employers' interests in individual and collective bargaining negotiations. The re-
establishment of electoral rules also meant that business groups could replace the
unsatisfactory Sarney administration through peaceful means, rather than a coup.
Thus, the existence of individual and collective channels of influence over policies
and decision makers enabled industrialists to adapt to the political transition.

Although many industrialists had been seriously concerned about the rise of the
left in 1964, their fear of the left had diminished considerably by the time the transition from authoritarian rule occurred. Thus, although the left and labor unrest resurfaced in the 1980s, industrialists' fears generally did not. They recognized the
Brazilian left and labor as legitimate participants in the political process, rather than
a subversive threat to the capitalist order. In addition, since 1964 most industrialists
had begun to view the left and the labor movement as relatively weak and moderate,
and, therefore, unlikely to threaten the capitalist order.

The gradual pace of liberalization during the New Republic also provided industrialists with sufficient time to adapt to the transformations under way, even when
those changes were inimical to their interests. For example, they generally accepted
political party reforms and the broad amnesty that ushered in the left after a long
hiatus, as well as liberalization of labor relations, which increased workers' demands and strike activity. Industrialists accepted the reforms because, during the
slow transition process, they had discovered their own methods of controlling the
perceived threat from workers and the left (e.g., support for political candidates,
financial assistance to conservative labor leaders, rigid positions in collective bargaining sessions, dismissal of labor activists, and campaigns against changes in labor relations), which reduced their dependence on the authoritarian state. Furthermore, they proved capable of retaining some authoritarian controls throughout
the political transition.

This analysis of industrialists' political attitudes and behavior during twenty-
five years of Brazilian history leads to the conclusion that most Brazilian industrialists are neither inherently democratic nor inherently authoritarian. Instead, they
evaluate governments according to the governments' capacity to ensure investment
stability. Unstable governments make them feel that their investments are vulner-

able. They fear that if the government lacks legitimacy (either de facto support from the public or a constitutional mandate to govern) the nation is vulnerable to anarchy, which would undermine their investment and production decisions. They also fear governments that are incapable of formulating and implementing effective policies, because their investment and production decisions depend on some minimal government competence and predictability in developing policies. They are also threatened by governments that threaten private property. Two additional factors—historical and international context, and business influence over government decisions—are also crucial in shaping industrialists' political attitudes. Their attitudes tend to mirror dominant international and domestic opinions. Additionally, when industrialists, whether individually or collectively, possess the means of defending their investments and their firms' production levels from unfavorable government policies, they are unlikely to advocate the overthrow of the government.

Protections from Industrialists' Pressure

There is ample evidence to suggest that Brazilian industrialists have potential political power. The profile of the industrialists I interviewed indicates that an industrial elite possessing social status, wealth, and significant political power exists in Brazil. The history of Brazilian business associations (particularly FIESP) further demonstrates that industrialists' associations have remained intact since the 1930s despite frequent political transformations. Brazilian business leaders, in short, possess the financial, social, and organizational resources with which to influence political outcomes. And they have used these resources during both authoritarian and democratic periods to influence political outcomes by shaping popular opinion, influencing the selection and attitudes of decision makers, and imposing sanctions on the government.

However, despite these sources of political power, Brazilian industrialists do not always influence change. Indeed, owing to traditional business-state relations, the innate character of the business community, and the nature of business elites' collective action, Brazilian governments are often immune from industrialists' mobilizations.

Patterns of Business-State Relations.   Brazilian industrialists' collective political action has often been constrained by their fear of retribution by the government. For example, although industrialists opposed the military regime's exclusive control over the economy, their protests were delayed and rather mild. Their cautious attitude resulted from their fear of government retribution. They believed that the military regime would retaliate by adopting prejudicial economic policies or by violently repressing private-sector dissent. During the New Republic, industrialists were generally exempt from government repression but took part only in mild forms of protest against the increasingly severe economic crisis. Industrialists still feared government retribution in the form of prejudicial policies. For example, FIESP, the strongest business association in the country, balanced its protests against the government's economic policies with accolades for the government, and asserted that caution was necessary to protect the majority of industrialists, who were both dependent on the government and incapable of surviving retaliation. FIESP argued that as long as the government controlled credit, import and export, and wage and pricing policies, industrialists' protests against government policies could backfire and produce even more unfavorable policies, thereby undermining industrialists' ability to produce, to invest, and to make profits. While this may be true, FIESP's cautious attitude imposed strict limitations on its capacity to confront any government, whether democratic or authoritarian, and influence change.

During the New Republic, the business community showed some signs of change. Industrialists demanded more autonomy from the state. They wanted less government intervention in price setting, wage setting, trade union organization, and negotiations with labor. Some members of FIESP criticized that organization's strategy of accommodation in order to obtain rewards. These industrialists believed that the industrial community would never achieve its demands if it remained dependent on, or acquiescent to, the government. They even formed parallel and alternative business associations to more aggressively defend their interests. Despite these changes, however, most industrialists continued to endorse the traditional business associations, as well as government intervention in strikes. In general, industrialists only want to surrender those aspects of corporatist business-state relations that are inimical to their interests, while preserving those that protect business from labor.

Despite their unusually dependent and subordinate relationship to the government, Brazilian industrialists have at times opposed it. The events of 1964 are illustrative. Nearly all industrialists felt threatened by some aspect of the Goulart government. They had no assurance that their interests would be protected, or that they could use existing political institutions to change policies or policy makers. By uniting to depose Goulart they felt they had much to gain in terms of protection of private property, channels of influence, and undisrupted production. They generally believed that these benefits far outweighed the costs of possible government retaliation.

In short, Brazilian industrialists have traditionally been dependent on and acquiescent to governments, including democratic regimes. But if industrialists perceive that a government or its policies seriously jeopardizes their interests, and if they consider the cost of rebellion less than the cost of cooperation or adaptation, they will rebel. Transitional governments could eliminate this potential threat by adopting only moderate policies that business leaders would accept. However, that strategy would limit the government's capacity to achieve democratic objectives, such as social and economic redistribution. Alternatively, as shown below, transitional governments could maximize the weak collective spirit within the business community.

Characteristics of the Business Community.   Business elites' political strength is limited by their inability to mount strong collective action. While business associations such as FIESP have survived political transformations and retained some influence over political outcomes, they often fail to represent the diverse needs, interests, and views of industrial leaders. The diversity of businesses and their needs, as well as the diverse ideological viewpoints of industrialists themselves, often prevent industrialists from working together to achieve collective ends. Nonetheless, at specific historical moments business associations have overcome these weaknesses. Industrialists' involvement in the 1964 coup is a case in point. They overcame fragmentation because the Goulart government threatened nearly all of them. These industrialists did not agree on the source of the threat, or on the proper alternative, but they agreed on the solution: ousting Goulart. They also realized that they could not achieve this goal by acting on their own, and that passivity would be suicidal. Therefore, owing to the nearly universally negative impact of Goulart's policies and the lack of alternative forms of political action, industrialists overcame their individualism, diversity, and political indifference and united to help undermine the government.

Crisis situations like that of 1964 are, fortunately, extremely rare and are unlikely to recur. Diversity within the business community ensures that industrialists will rarely agree that they are all threatened by a particular government or its policies. Moreover, industrialists' resources generally enable them to use alternative means of influencing the political system from within, rather than having to overthrow it. Thus a business rebellion is highly unlikely.

Industrialists' diversity also limits their influence over particular government policies or policy changes. Their efforts to defeat the inclusion of measures mandating a reduced work week in the 1988 Constitution provide an example. While industrialists generally opposed the mandated reduction of the work week, some had already reduced the work week in their firms, and others were capable of absorbing the increased cost. As a result, the business community lacked the unity needed to defeat the legislation. However, even when industrialists reached consensus to mobilize for a particular purpose, their political power was limited owing to the nature of their collective action.

The Nature of Collective Action by Brazilian Business Leaders.   When industrialists reach consensus and mobilize politically, they engage in defensive collective action. Rather than designing and implementing political initiatives or policy changes, they simply defend their own political and economic interests from unacceptable changes. When faced with particular threats, they may overcome the diversity of their views and needs to defend themselves against unfavorable governments or policies. However, diversity often prevents them from developing alternatives to those governments or policies. As a result, they often rely on other social sectors to design and implement alternatives. When that support from other social sectors is unavailable, business leaders' influence is extremely limited.

The 1964 coup and the attempts to influence the 1988 Constitution are examples of the successes and limitations, respectively, of business collective action. The Goulart government was unusual in that the extent of the political and economic crisis was so great that various groups within the business community and society at large agreed that Goulart should be ousted. The military felt that the Goulart government was undermining the hierarchy of the armed forces, the Constitution, the capitalist order, and social and political stability. Some politicians believed that Goulart would not hold presidential elections and thus would frustrate their political ambitions. Anticommunist middle-class groups believed that Goulart was threatening the nation by tolerating, and even encouraging, the spread of communism. Thus, industrialists' alliances with other social sectors, particularly the military and the technocracy, made the coup possible.

While industrialists generally agreed that their objective was to remove Goulart, they did not agree on his replacement. Some advocated new elections and a continuation of the democratic system, while others endorsed authoritarian rule. However, industrialists had little influence over the regime that replaced Goulart; their allies in the military and the technocracy made the decision to implant a military regime. The 1964 coup therefore suggests that industrialists' alliances with powerful social groups can prove extremely effective in bringing about political change. However, on their own business leaders lack the power to undermine political systems or to design replacements for those systems.

On the legislative level, business leaders also relied on defensive collective action and external support. For example, most agreed that the job security legislation would undermine their flexibility to hire and fire at will. They did not, however, agree on what kinds of protections from arbitrary dismissal workers should be given, or whether indeed workers should have any such protection. Thus, industrialists relied on the Centrão to formulate and implement an alternative to the legislation: the indemnity clause, which was acceptable to most industrialists (it merely increased the amount of indemnity employers were already obliged to pay). However, industrialists as a group could not have agreed to the indemnity alternative without the assistance of the Centrão, since many initially opposed the measure. Some argued that the new compensation level was too high. Others opposed the measure on the grounds that any form of indemnity raises firms' costs and reduces national growth and employment. Still others believed that indemnity did not protect workers sufficiently against arbitrary dismissal. In other words, consensus against the job security legislation was not sufficient to defeat it. Rather, the defeat of the legislation was also a result of the Centrão's lobbying in favor of alternative legislation, which industrialists did not endorse but which they preferred to job security.

Although during the New Republic industrialists also nearly universally opposed the unrestricted right to strike and the reduced work week, they proved incapable of defeating either proposal because of a lack of external support. The Constituent Assembly had already forged a compromise in response to labor's initial proposal of a forty-hour week, and as a result, industrialists could not convince conservative groups to lobby against the reduction. And although industrialists widely opposed the right-to-strike legislation, the Centrão had disbanded, and no other social sector mobilized on behalf of industrialists to defeat the provision or provide an alternative to it. Thus, industrialists' efforts failed.

These examples of industrialists' involvement in the 1964 coup and the 1988 legislative reforms emphasize a number of points about collective action on the part of Brazilian business. First, industrialists' political activities are primarily aimed at vetoing proposed changes rather than designing and implementing alternatives. Second, industrialists' success in political endeavors depends on whether or not the business community can reach a consensus to mobilize in collective self-defense. Success also depends on reinforcement from other social groups. These social groups bolster business leaders' political activities by providing alternatives to the governments or policies that business leaders veto. When business leaders lack internal consensus or external support, their political initiatives generally fail.

In short, the Brazilian case suggests that transitional political systems are likely to remain protected from disloyal opposition on the part of business elites (even if they face radical popular uprisings) if certain conditions are met. These governments must remain legitimate by guaranteeing established procedures and protecting political institutions. In addition, these governments must continue to regulate the economy, keeping the business community vulnerable to government retribution, and must guarantee sufficient individual and collective channels of influence for business elites, so as to allow them to participate in the political system. Business loyalty to transitional governments also depends on prevailing domestic and international contexts. If nations experience political amnesia and begin to view authoritarian rule as a panacea for political and economic uncertainty, Brazilian business leaders' opinions will no doubt shift in that direction. Finally, to prevent business elites from limiting social and economic redistribution and substantive democratic reform, democratic governments must prove adept at developing compromises and maintaining the natural fragmentation within the business community.

Brazilian Industrialists in Comparative Perspective

It is difficult to compare Brazilian industrialists' political attitudes and behavior to those of their counterparts in other countries for a number of reasons. First, only a few empirical studies of business elites exist. This is beginning to change, however; a growing number of scholars have recently begun to investigate business elites in Latin America.[2] Second, the studies that do exist focus primarily on business associations and interest groups rather than on individual business leaders' attitudes and behavior, and also often probe a different set of questions than those posed in this study. And third, political and economic development in other countries, as well as the organization of capital-labor relations, differs from that in Brazil.

Despite these limitations, three case studies of business elites in Argentina, Chile, and Spain—countries that have recently undergone similar transitions from authoritarian rule to greater political opening—confirm elements of the adaptive actor approach to business leaders' political attitudes and behavior. These studies also provide insights into the factors that differentiate these elites from one another with regard to attitudes and behavior.

The Political Preferences of Business Elites

In all of the cases selected for comparison, business leaders generally supported authoritarian regimes, at least initially. However, as in the Brazilian case, they did not derail the political liberalization process once it had begun. Instead, they adapted to it and even realized certain benefits from it. In particular, they endorsed increased participation by all social sectors in the new political system, thus enhancing the government's legitimacy. Yet, while accepting and adapting to the changes, they also feared liberalization, especially in the area of labor relations.

The Argentine Case.   In Argentina, business leaders lent strong support to the 1966 and 1976 military coups.[3] In both cases, they were reacting not only to the serious economic problems and increasing social disorder confronting them but also to the government's lack of legitimacy and its unresponsiveness to business needs. President Illía (1963–66) had only a weak base of social support, which further eroded over time. In business leaders' view, Illía's weak legitimacy was compounded by his failure to consult with the business community or in any way represent private sector interests. Frustration with the government led the business community to mobilize against Illía and embrace the coup and the initial years of the Onganía government. General Onganía provided business leaders with the political stability they believed Illía threatened; and Onganía, through his appointment of Adalberto Krieger Vasena as economics minister, contributed to the design and implementation of competent economic policies.

It was not long, however, before the Onganía government also began to lose legitimacy. Internal divisions within the government hindered effective decision making. Workers' and students' protests against the regime eroded its social support. Its inability to control the increasing number of assassinations and kidnappings, and the increasing amount of guerrilla activity, heightened popular insecurity about the regime's capacity to govern. Its economic program also failed to maintain support. It was perceived as having "sold out" to the transnational and big-business sectors, rather than encouraging national industry.

Business leaders' original consensus in support of the military regime deteriorated into intrabourgeois factionalism. Rural elites felt marginalized by the regime's support for urban industrial development. Regional business groups complained of discriminatory treatment by the regime. Local capital criticized the regime for "denationalizing" the economy. And competing business groups protested the regime's unresponsiveness to private sector needs.

Social discontent with the Onganía government exploded in a massive protest in Córdoba in 1969. The *cordobazo,* the regime's use of repression in squelching workers and students in Córdoba who were protesting national economic policy, began the government's ultimate demise. The regime was rent with internal tensions. The economy plummeted and guerrilla activity increased, proving the regime's economic and political incompetence. As a result of this incompetence, even the regime's strongest supporters in the transnational and big-capital sectors withdrew their support. However, although business leaders were dissatisfied with the Onganía government, their opinion of the military regime was divided. While some advocated making the government more authoritarian and strongly resisted political liberalization, others adopted a more flexible attitude. These divided opinions persisted even after a failed attempt to continue the military regime under General Levingston, and after General Lanusse's transition from authoritarian rule in 1971.

The Cámpora (1973) and Perón (1973–74) governments did little to reinforce the democratic elements within the business community. Both Peronist governments faced legitimacy problems. Radical guerrilla activity further eroded the government's control, and internal conflicts within the governing party undermined effective policy making. A power vacuum resulted from President Cámpora's isolation and ineffective leadership, President Juan Perón's death in office, and the weak leadership of Perón's successor and wife, Isabel Perón (1974–76). In addition to being plagued by weak leadership, these democratic governments were also threatened by the global economic crisis of the mid-1970s, which hindered their ability to manage the economy competently. As a result of such political and economic instability, the business class again united behind a military coup in 1976.

The coup installed a military regime under the successive leadership of Generals Videla (1976–81), Viola (1981), and Galtieri (1981–82). Rather than resolving the political and economic crises, these military governments exacerbated them. Incompetence and unpredictability marked the military regime's economic policies. Draconian economic orthodoxy under Videla alienated a good deal of the business class, leading to high rates of capital flight. Viola attempted—and failed—to restore the regime's base of societal support through populist measures, and did not try to regain business support. Galtieri returned to more orthodox policies, emphasizing the privatization of state enterprises. Despite the various attempts to restore economic order, however, the economy plummeted under the military regime.

The regime also proved incapable of producing competent political policies. Notorious among its acts was the "dirty war," in which more than fifteen thousand citizens disappeared into the hands of the military regime's repressive apparatus. Military authority was supplemented with state terror. The regime's violation of human rights received widespread attention both in Argentina and abroad, and brought mounting international and domestic pressure for political change. The regime's fatal error, however, was its initiation of the Malvinas (Falklands) War in 1982. The military's miscalculations in waging the war and assessing the chances of success, as well as its deceptive reporting on military victories and the economic and social costs of its ultimate defeat, eroded the public's already dwindling confidence in its capacity to govern.

Business leaders began to withdraw support from the regime because of its failed economic program, the disastrous Malvinas adventure, and widespread domestic and international protests over its "dirty war." In their eyes, the regime lacked legitimacy (i.e., legal, traditional, or charismatic authority), its military and economic policies were incompetent, and its overall stability was in doubt. Moreover, it did not allow business any influence over policy decisions. Business leaders believed that the regime both ignored business interests and attempted to control the business community through intervention in, and elimination of, business associations. Thus, business leaders perceived that the costs of democracy (e.g., increased trade union power and state control over the economy) were less threatening to their interests than continued ineffective and unchecked control by the armed forces would be.[4]

Despite their withdrawal of support from the military regime, however, business leaders provided only contingent support for the new civilian leaders.[5] They did not try to undermine the new democratic governments of Presidents Alfonsín and Menem, but neither did they embrace them. They continued to hedge their bets, engaging in capital flight and limiting their domestic investments.

Their uneasiness resulted in part from their recollection of threats prior to the 1966 and 1976 coups. Stridently radical popular movements are much more prominent in the history of Argentina than in the history of Brazil. The Peronist trade union and guerrilla movements were clearly stronger, more radical, and more successful at winning their demands than were the trade union movement or radical popular movements in Brazil under Goulart. Thus, Argentine business leaders' fears of the left and of labor were much greater than those of their Brazilian counterparts, and they therefore provided more cautious support for the transitions from authoritarian rule than did Brazilian business leaders.

Over time, Argentine business leaders' fears have subsided. With the victory of President Alfonsín and the Radical Party, the business community realized that political liberalization is not necessarily equated with increased trade union power, although the civilian government did assume more control over the economy than the military regime had done.[6] In other words, the Alfonsín government's policies "neutralized the costs" of democracy.[7] Under Menem, business leaders learned that civilian presidents, even Peronists, can offer effective political and economic leadership. Indeed, Carlos Acuña states that, regardless of the different shapes Argentine democracies might take, the bourgeoisie considers democracy "more functional and less risky" than an authoritarian option.[8]

As in the Brazilian case, most Argentine business leaders did not become involved in the demand for political liberalization. At the same time, they did not try to derail the transition from authoritarian rule once it was under way. Instead, they adapted to it. Acuña's study suggests that they provided stronger (although still passive) support for that transition than did their counterparts in Brazil, owing to the more extreme failure of the Argentine military regime's policies. Although Argentine business leaders felt more vulnerable to the liberalization of controls over trade unions than did Brazilian industrialists, because of the greater threat from the Peronist unions in the period prior to the 1966 and 1976 coups, their fears subsided when only moderate changes in capital-labor relations occurred under democratic rule. While investment stability is not guaranteed, the business community possesses new options for influencing outcomes. Moreover, broad domestic and international support for the transition has increased Argentine business leaders' tolerance. In other words, they, like their Brazilian counterparts, have accepted the transition and worked within it to defend their interests.

The Chilean Case.   Before his election in 1970, Chilean business leaders viewed socialist Salvador Allende as a threat and campaigned against his presidential candidacy. During Allende's first two years in office, however, business leaders appeared to accept him. They believed that their survival was guaranteed and that they possessed the political resources to work within the government, influence it through bargaining and negotiations, and neutralize Allende's challenges to the private sector.[9]

By 1972–73, however, business leaders had begun to collectively oppose the Allende government. They almost universally viewed Allende as a threat to the nation, to democracy, and to the traditional patterns of social relations. They feared that Allende would turn the country into a totalitarian, communist state.

Initially their forms of opposition were entirely consistent with the democratic political system. They mobilized to directly influence parliamentary elections, an entirely new political activity for Chilean business leaders. And although they were sufficiently successful to prevent Allende from instituting many of his reforms, they failed to elect the number of representatives necessary to impeach him. Thus, not only were they stuck with Allende but their electoral activities had heightened social tensions and created a parliamentary impasse.

Faced with their failure to oust Allende through democratic means, most business leaders, with the exception of a small group who endorsed Allende's Popular Unity government, began to favor a military coup. However, while nearly united in their opposition to Allende, these business leaders had no clear vision of an alternative government. As in the Brazilian case, some business leaders endorsed the coup but believed that the military would restore democracy under new leadership. Others believed that the military should remain in power and restructure the political system. Thus, while business leaders' widespread fear of the Allende government unified their political action against it, their ideological diversity and their heterogeneous needs and capacities prevented them from developing any consensus on an alternative to that regime. Thus, the anti-Allende business movement was vague, defensive, and reactive. Business leaders relied on their allies in the military and the technocracy to develop an alternative to the Allende government.[10]

Chilean business leaders, like their Brazilian counterparts, generally accepted the military regime installed after the 1973 coup. However, the diversity within the business community produced conflicts over the regime's specific policies and practices. Most of those who were opposed to the regime's policies were industrialists at small and medium-sized businesses who felt that they had lost their political and economic representation under General Pinochet's leadership. They particularly objected to the regime's efforts to control or disband business associations. Despite these tensions, however, business leaders generally accepted the military regime and its policies. Their fear of political instability under Allende, and their general belief that the military was managing the economy competently, guaranteed their loyalty. Indeed, despite their conflicts with the regime business leaders strongly backed General Pinochet in the 1980 plebiscite.

After the plebiscite, some business leaders engaged in antiregime protests. The economic recession and numerous bankruptcies led the business community to question the regime's competence to manage the economy and protect the capitalist order. Some business leaders openly criticized the regime and called for a political opening, including a liberalization of labor legislation and capital-labor relations. However, as in the Brazilian case, several characteristics inherent to the business community—specifically, internal diversity and fear of retribution by the government—prevented business leaders from mounting a successful opposition to the regime.

The regime adopted two strategies to stifle dissent from business groups. It both threatened to use force against rebellious entrepreneurs and modified some of its policies. While the threat of retribution kept some business leaders from protesting, the renewed sense of influence reassured others that they retained some influence over the regime. Either way, the regime effectively defused business opposition.

In addition, despite the severity of the economic crisis and the defection by some business leaders, some firms continued to strongly endorse the regime. Some believed in the regime's neoliberal economic policies and had sufficient resources to withstand the negative consequences of those policies. Most still feared political instability and thus endorsed the regime as a preferable option. These industrialists viewed increasing labor protests as a reason to end business-state conflicts and close ranks with the regime.

While Chilean business leaders' political attitudes and behavior mirror in many ways the attitudes and behavior observed in Argentina and Brazil, there is one striking difference: their attitude toward the military regime. The Pinochet regime was not as discredited domestically as its counterparts in Argentina or Brazil. Although international criticism for human rights abuses eroded some of the regime's legitimacy, the regime's economic management bolstered it. In business leaders' view, the regime was consistent in its policies, somewhat responsive to business needs, and competent in managing the economy. It instituted a successful free market system and removed most controls over the economy (e.g., price and wage controls were lifted, tariff rates reduced, and exchange controls eliminated), thus giving business leaders flexibility in production and investment strategies.[11] In addition, after a severe economic crisis in the early 1980s, the Chilean economy under Pinochet achieved levels of growth (an average of 3.5% per year from 1984 to 1989) that were high compared to the growth rates for the rest of Latin America.[12] In the 1988 plebiscite, therefore, a significant number of business leaders continued to support the regime because of its economic management and political stability. They simply ignored (or, indeed, benefited from) the authoritarian and repressive aspects of the regime.

Opposition to Pinochet from within the business community was limited to a minority of industrialists. This minority was composed of both supporters of Allende's Popular Unity government and disgruntled supporters of the coup against Allende. They argued that the regime's political opening was too slow and that its widespread economic and political exclusion had led to a potentially explosive social situation. These democratic businesspeople lacked power within the business community and, like their counterparts in Brazil, they failed to join the opposition movement in the country. In other words, they posed no true challenge to the acquiescent strategy of the majority of business leaders.

The pro-Pinochet business leaders mobilized to support the regime in the plebiscite. They advocated a continuation of Pinochet's economic strategy of modernization and development, suggested that the opposition would undermine those strategies, and tried to underplay the repressive and dictatorial aspects of the regime. When the polls indicated that the opposition might win, these pro-Pinochet business leaders began to alter their strategy. Rather than emphasize Pinochet's modernization and development projects, they rekindled fears of the social and political chaos that had existed prior to the Pinochet government. Despite their efforts, the opposition won the plebiscite.

After the plebiscite, business leaders, because of their close alliance with the dictatorship, feared retaliation from the political center and left. The political calm that followed the plebiscite eased their fears. It also led business groups to adopt various strategies. Many retreated to a preocupation with the concerns of their individual firms. Others, especially in those business sectors alienated during Pinochet's regime, became politically reactivated and advocated social and economic harmony. Still others mobilized around the 1989 presidential elections, again praising the neoliberal and modernizing policies of the military regime. While this appeared to be an attempt to develop a more proactive rather than defensive posture vis-à-vis the state, business leaders never achieved this goal. Guillermo Campero suggests three reasons why this strategy might have failed: business leaders' social prestige was weak owing to their close association with Pinochet; there was a lack of consensus within the business community with regard to the project; and there was a lack of strong political support.[13] In other words, business leaders lacked the social status, internal unity, and external support to carry out their project.

Chilean business leaders have proved more cautious in their acceptance of the political transition than have their counterparts in Brazil and Argentina for two principal reasons: the precoup threat, and the relative success of the military regime. Business leaders' precoup fears were more intense in Chile than in either Argentina or Brazil. As Ernest Bartell states, "Not only political instability, but also the memory of it and the fear of it, influence business perceptions in Chile."[14] Chilean business leaders feared any challenges to private property, such as agrarian reforms.[15] Unlike the Brazilians, they did not believe that the left had modified its position because of changing international trends or its experiences under military rule. On the contrary, these business leaders viewed political parties and their leaders as uncompromising ideologues. Chilean business leaders also feared trade union mobilization and hoped to restrict the politicization of trade union federations. While Bartell acknowledges business leaders' intolerance of radicalism in economic policies, political parties, and trade unions, he suggests that, at the very least, Chilean business leaders' attitudes toward workers may change, since several business leaders he interviewed stated that workers were becoming more concerned with their own economic interests (i.e., steady employment) and less focused on political involvement. In another contrast to their Brazilian counterparts, Chilean business leaders proved more reluctant to accept democracy and liberalization of the labor relations system. Moreover, their perceptions of ideological polarization continued to prevail, heightening their fear of prejudicial economic reforms and political instability.

In stark contrast to Brazil and Argentina, the Chilean military regime's economic model had not been as universally discredited among the business community. The Pinochet regime was much more successful at bringing about an economic restructuring than were the Brazilian and Argentine military regimes. As a result of this success and precoup fears, Chilean business leaders' support for the regime was much greater than that of their counterparts in Brazil and Argentina, and withstood serious economic crises. The factor that most effectively eroded the legitimacy of the regime in business leaders' view was international criticism. Indeed, international criticism appeared to be more significant in Chile than in Brazil and Argentina.[16] Its importance results no doubt from the absence of other delegitimizing factors and from the fact that Chile's transition from authoritarian rule occurred after most of the other countries in the region had already begun the transition process. Yet despite the general international consensus regarding the legitimacy of democratic government, business leaders still feared that democracy would destroy the neoliberal economic foundation built at great cost under Pinochet, and replace it with the excessive government intervention in the economy which had prevailed under earlier democratic regimes.

While their uneasiness with a democratic transition continues, Chilean business leaders have over time become increasingly tolerant of the political liberalization and are unlikely to derail the transition. In part this is because of the fragmentation within the business community. Not all industrialists benefited from the military regime. Indeed, some suffered a great deal under that system. As a result, not all business leaders are stalwart defenders of the Pinochet neoliberal project. Indeed, some advocate a reversal of Pinochet's project by demanding some government intervention and social and economic redistribution.

The Spanish Case.   Spanish business leaders, for the most part, supported General
Franco's regime. During its first three decades, it provided them with stability,
protection against external and internal competition among businesses, and control
over trade union demands. However, as in the Argentine and Brazilian cases, the
Franco regime eventually lost its high level of support from business leaders. During its second phase, in the 1960s, the regime implemented reforms in labor relations (e.g., social security benefits, pensions, plant committees, and protection
against arbitrary dismissal) to control pressure from trade unions. Some of these
reforms, particularly the restrictions on employers' right to discharge workers,
directly affected businesspeople's profits, since it limited their use of labor-saving
devices. In addition, the business community faced an increasingly unfavorable
economic climate owing to, among other things, a rising inflation rate and rising
balance-of-payments deficits. Moreover, business leaders perceived that the government had become less responsive to their needs. Finally, despite their illegality,
strikes erupted during the final years of the Franco regime, indicating to business
leaders that the regime's policy of providing popular sectors with social benefits in
exchange for political demobilization could not be sustained.[17] In the eyes of industrialists the Franco regime now lacked stability; its legitimacy was questionable because it could no longer command obedience from society and because its
economic policies were ineffective. Moreover, the regime excluded business leaders from its economic decision making.

Thus, when Franco died, and controlled liberalization began, industrialists neither protested the political transition nor attempted to derail it. At the same time,
their dissatisfaction with the latter years of the Franco regime did not translate into
active support for the transition to democracy. Instead, as in Brazil, business leaders
were confused and had mixed opinions about the transition. Some of them endorsed
it, or at least the opportunity it afforded for greater influence over policy decisions.
Others feared that because of the lack of strong business associations and the unre-
liability of political parties they had no effective representatives with which to defend their interests in an open political system.[18] Business leaders also feared
increased pressures from organized labor. Moreover, the results of a Spanish study
were similar to my findings regarding the early transition in Brazil: Spanish business leaders disagreed over the pace of the transition. Twenty-four percent demanded a faster pace of liberalization, 10 percent accepted the existing pace, 24
percent demanded a slower pace, and 22 percent desired an end to the transition and
a return to authoritarian rule.[19]

Nonetheless, once the transition was under way, business elites tolerated it.
Roberto Martinez refers to this adaptation as a "remarkable proclivity towards
change and flexibility."[20] Yet, he notes that they approached the transition with a
high degree of "conservatism and moderation."[21] In particular, they resisted

changes in labor relations, even those begun during the Franco era, such as the enactment of prohibitions against arbitrary dismissal and a loosening of controls over
strikes. However, Víctor Pérez Díaz suggests that, over time, business leaders even
accepted the liberalization of labor relations. Indeed, he states that they recognized
that although Spanish workers militantly fight for certain demands (e.g., increases
in real wages, increased levels of employment, and social benefits), the workers are
not fighting against "the company, . . . capitalism, or . . . the state."[22]

This realization resulted from business leaders' experience in negotiations with
labor and their overall observations of the labor movement. For example, as a result
of the social pact discussions of the 1970s and 1980s, the labor movement im-
plicitly accepted a reduction in its strike activity in exchange for government concessions on wages, higher employment, and social benefits. As a result, the
dramatically high level of strike activity of the early transition period (1975–77)
diminished. In addition, the socialist General Labor Union (UGT), which had taken
a more conciliatory role in negotiations, grew in strength, while the more combative Communist Party Workers' Commissions (CCOO) did not.[23] Although business leaders continued to view the CCOO as extremely radical, their overall
perception that organized labor was moderate in its demands and strategies assuaged their fears. This reduced fear translated into a high degree of satisfaction
with labor relations in their firms.[24]

In another parallel with the Brazilian case, Spanish business leaders' fear of the
left subsided despite the latter's revolutionary past and the electoral victories of the
Spanish Socialist Labor Party (PSOE). In fact, business leaders even praised some
specific policies of González's PSOE government. For example, although they
gave the socialist government lower grades than the center-right Union of the
Democratic Center (UCD) government of Suarez for its increase in public expenditures, they gave it higher marks for its labor and industrial policies.[25] Moreover, 80
percent of the business leaders interviewed by Pérez Díaz stated that they thought
PSOE brought political stability.[26] As in Brazil, a small minority of business lead-
e s supported the left (PSOE), although the majority voted for center-right and
right-wing parties (the UCD and the Popular Alliance [AP]).[27] Finally, as depicted
in table 6.1, a significant minority of Spanish and Brazilian business leaders identified with the left, although most considered themselves just right of center (4 on a
7-point scale, compared to 6 on a 10-point scale in the Brazilian case). Thus, as in
the Brazilian case, most business leaders did not consider the left or labor to be a
serious threat to their interests during the transition to democracy.

Both Pérez Díaz and Martinez suggest that Spanish business leaders are highly
adaptive, which has allowed them to accept such diverse governments as Franco's
authoritarian military regime, Suárez's center-right transitional government, and
González's socialist democracy. Martinez states that Spanish business leaders are

Table 6.1.   Percentage Distribution of Spanish
and Brazilian Business Leaders by Ideological
Self-Description

Ideology	Business Leaders' Nationality	
	Spanish ($N = 551$)	Brazilian ($N = 143$)
Moderately leftist	15	18
Centrist	23	27
Moderately rightist	51	48
Extremely rightist	11	6

Sources: The Brazilian data come from my 1987–88
interviews with industrialists (see Appendix). The
Spanish data come from Perez Díaz, *El retorno de la
sociedad civil,* 163.
Note: The no-responses have been excluded from both
sets of percentages.

basically prosystem and will work within the existing political framework, regardless of its orientation, to protect their interests.[28] This analysis mirrors the Brazilian
case. Brazilian industrialists also proved capable of adapting to both authoritarian
and democratic governments. While they have not had the opportunity to experience a socialist national government, they certainly adapted to a socialist mayor in
São Paulo.

Overview.   In short, business elites in Argentina, Chile, and Spain, like those in
Brazil, are neither inherently authoritarian nor inherently democratic. Business
leaders tolerated, rather than blocked the transition from authoritarian rule. However, the degree of acceptance of the transition varied, and depended on four factors: the seriousness of the threat they had perceived in the earlier democratic
period; the legitimacy and competence of the authoritarian regime, and its inclusion
of business in its decision making; business leaders' perceptions of government
and society during the transition; and the passage of time. For example, Argentine,
Brazilian, and Spanish business leaders all appeared to give greater support to the
democratic transition than did their Chilean counterparts. The first three groups had
experienced more problems during the military regime than had the Chileans, and
recognized that the transition might resolve the problems of political instability and
their lack of influence over government policies.

However, all of these business elites feared that the democratic transition would
unleash anew the labor movements and the radical left, which they felt had contributed to the earlier breakdown of democracy in their countries. Nonetheless, the

Argentine, Brazilian, and Spanish business elites' fears subsided over time, while the Chileans' remained constant. Indeed, Chilean business leaders' perceptions of the left and of labor have not changed substantially since the Allende period. This perception can be explained, in part, by the higher degree of fear Chilean business leaders felt during the period before the coup. Moreover, the pace of change was more rapid and less controlled in the Chilean case. In contrast, Brazilian and Spanish business leaders acquired experience negotiating with labor and observing the left during a gradual and controlled transition. These experiences and observations reduced their fear of radicalism. And in Argentina, business leaders' initial fear that democracy would inevitably bring increased trade union power was reduced when such power failed to materialize under Alfonsín. Thus, the attitudes of Chilean business leaders may also change as they accumulate nonthreatening experiences with labor and the left in the new democratic environment.

An additional factor also affects business leaders' attitude toward democracy: their ability to influence policies. In each of the countries discussed above, business elites, in part because they had lost influence over the decisions made by democratic governments, supported the military coups that replaced those governments. They subsequently withdrew support from, or criticized, the military regimes when those regimes excluded business leaders from decisions affecting them. The next section analyzes how these business elites have defended their interests during the democratic transitions.

Political Action by Business Elites

As in Brazil, the transition to democracy brought new channels of influence for business elites in Argentina, Chile, and Spain. In each of these cases, business leaders employed a variety of political strategies for defending their interests within the emerging democratic framework.

The Argentine Case.   Acuña's study of Argentine business associations sharply contrasts with the Brazilian case. He describes a highly independent and active system of business associations. Those business associations are not organized by the state, do not appear to be dependent on it, and do not seem to fear retaliation from it. They freely protest government policies. Moreover, these business associations are "functional" representatives of business interests. Unlike their Brazilian counterparts, they form or merge to defend specific interests within the business community. And they are able to achieve positions within the government's decision-making apparatus. Rather than representing the entire business community, they unite only those enterprises that share opinions on particular issues. And once they have achieved (or failed to achieve) their objective, these associations disband.[29]

Therefore, they are not permanent representatives of a particular faction, since the members of any given faction may disagree on future issues.

Despite the relative success of Argentine business associations, Acuña identifies several problems the Argentine business community has faced in defending its interests. First, although the Alfonsín government allowed for institutional representation of business interests on government commissions, those interests were not often reflected in the government's policies. Since the government's first priority was to adopt strategies that it believed would ameliorate the severe national crisis, business interests were sometimes adversely affected. Moreover, in formulating its policies the government weighed the competing demands of organized labor and business interests, not always acceding to the latter.

Second, the Argentine system of business representation fragmented the business community. Various business associations competed with each other for representation and influence in government. In an attempt to win representation, the excluded groups have criticized the decisions and strategies of the associations that are currently represented in government. A united business position is, therefore, rarely achieved, and because no business group can claim to represent the interests of the entire business community, the power and influence of all associations is diminished.[30]

In contrast, the key business association in Brazil, FIESP, has existed virtually unchanged since the 1940s. The specific and functional demands of sectors of industry are represented by autonomous and parallel associations that coexist with FIESP rather than competing with it. Ideological or class factions within the industrial community have formed independent associations (e.g., small business associations and the PNBE), but these organizations often act as interest groups within FIESP (e.g., seeking to increase FIESP's awareness of certain industrialists' needs) rather than competing with FIESP to represent the business class on national issues. Moreover, despite industrialists' complaints about FIESP's strategy and scope of representation, most industrialists recognize that FIESP provides the best method for defending their interests on the national level and in collective bargaining sessions. In other words, FIESP faces little competition and receives qualified, but nonetheless widespread, support from its constituents. However, its power is limited owing to its pattern of accommodation with the state, its dependence on the state for finances, the fragmentation of opinion among industrial leaders on specific issues, and competition with other social groups for influence over government policies. In addition, although FIESP engages in national politics, it is largely a regional and sectoral association, representing the interests of São Paulo industrialists. Few other regions or sectors have acquired the same degree of organizational strength.

The difference between the Brazilian and Argentine forms of business associations can be explained, at least in part, by the different traditions in the two countries. Brazilian business associations were for the most part organized by the state, and achieved a monopoly of representation through the corporatist system. Individual factions are not strong enough to compete with FIESP's overarching power. Individual industrialists are unwilling to undermine the organization's authority because it provides them with a highly respected, albeit often ineffective, voice to defend their interests on national issues. In the Argentine case, the state did not organize business associations, and business leaders, left to their own devices, formed ad hoc pressure groups to defend the consensus interests of various factions within the business community.

The Chilean Case.   Bartell's analysis of Chilean business leaders suggests that they use the party system more consistently than do either the Argentine or Brazilian elites. Bartell notes that Chilean industrialists firmly endorsed the right-wing party National Renovation, whose presidential candidate was the former finance minister responsible for the policies that had benefited much of the private sector. Bartell contends that these business leaders believed that only the right would guarantee their basic economic demand, namely, that the free enterprise system be protected.[31]

Chilean business leaders' recourse to political parties to protect their interests contrasts sharply with the weak support for parties among Brazilian business leaders. The difference stems no doubt from the stronger democratic tradition in Chile, which fostered stronger identification with political parties and ideologies. Moreover, the highly politicized and polarized political spectrum in Chile gave industrialists clearer choices between political candidates and between the candidates' positions. With the exception of parties on the left, the ideological components of most Brazilian political parties are amorphous, as are the parties' attitudes toward business.[32]

Also in sharp contrast with the Brazilian case, most Chilean business leaders supported collective bargaining via firm-level negotiations rather than through employers' associations. Bartell argues that Chilean business leaders believed that industrywide or regional bargaining would increase the role of trade union federations, thereby reducing employers' control over the workers in their firms.[33] This suggests that they believed the trade union movement was a stronger force than the employers' association. In contrast, Brazilian industrialists felt that negotiating through employers' associations would provide them with greater protection from trade unions' demands.

The difference between Chilean and Brazilian business leaders' attitudes toward collective bargaining stems from the historical differences between the trade

union movements in the two countries. The Chileans are understandably more concerned than the Brazilians about highly politicized and powerful trade union movements. Therefore, they attempt to minimize the involvement of the labor movement
in collective bargaining by negotiating directly with workers on a firm-by-firm
basis. On the other hand, Brazilians, who are less concerned with confronting a
radical labor movement, rely on centralized representation by their business associations to limit their losses in negotiations.

The Chilean case indicates that the success of collective action by business elites
depends in part on political options and traditions. If a political party clearly represents business interests, business leaders will defend it. Moreover, if a country has
had a tradition of party politics, its business leaders are more likely to use that
mechanism for defending their interests. Finally, the Chilean case suggests that the
representation of employers' interests in collective bargaining sessions will depend
on past, as well as current, experiences. Whereas Chilean business leaders avoided
negotiations via associations in order to limit the power of labor federations in collective bargaining, Brazilian business leaders opted for these negotiations because
they had proved successful in limiting labor's demands.

The Spanish Case.   Spanish business associations provide the strongest parallel
with the Brazilian case. Most Spanish business leaders, like their Brazilian counterparts, belonged to business associations (85% in Pérez Díaz's study, compared to
86% of the Brazilian industrialists I interviewed) and preferred them to political
representatives for defending their interests.[34] Spanish political parties' ambiguous
position with respect to business concerns rendered industrialists reluctant to support them. As in Brazil, Spanish industrialists used associations to lobby for the
protection of their interests during the writing of a new national constitution, although many questioned their effectiveness.[35] Some charged that these associations lacked experience, since they had been formed during the democratic
transition and shared few traits with their predecessors, which had pursued an acquiescent strategy vis-à-vis the state.[36] Brazilian business leaders also complained
about the lack of expertise within business associations. However, they often
blamed the business associations' historical pattern of acquiescence for the associations' failure to defend industrialists' interests. Moreover, like FIESP, Spanish
business associations faced difficulties in formulating and implementing consensus
policies.[37]

Despite these criticisms, business leaders in both Spain and Brazil had few alternative means of representing their interests. Referring to the Spanish Confederation
of Business Organizations (CEOE) and the Spanish labor federations, Pérez Díaz
argues that "even if the control these economic organisations had over their bases
seemed weak, their degree of representation and influence had become impor-

tant."[38] In the Brazilian case, industrialists frequently criticized FIESP but neither formed competitive organizations nor withdrew their support. They accepted FIESP's leadership, however flawed they perceived it to be.

Moreover, as FIESP and the CEOE gained experience, they proved increasingly effective in defending their constituents' interests, which increased those organizations' influence within the business community, as well as their overall strength. FIESP's collective bargaining and lobbying successes enhanced its role in the Brazilian business community. The CEOE proved even more effective, owing to its role in social pact discussions.[39] It repeatedly and effectively represented business leaders in successful pacts that benefited the business community as a whole.[40]

In sum, at the beginning of the transition from authoritarian rule in both Spain and Brazil, business associations were relatively weak. However, their institutional roles (e.g., in social pact negotiations in Spain, collective bargaining and lobbying in Brazil) enabled them to acquire experience in defending business interests. This experience, the success they achieved in their endeavors, and their monopoly of representation within the business community all increased their power and influence. Nevertheless, they remained burdened by fragmentation and individualism within the business community, which prevented the formation of consensus positions and left the associations vulnerable to competition from other social sectors as well as to the government's agenda.

Overview.   These comparative cases of business elites' collective action indicate several variables that determine the kind of political action business elites pursue. First, national political traditions often dictate business elites' channels of influence. For example, the traditional party system in Chile, with its ideological dimension, motivated business leaders to engage in party politics, whereas elites in other countries were less inclined to do so. Second, the traditional pattern of business association organization and behavior influences the types of business associations that evolve, as well as the strategies they choose. For example, while the corporatist tradition in Brazil had imposed permanent, monopolistic, state-controlled and state-financed business associations, the lack of such control in Argentina led the business community to form ad hoc interest groups that represented class factions, competed—often with each other—for power within the state, pursued specific goals, and dissolved once those goals were (or were not) achieved. Third, the state may create institutional roles for business associations. For example, when the state withdrew from labor negotiations in Brazil, FIESP began representing business interests in collective bargaining sessions. The social pact discussions in Spain created an institutional role for the CEOE with respect to national decisions. And Argentine business associations have competed for positions on government councils and advisory commissions. Fourth, business elites continue supporting existing associations as long as those associations effectively represent the business elites' interests. In the Spanish and Brazilian cases, for example, because the CEOE and FIESP proved somewhat successful in defending business elites' interests in social pact discussions and collective bargaining sessions, their power within the business community grew.[41]

Conclusion: Prospects for Democratic Consolidation

Social scientists could not have foreseen the military coups and military regimes that proliferated throughout Latin America during the 1960s and 1970s. Nor could they have predicted the democratic transitions in the 1980s and 1990s. It is similarly impossible to calculate whether, for how long, and with what specific constraints Latin America's incipient democracies will survive. Moreover, social scientists have not yet anticipated the kinds of political forces that might eventually displace these new democracies. In this study I have attempted to reduce the unpredictability inherent in these dramatic political changes. By analyzing Latin American business elites' political attitudes and behavior during crucial political moments, I have developed insights into how they might react to the consolidation of democracy.

Democratic consolidation, in my view, depends not only on the development of political institutions that allow for broad democratic representation and participation, but also on the redistribution of, and the establishment of equity in, political, economic, and social rights. In other words, it involves creating social democracies capable of ameliorating the endemic economic and political exclusion of the vast majority of Latin America's population.

The political role that business elites have historically played suggests a bleak future for this kind of democracy. My research, for example, confirmed an aspect of the theory of the bureaucratic-authoritarian state: its assumption that a faction within the Latin American business elite prefers authoritarian rule to democratic rule. This faction played an instrumental role in overthrowing the reformist democratic regimes of the 1960s and 1970s. Furthermore, it bolstered authoritarian regimes by financing the repressive apparatus, endorsing regressive economic policies, and providing one of the regimes' only bases of legitimacy within society. Because many of the conditions that prompted business elites' antidemocratic activity in the 1960s and 1970s have resurfaced, the new Latin American democracies appear nearly as vulnerable as their predecessors.

While recognizing the possibility of an authoritarian reversal, I have provided in this study some reasons to suggest that such an outcome is unlikely, at least in the short term. I have identified the conditions and motivations behind business elites' political actions which would lead them to accept democratic consolidation rather than participating once more in the overthrow of democratic regimes. I have also raised some questions with regard to business elites' capacity to engage in success-ful collective action against democratic regimes. On the basis of my analysis of business elites' motivations and capacities, I suspect that social democratic govern-ments have more flexibility in dealing with business elites and their constraints on policies than might otherwise be assumed.

Business Elites' Motivations for Rebellion

Some of the conditions that had—according to the theory of the bureaucratic-authoritarian state—prompted business elites to rebel against the old democratic regimes have resurfaced. Chief among these are economic stagnation, a radical left, and a combative labor force. In this study, however, I have argued that these factors alone are unlikely to mobilize business rebellions again. They only lead to business opposition if they threaten business elites' foremost political demand: investment stability. The more crucial factors undermining investment stability and thereby provoking business rebellions are political instability (i.e., lack of government le-gitimacy and competence) and the absence of business influence over government policies.

The theory of the bureaucratic-authoritarian state and the transitions literature also fail to emphasize the importance of business elites' perceptions in determining their political actions. I argue that these perceptions are much more significant than objective conditions of threat, and are often shaped by international and domestic political trends and values. In other words, whereas business elites may again mo-bilize against democratic regimes, their reasons for doing so will not be limited to the set of reasons identified in the theory of the bureaucratic-authoritarian state and the transitions literature, and will most likely include threats to political stability and to business influence over policy making.

The Threat of Political Instability

Business elites demand political stability, which they define as government compe-tence and legitimacy, in order to protect their investment and production decisions. There is nothing antidemocratic about such a demand. On the contrary, government legitimacy and competence are essential to the survival of democracy. They enable governments to establish the rules and procedures upon which democratic stability is built. They guarantee that the political order will not change dramatically in the short term. And they allow governments to negotiate compromises between diverse social groups and to enforce the resulting decisions.

There is no guarantee, however, that Latin American business elites' demands for competent, legitimate, and stable governments will be met. Indeed, the political history of the region illustrates the rarity of such regimes. Moreover, business elites themselves have often proved instrumental in eroding the legitimacy, competence, and stability of past Latin American governments.

Despite the region's history, however, business elites today appear increasingly confident about its democratic governments. This confidence results from the legitimacy and competence of those governments. Business elites perceive these new governments as legitimate—in part owing to the fact that previous governments, the authoritarian regimes, have been discredited, leaving business elites and other social actors with few alternatives but democratic systems for political stability. In addition, international opinion strongly supports democratic change. An increasing number of countries throughout the world are attempting to create or restore democratic rule, and international organizations and foreign governments are promoting such transformations. The new government's legitimacy is also based on their capacity to command obedience from their populations. Most have legal authority to govern. They have been elected in fair and open elections that allow for the peaceful transfer of power. They have successfully established rules and procedures for governing, including new constitutions written by democratically elected legislative bodies.

Moreover, business elites have confidence in the competence of these new regimes. Although economic crises continue to plague most of the region, business elites generally respect the economic policies adopted by these new governments. In particular, the international trend toward neoliberal strategies of development has taken hold in Latin America, reversing the well-entrenched pattern of state-sponsored development. In addition to providing the private sector with more economic resources by selling off shares of state-owned enterprises, these neoliberal strategies also reassure business elites that the new governments endorse capitalism and private sector development. This has reduced fears of threats to private property and has increased loyalty to the nascent democracies.

Whereas the legitimacy and competence of the newly emerging democratic regimes appear to protect them from rebellions by business elites, some remain vulnerable. The recent rejection of democratic rules and procedures by President Fujimori in Peru, and by the armed forces in Venezuela and Haiti, suggest that international trends toward democratic change may be fleeting. In addition, domestic and international collective amnesia may gradually eradicate the memory of the failure of authoritarian regimes, thus allowing some social groups to promote an authoritarian reversal. Business elites may join such a movement, if it occurs, when they perceive that the democratic government threatens their investment security. Their perception of such a threat is based not only on a lack of government legitimacy and competence but also on a lack of business influence over government policy making.

Threats to Business Influence over Policy Making

In order to have investment stability, business elites believe that in addition to government competence and legitimacy they also need access to information about government policies affecting the private sector, or participation in the making of those policies. Their demand for participation is not necessarily inconsistent with democratic stability. After all, business elites, like other social groups and individuals, are entitled to representation and participation in democratic systems. Indeed, as the case studies presented in this book suggest, such representation and participation frequently promote stability: the more access to or information about government policy decisions business elites have, the less likely they are to rebel against the state.

Because business elites' demands for participation appear to have been met by the new Latin American democracies, democratic stability has been fortified. On the one hand, these governments have established formal channels of representation and participation which business elites and other social sectors have used to effectively influence political outcomes. On the other hand, business elites have maintained the traditional informal channels of access to, and influence over, government officials. Thus, business elites have enjoyed both collective, formal opportunities and individual, informal opportunities for influencing outcomes in the new Latin American democracies.

The new democratic governments' adoption of neoliberal policies has reinforced business elites' perception of influence over policies. Business elites rarely pressured for these policies, and at times they even resisted them. Nonetheless, the neoliberal thrust of the new Latin American governments has reassured business elites that these governments consider the private sector crucial to development strategies. Thus, although government policies do not always reflect business elites' specific demands, business elites perceive that they have several peaceful options for influencing political outcomes and that the new democratic governments value the business community's contribution to national development.

While no doubt increasing political stability, the new influence that business elites enjoy may simultaneously constrain social democratic governments' attempts at social and economic redistribution. Private entrepreneurs increasingly own and manage essential economic enterprises upon which the foundation of viable democratic systems will be built. They also provide—and have the power to withhold—some of the factors necessary for redistributing wealth and political power: employment and wages, essential goods and services, and government revenues for social services. In other words, whereas business elites' demands for political participation are not necessarily inconsistent with democratic values, unchecked business power can make the democratic system a hostage to private sector interests. Business elites can easily undermine the public interest, threatening the rights and safety of workers and consumers, as well as social welfare, education, environmental protections, and access to health care.

In addition, although redistribution of wealth and power is long overdue in most Latin American countries, business elites have historically viewed any such attempts as a threat to private property; they have blocked reforms and have mobilized against governments that dared to implement reforms. There is no clear measure of the extent of redistribution that business elites will tolerate before feeling threatened. Indeed, business elites' perceptions of threat are no doubt more significant than the actual levels of redistribution. The cases presented in this book suggest that business elites' perceptions will be based on past experiences—and future predictions—regarding government threats to private property, and international trends toward expropriation.

Yet, in most cases, business elites appear to be less intolerant of social and economic reforms than they have been in the past. I attribute this attitude in large part to the cautious reforms implemented by the emerging democratic governments. Indeed, no bold reformers have appeared among the new democratic transition leaders. Yet tepid reforms do not always guarantee business loyalty. For example, because of the intensity of the precoup threat to their property and the relative stability under the military regime, most Chilean business leaders have continued to resist any threat of expropriation, such as agrarian reform. Because their experiences with the current democratic government are very recent, it is too early to assess how rigidly they will oppose redistribution policies.

In contrast to Chilean business leaders, the other business leaders analyzed in this book have tolerated recent reforms. This break with their past results as much from the tepidness of the reforms as from their past experiences and the current international climate. Business elites' experiences with economic and political exclusion during the military regimes prompted a significant and vocal number of them to warn against the dangers of ignoring social concerns. Such warnings, while self-serving in the sense that economic and political reforms will stimulate consumption and reduce social unrest, nevertheless indicate a degree of flexibility with regard to social and economic redistribution programs.

The end of the Cold War and the demise of the socialist bloc in Eastern Europe appear not only to have assuaged business elites' fears of leftist revolution but also (coupled with the neoliberal policy emphasis) to have led to more tolerance toward the new democratic governments' redistribution efforts. Moreover, as the number of leftist governments that take office and remain in power increases, business elites appear to fear such governments less than they did in the 1960s and 1970s. In Spain, for example, business leaders adapted to the socialist government and even applauded aspects of it. And São Paulo business leaders negotiated with and adapted to a socialist mayor. Business elites seem to have learned that private sector interests are not necessarily incompatible with leftist governments.

In short, the current incipient phase of democratization in Latin America provides us with too little information to accurately predict threats from business elites. It is likely, however, that formal political channels, informal forms of influence, the neoliberal thrust of economic policies, and the weakness of the international revolutionary left will be sufficient to convince business elites that their investments are secure. In this case, they are unlikely to mobilize against the new democratic governments even if these governments deny specific policy demands or implement social and economic redistribution. Nonetheless, it is possible over time that social reformers might take office, unravel neoliberal policies, and promote social and economic redistribution. In such a case, business elites' success in rebelling against the regime will depend on their capacity to mobilize.

Determinants of Business Elites' Capacity to Rebel

The transitions literature and the theory of the bureaucratic-authoritarian state emphasize business elites' capacity to join or to form opposition movements to successfully topple democratic governments. While agreeing that such mobilization is possible under unusual conditions, I have argued in this study that business elites normally cannot mobilize collectively. This failure results from their lack of consensus and their dependence on the government and on allies outside the business sector. These two characteristics of the Latin American business community help preserve democratic stability and social and economic redistribution initiatives.

Degree of Business Consensus

In most cases, business elites' diversity, individualism, and competitiveness will prevent them from mobilizing collectively. The democratic consolidation under way in Latin America illustrates these obstacles to collective action. First, the neoliberal strategies promoted throughout the region will probably exacerbate divisions within the business community. Whereas some business leaders, most likely those in domestic or multinational conglomerates, will benefit from these strategies, those dependent on government subsidies and incentives will suffer. Although the latter may wish to mobilize against the democratic government and its policies, they will lack one of the crucial conditions for mobilizing business elites: widespread consensus regarding a government threat to investment security.

Second, because the new democratic governments provide business elites not only with individual and collective channels for influencing political outcomes but also with regularly scheduled elections, they have created conditions that enable business elites to work within the system to promote change. Thus, the authoritarian faction within the business community would be hard pressed to convince the rest of the community to engage in collective action to overthrow a government, when less costly methods of promoting change are available. Rather than joining a collective opposition, most business elites will opt for formal and informal channels to influence or replace policy makers.

Degree of Business Dependence on the Government and on Nonbusiness Allies

I have shown in this study how business elites' dependence on the government tends to prevent them from becoming a disloyal opposition. A nation's business community relies on the government for favorable investment policies and conditions. The leaders of that community are therefore generally unwilling to jeopardize the community's relationship with the government, lest they provoke official sanctions. In addition, individual members of the business community rely on the government for subsidies, incentives, and credit. Accordingly, they also prefer more subtle forms of pressure rather than open confrontation toward the regime.

Despite this history of dependence, the cases analyzed in this book suggest a subtle shift toward greater business autonomy from the state. The neoliberal policies pursued by the new democratic governments should reduce business elites' traditional dependence on an interventionist state. Moreover, political liberalization seems to have generated dissension within traditional business associations. Members of the Latin American business communities have called for associations that represent, in a democratic manner, the diversity within their ranks. They challenge their old leadership's traditional acquiescence to government and backroom negotiations with policy makers and advocate more open and combative political strategies.

Despite the significance of these changes, however, Latin American business elites will no doubt continue to be incapable of mounting collective opposition to democratic governments. Both neoliberal policies and dissension within the business community over strategies are likely to exacerbate existing fragmentation and weakness rather than strengthen consensus and collective political power. And though new business leaders are likely to emerge, they are unlikely to transform the business community into a disloyal opposition, unless that community feels threatened by a government and its policies.

Moreover, even if authoritarian business leaders can organize their moderate colleagues against the state, their success in undermining a democratic government will depend in large part on support from other social sectors. At present, such support does not exist. Because of the failure of authoritarian regimes in most of Latin America, few individuals consider such regimes to be models for successful development or stability. The Latin American militaries with whom business elites allied in the past to overthrow democratic governments appear to have little interest in assuming the responsibility of governance. This results from broad recognition of their past failures in government, as well as from their present capacity to significantly influence the policies of the democratic governments without having to assume control. International trends in favor of democratic change have also reduced the appeal of authoritarian reversals.

Nonetheless, as the events of the past three decades in Latin America have demonstrated, domestic and international opinions change. If democratic governments generate intense threats to investment stability by becoming incompetent at solving internal problems, by losing domestic or international legitimacy, and by excluding business elites from decisions, it is likely that the authoritarian faction within the business community will mobilize business elites and other social sectors feeling similarly threatened. Although this is an unlikely scenario, there are steps the new democratic governments can take to make it an even more remote possibility.

Social Democratic Governments and Business Elites

The above scenario appears unlikely in the short term because of the kinds of governments which have emerged in the new democratic era in Latin America. Although these governments are not beholden to business elites and in most cases were not initially endorsed by the majority of the business community, they are conservative administrations. They have adopted policies consistent with business elites' demands and have avoided measures such as social and economic redistribution programs, which might have threatened investment security. Given the conservative nature of these governments, it is hardly surprising that business elites have not mobilized against them. On the other hand, will business elites prove as tolerant of, and as adaptive to, future social democratic governments intent on reducing the negative impact of poverty and powerlessness on national economic and political development?

I have implied throughout this study that business elites' attitudes depend on more than the ideological orientation of the government. That orientation, however, plays an important role in shaping business elites' perceptions of investment stability. Thus, it is imperative for the social democratic governments that might emerge in Latin America to adopt strategies that allow them to implement social and economic reforms while simultaneously offsetting business elites' perception of threat and capacity to undermine the government. Three broad strategies should provide social democratic governments with that security and flexibility.

First, social democratic governments must continue to provide opportunities for business elites to participate in government decisions. These opportunities should include formal channels of representation and participation similar to those used by other social sectors. They might also include informal discussions with individual members of the business community, business representatives, or business associations. Not only are these channels of participation consistent with democratic values, thereby strengthening the democratic system, but the case studies presented in this book also suggest that they can offset business elites' motivation to join a disloyal opposition.

Second, social democratic governments should exploit the natural divisions within the business community. For example, a government could increase its communication with one faction of the business community, such as the democratic business leaders. By soliciting assistance from this faction in developing non-threatening social and economic redistribution policies, this government would encourage participation from some business leaders and reassure the entire business community of the government's support for private enterprise. Social democratic governments should not, however, eliminate communication with the authoritarian elements of the business community. Such a policy might create a perception of threat among these elites. If exacerbated by other government policies or practices, this perception might be sufficient to mobilize these elites and their allies against the regime.

Third, social democratic governments must provide clarity and consistency in the redistribution policies they adopt. These policies must be clearly presented to the business community, carried out in ways consistent with existing rules and procedures, and accompanied by reassurances about the governments' commitment to capitalist economic development. Social democratic governments must guarantee business elites that the basic rules of the capitalist game are secure and will not be supplanted by prejudicial, arbitrary, and unpredictable policies.

The implications of these strategies for the future of social democracy in Latin America are twofold. Governments that pursue overtly anticapitalist policies are unlikely to survive because they will raise unappeasable fears within the private sector, causing business elites and their allies in the military, on the political right, and within the international community to effectively mobilize against them. On the other hand, socialist and social democratic governments that accept capitalist ground rules will most likely be able to avoid disloyal opposition from the business sector and its allies while promoting social and economic change. The success of these regimes, however, will depend on whether or not they enact clear and consistent policies, exploit natural divisions within the business community, and pursue specific strategies that allow for business participation. Their success will also depend n factors beyond their control—in particular, international trends and opinions, and business elites' past experiences with, and perceptions of, government expropriation policies. Although these regimes' survival and stability are tenuous, such regimes are long overdue in the region.

Appendix: The Research Methodology

In order to analyze Brazilian industrialists' political attitudes and behavior, I conducted three types of research. First, I reviewed documentary research on their political activities and their opinions on public issues. Second, I observed, firsthand, their activities. And third, I conducted detailed interviews with numerous industrialists.

The first research activity involved tracing industrial leaders' political activities over the twenty-five-year period from 1964 to 1989. I consulted the business association archives in the document center at the São Paulo Federation of Industries (FIESP). I also reviewed newspaper and magazine coverage of industrialists' involvement in political events. I am skeptical of the accuracy of newspaper and magazine accounts of events, but unfortunately they provide the only comprehensive record of industrialists' involvement in the historical events examined here. In addition, I benefited from several informative studies of business leaders' political activities prepared primarily by Brazilian scholars; I refer to these throughout the text. This documentary research enabled me to reconstruct industrialists' attitudes and behavior from 1964 to 1989.

My second type of research, firsthand observation of industrialists' activities, involved making numerous visits to, and attending several meetings at, various Brazilian business associations. I also observed industrialists' lobbying efforts in the Constituent Assembly in Brasília in 1987 and saw the results of these efforts. This firsthand observation provided me with insights into how industrialists make collective decisions and seek to attain their goals.

The third type of research I conducted involved in-depth interviews of 159 industrial leaders; 155 of these interviews were included in a data base.[1] I selected industrial leaders owing to their political salience during the period 1964–89. However, financial and agricultural elites should receive future scholarly attention.[2] I did not randomly select the individuals I interviewed, since I was interested only in the attitudes and behavior of industrialists who were engaged in politics and who therefore had some impact on the political system. I assume that most business leaders are not politically involved and are not even aware of many of the issues I hoped to discuss in my interviews. Thus, I selected my interview subjects carefully.

I deliberately focused the study on industrial leaders in São Paulo because they are the most politically powerful and politically active industrialists in the country. I also chose to interview industrialists who had played important political roles during the 1964 coup, the military regime, the early transition to democracy, and the New Republic.

I selected my initial list of interview subjects on the basis of the documentary research described above. This list included industrialists who had been outspoken on political issues or involved in political activities during the period 1964–88 and therefore were frequently cited in newspaper or magazine articles, business association archives, or secondary literature.

In order to interview the informal industrial leaders who were not necessarily in the public eye, I used a "snowball" technique. At the end of each interview, I asked the interviewee to identify other industrialists whom he or she considered to be leaders within the industrial community. Even after compiling a list of interview subjects from the documentary research and the "snowball" method, I still lacked the names of leaders in certain important industrial categories, primarily small and multinational enterprises. To remedy this deficiency I contacted several industrial associations representing these types of industries, and with their help identified the key leaders. Nearly every interview subject I contacted (first by letter and then with a follow-up telephone call) agreed to an interview. These interviews were conducted in Brazil between July 1987 and June 1988. A list of the industrialists I interviewed is provided in the Bibliography.[3]

Discussion of the Interview Sample

In tables A.1–4 I provide profiles of the industrialists whom I interviewed, and of their firms. These profiles illustrate two characteristics of the industrialists I interviewed. First, they comprise an elite group that possesses the political resources to influence political outcomes. Second, although they form a part of the Brazilian industrial elite, they are not homogeneous but are highly diverse, thereby confirming the assumption of fragmentation of business communities embodied in the adaptive actor approach.

Table A.1 illustrates that these individuals are part of a firmly entrenched industrial elite. The sample includes predominantly older and experienced industrialists, and industrialists from firms that have been in operation for more than two decades. However, the sample also includes the younger generation of industrial leaders, and individuals affiliated with newly founded firms. The majority of the industrialists in the sample are executives who have no family ties to the firms at which they work. This indicates that the firms have been in operation long enough to replace family management with professional management. However, a sizeable percentage of

Table A.1.   Profile of the Industrialists Interviewed:
Background

	Number	Percentage
Year of birth		
1900–10	3	1.9
1911–20	13	8.4
1921–30	33	21.3
1931–40	56	36.1
1941–50	40	25.8
1951–60	10	6.5
Initial experience in business		
Before 1964	98	63.2
After 1964	56	36.1
No response	1	0.7
Date of firm's foundation		
Before 1930	44	28.4
1930–54	64	41.3
1955–63	17	11.0
1964–88	26	16.8
No response	4	2.6
Relationship to founder		
Founder	32	20.6
Heir	40	25.8
Executive	81	52.3
No response	2	1.3
Position in firm		
Director	85	54.8
President	49	31.6
Vice-president	5	3.2
Manager	16	10.3
Father's occupation		
Industrialist	48	31.0
Other urban professional	63	40.6
Manual or rural worker	40	25.8
No response	4	2.6

Note: N = 155.

those I interviewed had family ties to family-owned, family-operated firms. Some (32) of these industrialists had founded their firms and continued to oversee operations. Others had inherited their firms, and many of these firms had been in the same family for several generations. Indeed, as table A.1 indicates, a significant proportion of these industrialists' fathers had also been industrialists. Finally, the vast majority of my interview subjects held top leadership positions in their firms (i.e., they were directors and presidents), although I also interviewed managers, primarily those who were responsible for decisions in the area of labor relations.

Table A. 2.   Profile of the Industrialists Interviewed:
Indicators of Social Status

	Number	Percentage
Immigration status		
Foreign	11	7.1
Immigrant	15	9.7
First-generation Brazilian	30	19.4
Second-generation Brazilian	33	21.3
More than second-generation Brazilian	33	21.3
No response	33	21.3
National origin[a]		
Mediterranean Europe	114	73.5
Western Europe	28	18.1
Eastern Europe	12	7.7
Middle East	9	5.8
Asia	4	2.6
United States	4	2.6
United Kingdom	2	1.3
Other	3	1.9
Religion		
Nonpracticing Catholic	47	30.3
Catholic	69	44.5
Jewish	15	9.7
Protestant	6	3.9
Other	8	5.2
No response	10	6.4
Type of products produced by firm		
Some consumer products	63	40.6
No consumer products	88	56.8
No response	4	2.6
Firm's production for export		
More than 50%	10	6.5
10–50%	67	43.2
Less than 10%	38	24.5
None	36	23.2
No response	4	2.6
Experience abroad		
Much	74	47.7
Some	36	23.2
Little	26	16.8
None	16	10.3
No response	3	1.9
Size of firm		
Small (<500 employees)	34	21.9
Medium (500–1,999)	30	19.4
Large (2,000–4,999)	35	22.6
Mega (>5,000)	56	36.1

Table A.2—Continued

	Number	Percentage
Education		
Less than college	12	7.7
College	112	72.3
Graduate school	31	20.0
Fathers' education		
Primary school or less	43	27.7
High school	54	34.8
College or graduate school	53	34.2
Do not know	1	0.6
No response	4	2.6

Note: N = 155.
[a]The total for this category adds up to more than 155, and
the percentages add up to more than 100%, because
interviewees provided multiple responses.

When rated according to a measure of Latin American industrialists' social status and political influence elaborated by Albert Hirschman, most of the industrialists I interviewed ranked quite high. According to Hirschman, Latin American industrialists' social status and the political power they derive from their position in society depend on three factors. First, native-born industrialists rank higher than foreigners, immigrants, or members of minorities, since the latter three groups lack prestige and status in society. Second, industrialists who experiment and whose products are innovative will achieve higher status in society than those who merely copy foreign products or import ideas, processes, and technology. Similarly, the production of producer goods is more prestigious than the production of consumer products. Third, industrialists who have gained recognition and contacts abroad (which are usually obtained by producing for the export market) also have greater national prestige.[4]

Hirschman argues that because Latin American industrialists generally do not rank high according to these three criteria, they have not developed either the prestige or the influence that their North American and Western European counterparts have earned in their own countries. Thus, their political power is highly limited. Yet the data on my interview sample indicate that there is within the Brazilian industrial community an elite that has acquired a high degree of social status as measured by Hirschman's scale, and therefore represents a politically influential social sector (table A.2).

With regard to the first criterion (national origin and ethnicity), only 7 percent of the industrialists I interviewed were foreign (all but one of those foreigners worked

Table A.3.   Profile of the Industrialists Interviewed:
Diversity of Industrialists and Firms

	Number	Percentage
Principal sectors of industry		
Metalworking	49	31.6
Chemical	21	13.5
Food and beverages	16	10.3
Electrical-electronic	15	9.7
Textile and clothing	13	8.4
Mechanical	8	5.2
Other	33	21.3
Nationality of firm		
Brazilian (private)	104	67.1
Western European	25	16.1
North American	24	15.5
Japanese	2	1.3
Type of firm		
Conglomerate	29	18.7
Firm (several plants)	88	56.8
Firm (one plant)	38	24.5
Principal stock ownership		
Family	62	40.0
Another firm	55	35.5
Self	12	7.7
One individual, or few	10	6.5
Publicly held	6	3.9
Brazilian government	4	2.6
Conglomerates	3	1.9
No response	3	1.9

Note: N = 155.

for foreign companies), and only 10 percent were immigrants. The majority (62%) had been born and raised in Brazil. Moreover, few can be considered members of racial minority groups: none of the industrialists were black or indigenous Brazilian, and only a few were Middle Eastern or Asian. The family backgrounds of most of those interviewed are derived from Mediterranean Europe (primarily Portugal and Italy) or from advanced industrial countries. And the religious profile shows that most of them, like most Brazilians, identified themselves as Catholics.

With regard to the second criterion (type of goods produced), the majority (57%) of the industrialists in my sample manufactured only producer goods, as opposed to consumer goods. But the proportion of industrialists who manufactured both consumer and producer goods (41%) suggests that an even higher number of industrialists were engaged in producer-goods production. Indeed, only a minority of the industrialists I interviewed produced only consumer goods. In addition, although

Table A.4.   Profile of the Industrialists Interviewed:
Self-Placement on the Ideological Scale

Position on the Scale[a]	Number	Percentage
The left (total)	26	18.2
1.0 or 1.5	0	0.0
2.0 or 2.5	0	0.0
3.0 or 3.5	3	2.1
4.0 or 4.5	23	16.1
The center		
5.0 or 5.5	39	27.3
The right (total)	78	54.6
6.0 or 6.5	33	23.1
7.0 or 7.5	21	14.7
8.0 or 8.5	15	10.5
9.0 or 9.5	5	3.5
10.0+	4	2.8

Note: N = 143. Twelve industrialists failed to respond to
this question in the interviews.
[a]Although the scale did not include decimals, at times
respondents placed themselves in between the integers
on the scale. These responses are reflected by the
decimals.

the majority of Brazilian businesses still copy foreign products and are concentrated in traditional industrial sectors, several of the industrialists I interviewed had produced innovative products, particularly in the areas of alternative energy, aeronautics, computer technology, and weaponry.

Finally, regarding the third criterion (experience abroad), while the vast majority (91%) of the industrialists I interviewed continued to produce primarily for the domestic market, this does not imply that they lacked contacts and prestige abroad. As table A.2 demonstrates, their foreign experience was extensive. Moreover, this experience included not only vacation travel but also foreign study and business trips. In addition, many of the industrialists I interviewed sat on the boards of foreign enterprises.

Additional characteristics of the industrialists I interviewed, which Hirschman does not include in his scale, further confirm their elite status. As table A.2 illustrates, these individuals were predominantly from large firms. Whereas the majority of Brazilian businesses are small (according to official statistics, 90 percent of Brazilian businesses employ fewer than ten workers), the industrial elite in Brazil is concentrated in larger firms, and my sample reflects that tendency. In addition, these individuals were highly educated. The vast majority of the industrialists I interviewed, as well as their fathers, had attended college. A significant minority had even pursued postgraduate studies.

In short, my sample comprises an industrial elite with substantial social prestige and, presumably, considerable influence over government policies and practices. The data in these tables also indicate that this elite is heterogeneous. Thus, my sample confirms that even among the industrial elite in Brazil there is diversity. These industrialists have different personal and institutional backgrounds and experiences.

Table A.3 further illustrates the diversity of the industrialists included in the sample. The table indicates the wide variety of industrial sectors represented, the diverse nationalities of the firms, the various types of firms included in the sample, and their various forms of stock ownership.

An additional indication of the diversity of the industrialists I interviewed is their ideology. I asked the industrialists to identify their political attitudes on a 10-point ideological scale, with 1 representing the extreme left and 10 representing the extreme right. Table A.4 summarizes their responses. The average of these responses was 6, or just right of center. However, as the table indicates, industrialists placed themselves on the left (18%), center (27%), and right (55%), illustrating a variety of political perspectives (with the predictable exception of the extreme left).

Discussion of the Interviews

The interviews I conducted were extremely comprehensive and gave me new insights into industrialists' attitudes. The average length of my interviews was two hours. (The shortest interview was completed in forty-five minutes, and the longest lasted five hours.) The interview questionnaire I developed included closed-ended questions that referred primarily to the background of the industrialist and his or her firm. I also asked in-depth, open-ended questions to allow the interviewees to articulate their views without restriction. Given the length of the interviews, not all subjects were able to answer the entire questionnaire. This fact is reflected in the varying number of respondents to different questions. I later systematically coded the responses to the open-ended questions for purposes of quantitative analysis.

The questionnaire I used allowed me to explore industrialists' individual attitudes on a broad range of issues. It consisted of five parts. In part 1, I asked the industrialists to answer questions regarding changes in labor relations since 1978: what were the changes, what caused them, and how successfully had industrial organizations, as well as individual business leaders and firms, adapted to those changes? In part 2, I explored their attitudes about political and labor issues that were being debated at that time in the Constituent Assembly, trade unions, and business associations. These issues fell into the following categories: labor legisla-

tion; the representation and participation of labor and business in government decision making; and conflict resolution. In parts 3 and 4, I asked the industrialists about
their personal backgrounds and about their firms. I have included much of this
background information in tables A.1–4. In part 5, I explored the industrialists' political attitudes by asking questions that dealt with their ideology, their support for
the 1964 coup, and their evaluations of the military regime and the transition from
authoritarian rule. In doing so, I asked the industrialists to place themselves; the
workers in their firms; business and labor organizations; and individual politicians
on the same 10-point ideological scale discussed above.

I promised the industrialists anonymity in these responses, and in order to create
an atmosphere of trust I did not record the interviews electronically. Instead, when
an individual's responses were particularly interesting I wrote down those responses verbatim. When I have included these quotations in the text, I have tried to
provide the reader with some information on the respondent, while concealing his
or her identity.[5]

I have used the interview material extensively throughout the text, providing
specific quotations to illustrate various points made in the interviews, and using the
quantitative data to substantiate my claims. This interview material greatly en-
riches the study. I had anticipated that the industrialists would not be forthcoming
on politically charged questions; yet after having conducted and analyzed the interviews, I am satisfied with the range of responses I received, and confident that most
of the interviewees provided honest answers even to the most sensitive questions.

Nonetheless, the data have limitations. First, the industrialists' responses were
highly contingent on the events under way in Brazil during my field research. I
asked the industrialists their opinions on issues that were currently under debate in
the country. If I asked them about the same issues today, I would probably receive
different responses, for their opinions would have changed with new information
and experiences. For example, at the time of the interviews, much new labor legislation was evolving, and the industrialists could not anticipate how that legislation
might affect them. After they had positive or negative experiences with the new
legislation, their views may have shifted. Thus, the responses to these questions reflect the industrialists' opinions during a specific period. In addition, as I mentioned
before, because the industrialists I interviewed are an elite within the business community, their responses are more informed and articulate than one might find in a
random sample of Brazilian business executives.

Notes

Introduction

1. See Ernest Bartell, "Business Perceptions and the Transition to Democracy in Chile," in *Business and Democracy in Latin America,* ed. Ernest Bartell and Leigh A. Payne (Pittsburgh: University of Pittsburgh Press, forthcoming); and Carlos H. Acuña, "Business Interests, Dictatorship, and Democracy in Argentina: Why the Bourgeoisie Abandons Authoritarian Strategies and Opts for Democratic Stability," in ibid.

2. See Blanca Heredia, "Mexican Business and the State: The Political Economy of a 'Muddled' Transition," in Bartell and Payne, eds., *Business and Democracy in Latin America;* and Catherine M. Conaghan, "The Private Sector and the Public Transcript: The Political Mobilization of Business in Bolivia," in ibid.

3. Albert O. Hirschman, "The Political Economy of Import-Substituting Industrialization in Latin America," in *A Bias for Hope: Essays on Development in Latin America,* ed. Albert O. Hirschman (New Haven: Yale University Press, 1971), 85–123. See also the dependencia literature, especially Fernando Henrique Cardoso and Enzo Faletto, *Dependency and Development in Latin America* (Berkeley and Los Angeles: University of California Press, 1979); and Peter Evans, *Dependent Development: The Alliance of Multinational, State, and Local Capital in Brazil* (Princeton: Princeton University Press, 1979).

4. See Guillermo O'Donnell, *Modernization and Bureaucratic-Authoritarianism* (Berkeley and Los Angeles: University of California Press, 1973); and David Collier, "An Overview of the Bureaucratic-Authoritarian Model," in *The New Authoritarianism in Latin America,* ed. David Collier (Princeton: Princeton University Press, 1979), 26–27.

5. Guillermo O'Donnell and Philippe C. Schmitter, *Transitions from Authoritarian Rule: Tentative Conclusions about Uncertain Democracies* (Baltimore: Johns Hopkins University Press, 1986), 27.

6. Thomas E. Skidmore, *Politics in Brazil, 1930–1964: An Experiment in Democracy* (New York: Oxford University Press, 1967).

7. Adriano Campanhole and Hilton Lobo Campanhole, eds., *Consolidação das leis do trabalho e legislação complementar* (São Paulo: Editora Atlas, 1983).

8. For more information on the CLT, see Kenneth Paul Erickson, *The Brazilian Corporative State and Working-Class Politics* (Berkeley and Los Angeles: University of California Press, 1977); Kenneth S. Mericle, "Conflict Regulation in the Brazilian Industrial Relations System" (Ph.D. diss., University of Wisconsin, 1974); and idem, "Corporatist Control of the Working Class: Authoritarian Brazil since 1964," in *Authoritarianism and Corporatism in*

Latin America, ed. James M. Malloy (Pittsburgh: University of Pittsburgh Press, 1977), 303–38.

9. See M. Antonieta P. Leopoldi, "Industrial Associations and Politics in Contemporary Brazil" (Ph.D. diss., St. Antony's College, 1984); Marisa Saens Leme, *A ideologia dos industriais brasileiros, 1919–1945* (Petrópolis: Vozes, 1978); Eli Diniz and Renato Raul Boschi, *Empresariado nacional e estado no Brasil* (Rio de Janeiro: Editora Forense Universitária, 1978); and Philippe C. Schmitter, *Interest Conflict and Political Change in Brazil* (Stanford, Calif.: Stanford University Press, 1971).

10. In its literal sense, the term *pelego* refers to the cushion between the horse and the saddle.

11. Joan Dassin, ed., *Torture in Brazil: A Report by the Archdiocese of São Paulo,* trans. Jaime Wright (New York: Vintage Books, 1986), 58–59. For the complete Brazilian version, see *Brasil, nunca mais* (Petrópolis: Vozes, 1985).

12. Sarney had defected from that party shortly before the 1985 elections to form a conservative opposition party, the Liberal Front Party (PFL), that joined the PMDB's "democratic alliance."

Chapter 1. The Adaptive Actor Approach to Business Elites

1. See Alfred Stepan, *Rethinking Military Politics: Brazil and the Southern Cone* (Princeton: Princeton University Press, 1988); and Ben Ross Schneider, *Politics within the State: Elite Bureaucrats and Industrial Policy in Authoritarian Brazil* (Pittsburgh: University of Pittsburgh Press, 1991).

2. Guillermo O'Donnell, *Modernization and Bureaucratic-Authoritarianism* (Berkeley and Los Angeles: University of California Press, 1973).

3. The main critiques of the theory of the bureaucratic-authoritarian state can be found in David Collier, *The New Authoritarianism in Latin America* (Princeton: Princeton University Press, 1979).

4. Guillermo O'Donnell and Philippe C. Schmitter, *Transitions from Authoritarian Rule: Tentative Conclusions about Uncertain Democracies* (Baltimore: Johns Hopkins University Press, 1986), 27.

5. For the most widely utilized literature on dependencia in Latin America, see Fernando Henrique Cardoso and Enzo Faletto, *Dependency and Development in Latin America* (Berkeley and Los Angeles: University of California Press, 1979); and Peter Evans, *Dependent Development: The Alliance of Multinational, State, and Local Capital in Brazil* (Princeton: Princeton University Press, 1979).

6. Guillermo O'Donnell, "Reflections on the Patterns of Change in the Bureaucratic-Authoritarian Regimes in Latin America," *Latin American Research Review* 13, no. 1 (1978): 8, 20–22.

7. O'Donnell, *Modernization and Bureaucratic-Authoritarianism,* 72.

8. O'Donnell, "Reflections on the Patterns of Change in the Bureaucratic-Authoritarian Regimes in Latin America," 8, 20–22.

9. Nicos Poulantzas, *Political Power and Social Classes*, trans. Timothy O'Hagen (London: Verso Editions, 1968). See also Theda Skocpol, "Political Responses to Capitalist Crisis: Neo-Marxist Theories of the State and the Case of the New Deal," *Politics and Society* 10, no. 2 (1980): 170–71.

10. James Scott, *Domination and the Art of Resistance: Hidden Transcripts* (New Haven: Yale University Press, 1990), 79.

11. For a discussion of these resources, see Fred Block, "The Ruling Class Does Not Rule: Notes on the Marxist Theory of the State," in *The Political Economy: Readings in the Politics and Economics of American Public Policy*, ed. Thomas Ferguson and Joel Rogers (Armonk, N. Y.: M. E. Sharpe, 1984), 36–37; Charles E. Lindblom, *Politics and Markets: The World's Political-Economic Systems* (New York: Basic Books, 1977), 171–78; Ralph Miliband, *The State in Capitalist Society* (New York: Basic Books, 1969), 146; Skocpol, "Political Responses to Capitalist Crisis," 160; and David Vogel, "The Power of Business in America: A Re-Appraisal," *British Journal of Political Science* 13 (1983): 29–42.

12. Juan J. Linz, *Crisis, Breakdown, and Reequilibration*, in *The Breakdown of Democratic Regimes*, ed. Juan J. Linz and Alfred Stepan (Baltimore: Johns Hopkins University Press, 1978), 20.

13. For a discussion of sanctions, see Block, "Ruling Class Does Not Rule," 36–40; and Charles E. Lindblom, "The Market as Prison," in Ferguson and Rogers, eds., *Political Economy*, 4–6.

14. Juan J. Linz and Amando de Miguel, *Los empresarios ante el poder público: El liderazgo y los grupos de intereses en el empresariado español* (Madrid: Instituto de Estudios Políticos, 1966), 107–21.

15. While it is true that powerful individual investors are capable of autonomously influencing political outcomes, concerted business efforts have a greater impact in Latin America because of the threat of collective sanctions on the state. This contrasts with the assertions in Claus Offe and Helmut Wiesenthal, "Two Logics of Collective Action: Theoretical Notes on Social Class and Organizational Form," *Political Power and Social Theory,* 1 (1980): 67–115.

16. Nathaniel H. Leff, *Economic Policy-Making and Development in Brazil, 1947–1964* (New York: John Wiley and Sons, 1968), 116; Adam Przeworski, *Capitalism and Social Democracy* (Cambridge: Cambridge University Press, 1985); and David Vogel, "Why Businessmen Distrust Their State: The Political Consciousness of American Corporation Executives," *British Journal of Political Science,* 8 (1978): 65–69.

17. Linz and Miguel, *Los empresarios ante el poder público,* 120.

18. For information on Brazilian business leaders, see Fernando Henrique Cardoso, "O papel dos empresários no processo de transição," *Dados* 26, no. 1 (1983): 21; Eli Diniz, "Post-1930 Industrial Elites" (Rio de Janeiro: Instituto Universitário de Pesquisas do Rio de Janeiro [IUPERJ], n.d., Mimeo), 188–89; and Leff, *Economic Policy-Making and Development,* 115–16. For information on the fragmentation of business elites in other countries, see Raymond A. Bauer, Ithiel de Sola Pool, and Lewis Anthony Dexter, *American Business and Public Policy: The Politics of Foreign Trade* (New York: Atherton Press, 1964); Paolo Farneti, *Imprenditore e societá* (Turin: Editrice L'imprensa, 1970); Linz and Miguel, *Los em-*

presarios ante el poder público; and Harry Mark Makler, *A elite industrial portuguesa* (Lisbon: Centro de Economia e Finanças, 1969).

19. Linz and Miguel, *Los empresarios ante el poder público,* 117–20.

20. Albert O. Hirschman, "The Political Economy of Import-Substituting Industrialization in Latin America," in *A Bias for Hope: Essays on Development in Latin America,* ed. Albert O. Hirschman (New Haven: Yale University Press, 1971), 96–98. For further discussion of Hirschman's analysis, see the Appendix.

21. Ibid., 109.

22. Philippe C. Schmitter, "Still a Century of Corporatism?" *Review of Politics* 36, no. 1 (1974): 85–121; and Leff, *Economic Policy-Making and Development,* 116–18.

23. Leff, *Economic Policy-Making and Development,* 116–18.

24. This link between interest groups and government agencies is called "bureaucratic rings." Fernando Henrique Cardoso, *Autoritarismo e democratização* (Rio de Janeiro: Paz e Terra, 1975).

25. Leff, *Economic Policy-Making and Development,* 116; and Philippe C. Schmitter, *Interest Conflict and Political Change in Brazil* (Stanford, Calif.: Stanford University Press, 1971).

26. Although import-substitution policies had enabled Latin American countries to reduce certain imports, it increased their dependence on other, more costly imports: the intermediate and capital goods that industries required in order to manufacture consumer goods.

27. Investment and expansion would come primarily from multinational corporations and international lending agencies. However, Latin American countries could divert the capital, technology, and "know-how" from these foreign sources in order to develop the intermediate-goods and capital-goods sectors of their economies. O'Donnell, *Modernization and Bureaucratic-Authoritarianism,* 60–70. See also David Collier, "Overview of the Bureaucratic-Authoritarian Model," in *The New Authoritarianism in Latin America,* ed. David Collier (Princeton: Princeton University Press, 1979), 26–27.

28. O'Donnell, *Modernization and Bureaucratic-Authoritarianism,* 70–72.

29. Ibid., 72.

30. O'Donnell and Schmitter, *Transitions from Authoritarian Rule,* 27.

31. Block, "Ruling Class Does Not Rule," 38–39; Diniz, "Post-1930 Industrial Elites"; and Vogel, "Why Businessmen Distrust Their State."

32. "Satisficing" behavior is also a close, but imperfect, description of the type of business elite behavior to which I am referring. "Satisficing" managers recognize that the cost of investing time and money in researching all of the available options may outweigh the benefits. Therefore, managers take a more cost-effective route, selecting the first action that occurs to them which will satisfy their goal, even though they might do better with a different strategy. In other words, rather than choosing the best alternative, they accept a tolerable situation. Jon Elster, "Introduction," in *Rational Choice,* ed. Jon Elster (Oxford: Basil Blackwell, 1986), 25.

33. Linz, *Crisis, Breakdown, and Reequilibration,* 16.

34. Max Weber, *The Theory of Social and Economic Organization,* ed. Talcott Parsons, trans. A. M. Henderson and Talcott Parsons (New York: Free Press, 1947), 328.

35. Linz, *Crisis, Breakdown, and Reequilibration,* 22.

36. Scott Mainwaring, "The Transition to Democracy in Brazil," *Journal of Interamerican Studies and World Affairs* 28, no. 1 (1986): 149–79; and William C. Smith, "The 'New Republic' and the Brazilian Transition: Elite Conciliation or Democratization?" (Paper presen ed at the Eighth International Congress of the Latin American Studies Association, Boston, 23–26 October 1986).

37. This concept of predictability is similar to Juan Linz's view of "efficacy"; see Linz, *Crisis, Breakdown, and Reequilibration,* 20–21.

38. Ibid., 20.

39. Hirschman, "Political Economy of Import Substitution," 120.

40. See Alfred Stepan, "Political Leadership and Regime Breakdown: Brazil," in *The Breakdown of Democratic Regimes: Latin America,* ed. Juan J. Linz and Alfred Stepan (Baltimore: Johns Hopkins University Press, 1978), 110–37; and Larry Diamond and Juan J. Linz, "Introduction: Politics, Society, and Democracy in Latin America," in *Democracy in Developing Countries: Latin America,* ed. Larry Diamond, Juan J. Linz, and Seymour Martin Lipset (Boulder, Colo.: Lynne Rienner Publishers, 1989), 1–58.

41. James G. March and Johan P. Olsen, *Rediscovering Institutions: The Organizational Basis of Politics* (New York: Free Press, 1989), 160–66.

42. Elster, "Introduction," 11.

43. March and Olsen, *Rediscovering Institutions,* 44; Jon Elster, *Sour Grapes: Studies in the Subversion of Rationality* (Cambridge: Cambridge University Press, 1983), 40.

44. George Tsebelis, *Nested Games: Rational Choice in Comparative Politics* (Berkeley and Los Angeles: University of California Press, 1990), 46; March and Olsen, *Rediscovering Institutions,* 39.

45. Linz, *Crisis, Breakdown, and Reequilibration,* 18.

46. March and Olsen, *Rediscovering Institutions,* 17.

47. Elster, "Introduction," 6–7.

48. The argument is that it is not rational for businesspeople to engage in collective action because it is too costly in terms of opportunity costs and competitive advantage. While all members have an interest in obtaining certain collective benefits, some will not pay the cost of providing collective goods. Instead, they allow others to bear the cost (the "free rider" problem). Mancur Olson, *Logic of Collective Action: Public Goods and the Theory of Groups* (Cambridge: Harvard University Press, 1965).

49. This directly contradicts some assumptions in the theory of collective action. See Mancur Olson, *The Rise and Decline of Nations: Economic Growth, Stagflation, and Social Rigidities* (New Haven: Yale University Press, 1982), 50.

50. Elster, "Introduction," 7.

51. Ibid., 10.

Chapter 2. When Industrialists Rebel

1. Phillip Siekman, "When Executives Turned Revolutionaries, a Story Hitherto Untold: How São Paulo Businessmen Conspired to Overthrow Brazil's Communist-Infested Gov-

ernment," *Fortune* 70, no. 3 (1964), 147. When most interview material (e.g., quotations) is used in the text, it is identified only by a general description of the interviewee, and the date of the interview (in brackets). One interviewee, Paulo Ayres Filho, gave permission for the use of his name. Translations of interview material and other Portuguese sources are mine unless otherwise noted.

2. The most extensive study of IPES is found in René Armand Dreifuss, *1964: A conquista do estado: Ação política, poder e golpe de classe* (Petrópolis: Vozes, 1986).

3. Philippe C. Schmitter, *Interest Conflict and Political Change in Brazil* (Stanford, Calif.: Stanford University Press, 1971), 218.

4. These groups include the American Chamber of Commerce; CONCLAP; the Anticommunist Movement (MAC); the Brazilian Democratic Movement (MDB), not to be confused with the MDB political party formed in 1966; the Anticommunist Organization of Paraná (OPAC); the Liberating Cross of Military Democracy (CLMD); Centro Dom Vital; Opus Dei; Parliamentary Democratic Action (ADP); and the Brazilian Democratic Institute (IDB).

5. Dreifuss, *1964*, 163.

6. Paulo Ayres Filho, "The Brazilian Revolution" (Paper presented at the Georgetown University Center for Strategic Studies, Washington, D. C., July 1964), 10. A condensed version of this paper was published in *Latin America: Politics, Economics, and Hemispheric Security*, ed. Norman A. Bailey (New York: Frederick A. Praeger, 1965), 239–60.

7. Dreifuss, *1964*, 163–64, 178.

8. Ibid., 163.

9. Dreifuss writes that the São Paulo branch of IPES was the headquarters for clandestine operations, while the Rio de Janeiro branch carried out more public debates. Ibid., 179.

10. Clarence W. Hall, "The Country That Saved Itself," *Readers' Digest*, November 1964, 142. While not an academic source, this is one of the few accounts by an IPES sympathizer published at the time of the coup.

11. Dreifuss, *1964*, 173.

12. Hall, "Country That Saved Itself," 138.

13. Jan Knippers Black, *United States Penetration of Brazil* (Philadelphia: University of Pennsylvania Press, 1977), 84.

14. Ayres, "Brazilian Revolution," 12; and Dreifuss, *1964*, 184–99.

15. Black, *United States Penetration of Brazil*, 73–75; and Eloy Dutra, *IBAD: Sigla da corrupção* (Rio de Janeiro: Civilização Brasileira, 1963), 14.

16. Yet only 5% said that they themselves had belonged to a political party. Schmitter, *Interest Conflict and Political Change in Brazil*, 278–79.

17. Solange de Deus Simões, *Deus, patria e familia: As mulheres no golpe de 1964* (Petrópolis: Voces, 1985).

18. Black, *United States Penetration of Brazil*, 111–24.

19. Dreifuss, *1964*, 317.

20. Ivan Hasslocher, *As classes produtoras diante do comunismo*, quoted in Dreifuss, *1964*, 165–67.

21. Some evidence exists that IPES assailed particular industrialists and members of the press who opposed IPES's ideals or who supported political candidates who opposed IPES's ideals. Dreifuss, *1964,* 167.

22. Siekman, "When Executives Turned Revolutionaries," 149.

23. For a description of the contacts between IPES and the armed forces, see Dreifuss, *1964,* 179, 361–415.

24. Ayres, "Brazilian Revolution," 16.

25. Ibid.

26. Hall, "Country That Saved Itself," 150.

27. Alfred Stepan, *The Military in Politics: Changing Patterns in Brazil* (Princeton: Princeton University Press, 1971); and Carlos Castello Branco, "Da conspiração á revolução," in *Os idos de março: A queda em abril,* ed. Alberto Dines et al. (Rio de Janeiro: José Alvaro Editor, 1964), 277–306.

28. Alfred Stepan, "Political Leadership and Regime Breakdown: Brazil," in *The Breakdown of Democratic Regimes: Latin America,* ed. Juan J. Linz and Alfred Stepan (Baltimore: Johns Hopkins University Press, 1978), 110–37. See also Almino Affonso, *Raizes do golpe: Da crise da legalidade ao parlamentarismo (1961–1963)* (São Paulo: Marco Zero, 1988).

29. Black, *United States Penetration of Brazil* and Phyllis R. Parker, *Brazil and the Quiet Intervention, 1964* (Austin: University of Texas Press, 1979). See also Moniz Bandeira, *O governo João Goulart: As lutas sociais no Brasil (1961–1964)* (Rio de Janeiro: Civilização Brasileira, 1977), 75–162.

30. Dreifuss, *1964,* 163; Black, *United States Penetration of Brazil,* 82–94; and Bandeira, *O governo João Goulart,* 64–74.

31. Dreifuss, *1964,* 163.

32. Black, *United States Penetration of Brazil,* 65–72.

33. Dreifuss, *1964,* 146.

34. All differences discussed in this manuscript were statistically significant at the p less than .09 level. Other variables that proved statistically significant in analyzing support for the coup were affiliations with business associations and community organizations, perceptions of threat from the New Republic government, and the type of firm that employed the interview subject. For a discussion of these variables, see Leigh Ann Payne, "Pragmatic Actors: The Political Attitudes and Behavior of Brazilian Industrial Elites" (Ph.D. diss., Yale University, 1990), chap. 3.

35. Fifty-eight (52%) gave only one explanation, 35 (32%) gave two, 13 (12%) gave three, and 5 (4%) gave all four explanations.

36. Four factors proved significant in determining which industrialists claimed to have supported the 1964 coup because of political instability: position in the firm; the sector of industry; community ties; and experience abroad. For a discussion of these variables, see Payne, "Pragmatic Actors," chap 3.

37. Stepan, "Political Leadership and Regime Breakdown," 118; and Affonso, *Raizes do golpe.*

38. These leaders include Miguel Arraes, governor of Pernambuco; Luís Carlos Prestes, leader of the Brazilian Communist Party (PCB); Francisco Julião, leader of the Peasant

Leagues; and Leonel Brizola, Goulart's brother-in-law and adviser. Stepan, "Political Leadership and Regime Breakdown," 124–25.

39. Ironically, IPES had helped to organize some of these "spontaneous" protests. In particular, on 19 March a middle-class women's movement in São Paulo led a "March of the Families" that allegedly brought five hundred thousand people into the street to protest Goulart's reforms. Thomas E. Skidmore, *Politics in Brazil, 1930–1964: An Experiment in Democracy* (London: Oxford University Press, 1967), 298.

40. Stepan, "Political Leadership and Regime Breakdown," 119.

41. Skidmore, *Politics in Brazil,* 284.

42. Stepan, "Political Leadership and Regime Breakdown," 128.

43. Quote from "Introduction to the Annual Presidential Message to Congress," 15 March 1964, reproduced in Skidmore, *Politics in Brazil,* 290.

44. These political factors partially resemble the critique of Goulart's leadership ability in other analyses of the period. Stepan, "Political Leadership and Regime Breakdown," 110–111; and Skidmore, *Politics in Brazil,* 253–302.

45. Ayres, "Brazilian Revolution," 3.

46. Many industrialists refused to place Goulart on the ideological scale (although they did not hesitate to place other politicians on the scale). Indeed, of the fourteen personalities and groups I asked industrialists to place on the scale, Goulart had the highest number of "no responses" and the highest standard deviation. One industrialist I interviewed stated that he assumed I took the scale seriously and therefore he would not put Goulart on the scale, because he did not consider Goulart to be a serious man.

47. Ayres, "Brazilian Revolution."

48. Ibid., 6–7, 9. Ayres appended a list of Brazilian "front organizations" and the international organizations that controlled them "though some of their leaders may not fully realize this." He believed that the unions on his list were run by the World Federation of Trade Unions in Prague.

49. Ayres, "Brazilian Revolution," 7.

50. Dr. Glycon de Paiva, quoted in Hall, "Country That Saved Itself," 140.

51. Hall, "Country That Saved Itself," 140.

52. Ayres, "Brazilian Revolution," 7.

53. As Skidmore states, "To refer to 'Communist' infiltration in order to explain the new life on the left was seriously misleading." Skidmore, *Politics in Brazil,* 282–83. Skidmore provides an in-depth discussion of the left in the 1960s in *Politics in Brazil,* 218–19, 225–26, 276–84. See also Dênis de Moraes, *A esquerda e o golpe de 64* (Rio de Janeiro: Espaço e Tempo, 1989).

54. Industrialists' family ties to their firms also proved statistically significant. For a discussion, see Payne, "Pragmatic Actors," chap. 3.

55. Certain leaders in the United States labor movement appeared to be more concerned about communist infiltration than heads of Brazilian businesses were. See Parker, *Brazil and the Quiet Intervention, 1964,* 19.

56. Leôncio Martins Rodrigues, "Sindicalismo e classe operária (1930–1964)," in *História geral da civilização brasileira, vol. 3, O Brasil republicano: Sociedade e política (1930–1964),* ed. Boris Fausto (Rio de Janeiro: Difusão Editorial, 1981), 542.

57. Skidmore, *Politics in Brazil,* 262.

58. Ibid., 219.

59. Ibid., 225.

60. Ibid., 228.

61. Community ties also proved statistically significant; see Payne, "Pragmatic Actors," chap. 3.

62. Two variables proved statistically significant in analyzing those industrialists who mentioned the economy as a primary reason for supporting the coup: their places of birth and their fathers' education. For a discussion of these variables, see ibid.

63. Black, *United States Penetration of Brazil,* 37–53; Parker, *Brazil and the Quiet Intervention,* 87–100; and Bandeira, *O governo João Goulart,* 43–45.

64. Joan Dassin, ed., *Torture in Brazil: A Report by the Archdiocese of São Paulo,* trans. Jaime Wright (New York: Vintage Books, 1986), 47.

65. Parker, *Brazil and the Quiet Intervention,* 9–10, 16–17.

Chapter 3. Industrialists and Dictatorships

1. Thomas E. Skidmore, *The Politics of Military Rule in Brazil, 1964–85* (New York: Oxford University Press, 1988), 23.

2. René Armand Dreifuss, *1964: A conquista do estado (Ação política, poder e golpe de classe)* (Petrópolis: Vozes, 1986), 421–79.

3. In 1974, 68% of all Bank for National Economic Development (BNDE) resources were allegedly provided to Brazil's southeast, and 47% to São Paulo alone. The Caixa Econômica Federal, a state-owned bank, provided 64.5% of its funds to the southeast, and 35.4% to São Paulo alone. The Council for Industrial Development provided 77% of its resources to São Paulo.

4. These bonuses were eventually authorized. See "Deputados investigam desgaste salarial," *Folha de São Paulo,* 27 April 1968.

5. General Golbery do Couto e Silva, who had been in charge of IPES's intelligence operations, was appointed head of the National Intelligence Service (SNI). Dreifuss, *1964,* 421–24.

6. Humberto Dantas, quoted in "Nova lei de greve prende o interesse dos convencionais," *Diario de São Paulo,* 19 May 1965.

7. Arthur Cezar Ferreira Reis, "Direito de greve" (Rio de Janeiro: Confederação Nacional da Indústria-Conselho Econômico, 1967, Mimeo). For a similar opinion voiced by FIESP see "Nôvo projeto sôbre direito de greve é inconveniente e danoso," *Boletim Informativo,* no. 962 (1968).

8. *Estado de São Paolo,* 20 July 1960, 12.

9. A fully developed democracy was never achieved in Brazilian history. Alfred Stepan, "Political Leadership and Regime Breakdown: Brazil," in *The Breakdown of Democratic*

Regimes: Latin America, ed. Juan J. Linz and Alfred Stepan (Baltimore: Johns Hopkins University Press, 1978), 110. Skidmore also refers to Brazil's government during the 1950s as a "democratic experiment" rather than a full-fledged democracy. Thomas E. Skidmore, *Politics in Brazil, 1930–1964: An Experiment in Democracy* (London: Oxford University Press, 1967).

10. Castello Branco's government is discussed in greater detail below. For a discussion of Kubitschek, see Kathryn Sikkink, *Ideas and Institutions: Developmentalism in Brazil and Argentina* (Ithaca, N. Y.: Cornell University Press, 1991).

11. A description of the historical pattern of Brazilian military intervention is provided in Alfred Stepan, *The Military in Politics: Changing Patterns in Brazil* (Princeton: Princeton University Press, 1971), 115–21.

12. Paulo Egydio Martins, quoted in "Chega de intereses carismáticos," *Senhor,* 15 April 1986.

13. Clarence W. Hall, "The Country That Saved Itself," *Readers' Digest,* November 1964, 156.

14. For example, on 9 April 1964 he decreed an Institutional Act that stripped 378 individuals of their official positions and revoked their political rights. The list included three former presidents (Juscelino Kubitschek, Jânio Quadros, and João Goulart), six state governors, two senators, sixty-three federal deputies, and more than three hundred state deputies and city council members. In addition, approximately 122 officials of the three branches of the armed forces were forced into "retirement," and ten thousand civil servants were fired. For more information, see *Brasil, nunca mais* (Petrópolis: Vozes, 1985). An abridged compilation in English also provides this data: Joan Dassin, ed., *Torture in Brazil: A Report by the Archdiocese of São Paulo,* trans. Jaime Wright (New York: Vintage Books, 1986), 50.

15. Boilesen was a Brazilian of Danish extraction. He was the chief executive officer at the liquid gas company Ultragas.

16. Antonio Carlos Fon, *Tortura: A história da repressão política no Brasil* (São Paulo: Global, 1979), 56–57.

17. A. J. Langguth, *Hidden Terrors* (New York: Pantheon Books, 1978), 123.

18. Moniz Bandeira, *Cartéis e desnacionalização: A experiência brasileira, 1964–1974* (Rio de Janeiro: Civilização Brasileira, 1975), 205. See also Dassin, ed., *Torture in Brazil,* 64.

19. See Bandeira, *Carteis e desnacionalização,* 205; *Veja,* 15 January 1986, 27; and *Latin America,* 30 January 1976, 36–37.

20. Fon, *Tortura,* 60.

21. Ibid., 58–59.

22. *Latin America,* 27 August 1976, 257. This newsletter covers the activities of the AAB during October and November 1976.

23. Fon, *Tortura,* 57.

24. Alfredo Syrkis, *Os carbonários: Memórias da guerrilha perdida* (São Paulo: Global, 1980), 295.

25. Robert Dahl, *Polyarchy: Participation and Opposition* (New Haven: Yale University Press, 1971), 4.

26. Raphael Noschese, quoted in "A industria ante a revolução de março" *Estado de São Paulo,* 17 December 1964. See also "A indústria quer ser co-responsável pelas decisões do govêrno," *O Globo,* 10 March 1965; and "Posição de coerência da indústria," *Diario de São Paulo,* 30 March 1965.

27. Renato Raul Boschi, "National Industrial Elites and the State in Post-1964 Brazil: Institutional Mediations and Political Change" (Ph.D. diss., University of Michigan, 1978), 283–86. See also the Brazilian version, Renato Raul Boschi, *Elites industriais e democracia: Hegemonia burguesa e mudança política no Brasil,* trans. Patrick Burglin (Rio de Janeiro: Edições Graal, 1979), 162–79.

28. Fernando Henrique Cardoso, "Associated-Dependent Development: Theoretical and Practical Implications," in *Authoritarian Brazil: Origins, Policies, and Future,* ed. Alfred Stepan (New Haven: Yale University Press, 1973), 148.

Chapter 4. Industrialists and Political Liberalization

1. Mario Amato, quoted in Mino Carta, "Termos de nos acostomar com greves," *Senhor,* 2 June 1982.

2. The official opposition party, the MDB, doubled its representation in the House of Deputies, from 87 to 165 seats, while ARENA dropped from 223 to 199 seats. In the Senate, the number of seats held by the MDB increased from 7 to 20, and the number of seats held by ARENA fell from 59 to 46. Thomas E. Skidmore, *The Politics of Military Rule in Brazil, 1964–85* (New York: Oxford University Press, 1988), 172–73.

3. For an overall discussion of the democratizing pressures from below, see various articles in Alfred Stepan, ed., *Democratizing Brazil* (New York: Oxford University Press, 1989).

4. "Businessmen stride on to Political Stage," *Latin America Weekly Report,* 25 July 1980, 10. I hesitate to draw any particularly meaningful conclusions from this survey because I have no information on the sampling size or the polling procedure employed.

5. Cláudio Bardella, quoted in Aluizio Maranhão and Luiz Roberto Serrano, "Quem mandou pedir feitiço?" *Istoé,* 9 November 1977, 85.

6. "Onde estão os liberais?" *Istoé,* 30 April 1980, 14–15.

7. *Istoé,* 22 March 1978, 44.

8. In 1984 the prodemocracy Christian groups publicly defended a social pact to combat inflation; reactivate the economy; expand the internal market; repay the debt without negative consequences for national development; and more equitably distribute income, in part through increased wages. *Jornal do Brasil,* 3 June 1984, 35.

9. The formal title of the document which was published in July 1978 as a pamphlet by *Gazeta Mercantil,* is "Primeiro documento dos empresários."

10. Ten leaders were chosen by the poll, but two of those leaders declined the invitation to sign the declaration in favor of democracy. In interviews, one of the signers explained that one leader declined because "he never signs anything" and the other because "he's right-wing and did not support a transition to democracy" [3 Nov. 1987].

11. *Latin America,* 11 June 1976, 182.

12. The film *Pra frente Brazil* depicts a case of a small businessman who, although innocent of any political involvement, is detained by the police, tortured, and eventually killed because he shared a cab ride from the airport with a suspected subversive.

13. Antonio Carlos Fon, *Tortura: A história da repressão política no Brasil* (São Paulo: Global, 1979), 61. However, the British journal *Latin America* reported that General Ednardo D'Avila, the officer in charge of the torture and death of journalist Vladimir Herzog in 1975, and of metalworker Manoel Fiel Filho in 1976, had received financial rewards from industrialists. *Latin America*, 30 January 1976, 36–37.

14. *Jornal do Brasil*, 10 May 1978, 1, 4; and 2 June 1978, 5.

15. Paulo Maluf, quoted in *Latin America Political Report*, 19 August 1977, 253.

16. José Mindlin, quoted in Armando V. Salem and Tão Gomes Pinto, "Recados ao presidente," *Istoé*, December 1976, 46.

17. Skidmore, *Politics of Military Rule*, 254.

18. Ibid., 238.

19. Luiz Carlos Bresser Pereira, *O colapso de uma aliança de classes: A burguesia e a crise do autoritarismo tecnoburocrático* (São Paulo: Editora Brasilense, 1978), 120.

20. *Latin American Political Report*, 14 January 1977, 14.

21. Skidmore, *Politics of Military Rule*, 201.

22. The campaign was not a complete failure. Although the Geisel government did not divest itself of its holdings, it promised to refrain from making future public investments in productive enterprises. This guarantee was provided in a document called "Ação para a empresa privada nacional," 15 June 1976. See Pereira, *O colapso de uma aliança de classes*, 113–24.

23. I cannot personally vouch for the reliability of these data because I have no information on the number of individuals polled or on the sampling or polling procedure used. *Latin America Regional Report: Brazil*, 20 April 1984, 4–5.

24. "Primeiro documento dos empresários," 8.

25. In addition, Peter Wicknertz, of the Swedish company Sandvik, lamented the low wages for workers. "Empresário diz que salário medio do país é muito baixo," *Jornal do Brasil*, 30 September 1976. In 1977, a group of seventeen industrial leaders headed up by Domício Veloso da Silveira, president of CNI, called for wage increases above the rate of inflation.

26. Theofilo de Azeredo Santos, quoted in *Latin America Political Report*, 14 January 1977, 14.

27. "Carta do Rio de Janeiro" (Report by the Fourth Conference of the Conselho Nacional das Classes Produtoras, November 1977). For a summary, see Maranhão and Serrano, "Quem mandou pedir feitiço?" 82–86.

28. Pereira, *O colapso de uma aliança de classes*, 117.

29. For more information on these strikes, see Maria Helena Moreira Alves, *State and Opposition in Military Brazil* (Austin: University of Texas Press, 1985), 194–95.

30. Eugenio Staub, quoted in *Jornal do Brasil*, 16 May 1978, 29.

31. President of FIESP, Theobaldo deNigris, quoted in *Gazeta Mercantil*, 31 October 1978, 1.

32. "FIESP: Negociação direta só sem controle de preço," *O Globo,* 19 June 1978.

33. *Jornal do Brasil,* 26 January 1981, 5.

34. Paulo Francini, quoted in "Federação não quer juntas do ABC negociando," *Folha de São Paulo,* 29 January 1981.

35. "FIESP só negocia com a junta que governo designar," *Jornal do Brasil,* 30 January 1981.

36. The first plant committees of the 1970s were established in Saab-Scania, Radio Frigor, Termomecânica, and Hevea.

37. Alves, *State and Opposition in Military Brazil,* 200.

38. Luis Eulálio Bueno Vidigal Filho, quoted in "A aposta da Volks," *Veja,* 17 October 1980, 116.

39. "Os empresários ameaçam entrar no páreo em 82," *Istoé,* 22 October 1980, 17.

40. See "As grandes liçoes da greve dos metalúrgicos," *Exame,* 21 May 1980, 19–21; and "O dialogo com os metalúrgicos," *Gazeta Mercantil,* 21 May 1980.

41. "Empresário acha FIESP madura para estimular commissão de trabalhador," *Jornal do Brasil,* 24 September 1981, 8.

42. Indications of support for the idea of direct negotiations can be found in a poll conducted by *Exame:* 51 percent of the members of the business community who responded to the poll stated that they were in favor of "free wage negotiations without government intervention." The results of the poll indicated that preference for direct negotiations was slightly greater among large firms (51%) than among medium-sized and small firms (49%), and was also greater among multinational firms (73%) than among Brazilian firms. However, because no information is provided on the size or nature of the sample, these figures must be viewed accordingly. "Os nomes que os empresários querem no ministério," *Exame,* 25 January 1978, 12–15. Also, in July 1980 254 businesspeople issued a statement in favor of free and direct negotiations between employers and employees, stating that this was the best system for Brazil. "Empresários debatem com Delfim eliminação do reajuste salarial," *Jornal do Brasil,* 30 July 1980, 19.

43. The minister of planning, João Reis Velloso, stated, "The government's position is not to intervene in direct negotiations, but to continue to stress that wage increases above the official index will not be passed on to consumers, or else large inflationary problems will arise." *Gazeta Mercantil,* 28–30 October 1978, 3.

44. Up to the very end of the strikes, Simonsen instructed managers not to offer more than a 60-percent increase (even though the union reduced its demand to 68%) and to refuse to make retroactive payments for strike days.

45. "FIESP sugere ao governo concessão de aumento para os trabalhadores com caráter de excepcionalidade," *Carta Semanal,* 23 June 1978.

46. Jorge Duprat Figueiredo, quoted in "Quem muda o assunto," *Veja,* 21 June 1978, 98.

47. "FIESP não reabre negociação," *Jornal do Brasil,* 11 May 1982, 17.

48. The police used horses, tear gas, billy clubs, and stones to break up the picket lines. The town square in São Bernardo became a virtual war zone. The state also forcibly intervened in three unions (the metalworkers' unions of São Bernardo, Santo André, and São Caetano de Sul). It also closed the sites used for mass meetings, deposed union leaders, cut

off communications facilities needed to keep in touch with the rank and file, seized union funds, and threatened leaders with imprisonment. When workers met in churches, these churches were stormed by shock troops. Alves, *State and Opposition in Military Brazil,* 198–204.

49. The regime put São Paulo under the command of the Second Army Division, allowing the commanding general to serve as an ad hoc governor-administrator. Helicopters filled with armed soldiers lingered overhead while workers met in assemblies in the soccer stadium. When the regime banned mass meetings, the security forces occupied the soccer stadiums and public square where workers had met. The army moved tanks into the streets to keep order. The regime charged the strike leaders with violation of the National Security Law and ordered their arrest and imprisonment. It took over the union and replaced the leaders with government appointees. The security forces forcibly dragged the union leaders out of churches—and out of the cars of prominent politicians—where they had sought protection. Alves, *State and Opposition in Military Brazil,* 204.

50. "Ministro intervem nos sindicatos em greve no ABC," *O Globo,* 18 April 1980.

51. Luis Eulálio Bueno Vidigal Filho, quoted in "FIESP instruiu as indústrias a chamar PM para deter greve," *Jornal do Brasil,* 22 August 1983, 8.

52. Alves, *State and Opposition in Military Brazil,* 244.

53. Luis Eulálio Bueno Vidigal Filho, quoted in "A posição da FIESP na greve," *Indústria e Desenvolvimento,* no. 8 (1983).

54. In 1978 Lula accused companies of firing striking workers. When Wolfgang Sauer, Volkswagen chairman, denied the charge, Lula presented him with a list of eleven leading labor negotiators who had been fired by Volkswagen. *Latin America Economic Report,* 22 December 1978, 400.

55. *Gazeta Mercantil,* 9 January 1979, 5.

56. In addition to threatening to lay off workers who did not return to work, these advertisements also listed the firms where the strike had failed and reminded workers how many paydays they had lost. The advertisements included warnings to workers such as "You won't be able to explain to your family later that you lost your job because you were not informed of the law" and "You know that a good worker is never fired; return to work." After the Metalworkers of São Caetano, a union led by Lula's brother, José Ferreira da Silva ("Frei Chico"), agreed to return to work after a strike, industrialists launched a campaign with advertisements saying, "Be like Lula's brother; end this strike." *Estado de São Paulo,* 1–30 April 1980.

57. He added that such actions, instigated by clandestine political groups, threaten democracy by provoking a coup from the right. "Antônio Ermírio ameaça de demissão operário em greve," *Jornal do Brasil,* 26 December 1984.

58. "Comissões de fábrica em São Paulo," *Reconstrução de Lutas Operárias,* no. 6 (May 1985): 3.

59. The braço cruzado strike, in which workers entered the firm and turned on their machines, but refused to work, was one of the most frequent forms of strike action used by the workers during this period.

60. The owner was João Roberto de Mello, of Alfa Industry. For a description of this incident and other acts of intimidation by employers in the 1978 strike, see Maria Christina Pinheiro, "O empresário puzou o revólver e . . . ," *Istoé,* 19 July 1978, 72.

61. This may reflect an interest in appearing to have consistent views. Two of those who stated that industrialists' attitudes had not changed made the following observations: the director of a small business stated, "Industrialists never changed . . . They were forced to wake up by the labor movement, but that doesn't mean they changed" [16 May 1988]. And the vice-president of a very large Brazilian company stated, "There wasn't any change. Strikes are no indication of progress" [18 Nov. 1988].

62. Henry Maksoud, "Sindicalismo, uma ameaça totalitaria," *Visão,* 13 November 1978, 45–58.

63. Adalberto Coelho, quoted in Luiz Roberto Serrano, "Cuidado, muito cuidado," *Istoé,* 27 December 1978, 27.

64. *Latin America Economic Report,* 23 June 1978, 188.

65. Laerte Setúbal, quoted in Salem and Pinto, "Recados ao presidente," 45.

66. Mario Garnero, quoted in Salem and Pinto, "Recados ao presidente," 55.

67. Luis Eulálio Bueno Vidigal Filho, quoted in *Gazeta Mercantil,* 23 March 1979, 1. I have cited Vidigal here because his statement reflected the views of democratic industrialists. Nonetheless, given statements he made subsequent to this one, he is better identified as one of the "uncommitted." Industrialist Paulo Francini's similar concern is also reflected in this article.

68. Responding to the successful negotiation sessions at the end of 1978, Luis Eulálio Bueno Vidigal Filho praised FIESP's role and remarked, "The great secret of this agreement was that the members of the business community worked as one entity." An editor of *Gazeta Mercantil* stated, "FIESP played a decisive role in the discussion and elaboration of a series of norms and joint action with management." SINFAVEA, the association representing automobile manufacturers, also considered FIESP's role crucial to the rapid resolution of the strike. *Gazeta Mercantil,* 11–13 November 1978, 3.

69. For a description of this debate, see "Acordo com metalúrgicos rompe a unidade da FIESP," *Folha de São Paulo,* 15 April 1982.

70. John Humphrey, *Capitalist Control and Workers' Struggle in the Brazilian Auto Industry* (Princeton: Princeton University Press, 1982).

71. Renato Raul Boschi, "National Industrial Elites and the State in Post-1964 Brazil: Institutional Mediations and Political Change" (Ph.D. diss., University of Michigan, 1978), 265–74. See also the Brazilian version, Renato Raul Boschi, *Elites industriais e democracia: Hegemonia burguesa e mudança política no Brasil,* trans. Patrick Burglin (Rio de Janeiro: Edições Graal, 1979), 151–55.

72. "O que pretendem, de fato, os empresários," *Exame,* 23 February 1977, 14.

73. Guillermo O'Donnell, "Tensions in the Bureaucratic-Authoritarian State and the Question of Democracy," in *The New Authoritarianism in Latin America,* ed. David Collier (Princeton: Princeton University Press, 1979), 285–318. See also Guillermo O'Donnell and Philippe C. Schmitter, *Transitions from Authoritarian Rule: Tentative Conclusions about Uncertain Democracies* (Baltimore: Johns Hopkins University Press, 1986), 50.

74. For these quotes, see *Latin America Political Report,* 9 September 1977, 278. This report does not mention the context in which these statements were made. See also Luiz Roberto Serrano, "Democracia já," *Istoé,* 7 September 1977, 12.

75. "Nigris convoca empresários para lutar contra os que se aproveitam da abertura," *Jornal do Brasil,* 20 December 1979, 2.

76. See "Empresários de São Paulo aplaudem advertencia do presidente da FIESP contra subversão," *Jornal do Brasil,* 21 December 1979.

77. In the first elections, on 21 August 1980, neither candidate won a majority: Vidigal won 54 and deNigris won 52 of the 108 votes. By the runoff election on 4 September 1980, Vidigal had acquired enough votes to defeat deNigris: Vidigal won 61 (56%) and deNigris won 45 (42%) of the 108 votes.

78. *Jornal do Brasil,* 14 February 1978, 5.

79. Cláudio Bardella, quoted in *Latin America Regional Report,* 17 October 1980, 7.

80. O'Donnell and Schmitter, *Transitions from Authoritarian Rule,* 50; and Fernando H. Cardoso, "Entrepreneurs and the Transition Process: The Brazilian Case," in *Transitions from Authoritarian Rule: Comparative Perspectives,* ed. Guillermo O'Donnell, Philippe C. Schmitter, and Laurence Whitehead (Baltimore: Johns Hopkins University Press, 1986), 147.

81. O'Donnell and Schmitter, *Transitions from Authoritarian Rule,* 27; and Cardoso, "Entrepreneurs and the Transition Process," 146–53.

Chapter 5. Industrialists and the New Republic

1. Aldo Lorenzetti, quoted in "FIESP decide ampliar apoio a Sarney e intensificar 'lobby' no Congresso," *Folha de São Paulo,* 15 October 1987, 30.

2. For example, before the Summer Plan the government promised not to freeze prices and wages. However, when the Summer Plan was implemented it included price and wage freezes.

3. Walter Sacca, director of the Economics Department of FIESP, quoted in "Empresarios acham que Cruzado II ja está demorando," *Jornal da Tarde,* 20 November 1986, 13.

4. "Indústria critica 'industabilidade' de política econômica," Folha de São Paulo, 30 December 1986, 25.

5. Mario Amato, quoted in "Empresários pedem regras mais claras," *Folha de São Paulo,* 9 July 1987, 23.

6. Walter Sacca, director of the Economics Department of FIESP, quoted in "Empresarios acham que Cruzado II ja está demorando," 13.

7. Thomas E. Skidmore, *The Politics of Military Rule in Brazil, 1964–85* (New York: Oxford University Press, 1988), 305.

8. For example, while these economic policies often froze wages after they had been averaged over a previous period, prices were never averaged. They were simply frozen at their current rate or, at times, they were allowed to increase before they were frozen. Leigh A.

Payne, "Working Class Strategies in the Transition to Democracy in Brazil," *Comparative Politics,* 23, no. 2 (1991): 224–27.

9. Peter Flynn, "Brazil: The Politics of the Cruzado Plan," *Third World Quarterly* 8, no. 4 (1986): 1176–77.

10. William C. Smith, "Heterodox Shocks and the Political Economy of Democratic Transition in Argentina and Brazil" (Paper presented at the Fourteenth International Congress of the Latin American Studies Association, New Orleans, 17–19 March 1988), 14. See also Skidmore, *Politics of Military Rule in Brazil,* 281.

11. Sarney responded by calling businesspeople "anarchists." See "Sarney acusa empresários de pegar anarquia," *Folha de São Paulo,* 10 January 1987, 17; and "Empresários ameaçam desobedecer governo," ibid., 22 August 1987, 17.

12. Matias Machline, quoted in "Machline defende fortalecimento do mercado interno," *Folha de São Paolo,* 6 August 1987, 25.

13. José Mindlin, quoted in *Estado de São Paulo,* 12 November 1986, 32.

14. Only 15% of the industrialists I interviewed rejected the concept of a national minimum wage. This minority argued that the market, not the government, should determine all wages. The vast majority (82%) of my interviewees believed that a minimum wage was necessary to protect workers from employers who could not be trusted to pay even a subsistence wage. Those industrialists who supported minimum wage legislation tended to have had substantial experience abroad. In addition, only 5%—primarily industrialists at non-United States foreign firms, and founders of firms—considered the level of the minimum wage during the New Republic adequate. See Leigh Ann Payne, "Pragmatic Actors: The Political Attitudes and Behavior of Brazilian Industrial Elites" (Ph.D. diss., Yale University, 1990), chap. 7.

15. The remaining 1% stated that they paid above the minimum wage but did not know exactly how much. The industries that paid the official minimum wage were primarily Brazilian firms owned by families or individuals. None of the firms with any foreign capital, and none of the firms that were owned by institutions or were publicly held, paid the minimum wage. All of the industrialists who paid the highest base salary (five to seven times the minimum wage) were college educated.

16. Forty-five percent believed that their base wages were high enough. An additional 8% did not have an opinion. The industrialists who believed that they paid high enough wages tended, logically, to be those who paid five to seven times the minimum wage. For an in-depth discussion of industrialists' attitudes toward the minimum wage, see Payne, "Pragmatic Actors," chap. 7.

17. Several industrialists told me in interviews that even with a minimum wage, employers frequently circumvented the law by failing to register workers, and that given the chance, many employers would use slave labor.

18. In addition, 8% advocated a variety of other strategies for setting the minimum wage, and 2% had no opinion.

19. The industrialists who believed that only the government should set wages tended to be from non–United States foreign firms. See Payne, "Pragmatic Actors," chap. 7.

20. The industrialists who advocated government intervention in wages tended to see themselves as being on the left. They advocated government wage setting because, given the surplus of unskilled labor in Brazil and the political weakness of organized labor, they believed the market would depress wages. See Payne, "Pragmatic Actors," chap. 7.

21. "Empresários fazem acordo em varios estados," *Folha de São Paulo,* 14 August 1987, 26; and "Empresas ignoram o Plano Bresser e antecipam residuo," ibid., 4 October 1987, 46.

22. "FIESP sugere abono para assalariados," *Folha de São Paulo,* 18 June 1987, 25; and "FIESP preve uma redução no rendimento do assalariado," ibid., 19 June 1987, 19.

23. "Empresários admitem apoiar a paralisação," *Folha de São Paulo,* 28 July 1987, 21.

24. *Latin America Weekly Report,* 4 October 1985, 8.

25. Boris Tabacof, "A oportunidade do pacto social," *Folha de São Paulo,* 12 December 1986, 20.

26. The only statistically significant variable I found in analyzing industrialists' responses to a social pact was their fathers' occupation: 23% of the industrialists whose fathers were also industrialists believed that a social pact was possible, compared to 12% whose fathers had other occupations.

27. Interestingly, the minority who did feel threatened represented approximately the same percentage as those who had felt threatened by the economic crisis in 1964: 21% in 1964 (a total of eighteen), and 25% (a total of sixteen) during the New Republic. Yet these were not the same industrialists during both periods. Of the thirty-four industrialists who were threatened by the economy, only 15% felt threatened by the economy in both periods.

The relationship between various characteristics of the industrialists and their fear of economic decline was random, with one exception. Eight industrialists, or half of those who felt threatened by the economy, were from small firms with less than five hundred employees. In other words, it appears as though industrialists from larger firms continued to have options that enabled them to ride out the economic crisis.

28. Feres Abujamra, quoted in "FIESP decide ampliar apoio a Sarney e intensificar 'Lobby' no Congresso," 30.

29. Clovis Rossi, "98% dos empresários não confiam no governo Sarney," *Folha de São Paulo,* 9 February 1988, 5.

30. Analysis of my interviewees' responses to the threat from the political situation produced only two statistically significant variables: religion, and interviewees' fathers' occupations. Twenty-eight percent of those who were not religious, but only 15% of those who were religious felt threatened by the political situation. In addition, 27% of those whose fathers were industrialists, but only 17% of those whose fathers had other occupations, felt threatened by the political situation.

For the most part, the same individuals did not feel threatened in both periods: only 14% fell into that category, whereas 30% felt threatened by the political situation in 1964 but not during the New Republic, and 6% felt threatened during the New Republic but not during 1964.

31. For more information on political corruption in the New Republic, see Skidmore, *Politics of Military Rule in Brazil,* 263–64.

32. Nildo Masini, quoted in "FIESP não assume tese de Masini de renuncia de Sarney," *Folha de São Paulo,* 18 November 1987, 4.

33. Rossi, "98% dos empresários não confiam no governo Sarney," 5.

34. Of the sixty-six industrialists who felt threatened by the left, only 12% felt threatened during both periods.

35. My analysis of this ideological diversity revealed two statistically significant variables: education and religion. All of the interviewees who placed themselves on the left were college educated, while only one-third of those who placed themselves on the extreme right had college educations. Nonetheless, of those with college educations, the largest proportion (49%) considered themselves to be on the moderate right. With regard to religion, 78% of those who considered themselves to be on the extreme right and 75% of those who considered themselves to be on the moderate right were religious, compared to 42% of those who considered themselves to be on the left. I also found that all of the industrialists who defined themselves as being on the extreme right were from firms that had been founded before 1955; however, this was not statistically significant.

36. Flynn, "Brazil," 1166–68.

37. For information on the support for the PT among business leaders, see *Folha de São Paulo,* 24 June 1987, 4; 5 July 1987, 6; and 19 June 1988, 8. Some business leaders voted for the PT in the 1988 mayoral elections "out of respect for its idealism and outrage over the blatant opportunism displayed by more conservative parties since civilian rule returned here [to Brazil] in 1985." Alan Riding, "New Star Player in Brazil Politics," *New York Times,* 23 November 1988, 14. Some considered the PT "to be the most honest and idealistic of the groups seeking power." Alan Riding, "A Mayor Bent on Inverting Priorities," *New York Times,* 18 March 1989, 4. For more information on the PT, see Margaret E. Keck, *The Workers' Party and Democratization in Brazil* (New Haven: Yale University Press, 1992).

38. For an expanded discussion of the political actors chosen and the scale, see Payne, "Pragmatic Actors," chap. 6.

39. I found no statistically significant variables in my analysis of these industrialists. However, I did discover that they were not from large firms: among those I interviewed, no industrialist from a firm with more than two thousand employees feared the left, and only one industrialist from a conglomerate expressed such fear.

40. These three industrialists all shared the following characteristics: (1) they were of Brazilian nationality; (2) they were born in capital cities; (3) they were college educated; (4) they were religious; (5) they had some experience abroad; (6) they became industrialists after the 1964 coup; and (7) they defined themselves as right-wing (although not extremely so). All three feared the New Republic and viewed labor as being on the extreme left, but they did not fear labor during the New Republic.

41. For an expanded discussion of these findings, see Payne, "Pragmatic Actors," chap. 6.

42. "Luís Eulálio critica os partidos," *Jornal do Brasil,* 26 January 1985, 18.

43. An example of this view is the attack on trade unions by Roberto Della Manna, the director of FIESP's labor negotiating department, during the strikes to protest the first Cruzado Plan in 1986. He stated that the union leadership had distanced itself from its base

and had brought about "union anarchy." "FIESP mobilizada contra as greves," *Jornal da Tarde,* 11 July 1986. He also commented, with regard to the declaration of the 1986 strikes against the second Cruzado Plan, "In the factories on the eve of the 'protest movement,' we felt that the workers were upset. The climate was sad. Union leaders had forced the situation. Today, in Brazil, some sectors have decided to have a strike, as if it were a simple decision. This attitude is irresponsible . . . They made the decision as if it were as easy as deciding to go on a picnic." "O movimento de protesta," *O Globo,* 14 December 1986.

44. Industrialists at Brazilian firms were more likely than those at multinational corporations to place labor federations on the extreme left, probably owing to their limited exposure to labor movements. Moreover, older industrialists were more likely to place the CGT on the extreme left, probably because they had not altered their view of the CGT since the 1960s.

45. Forty-six percent listed other obstacles, including poor leadership, lack of experience, and fragmentation. For an in-depth discussion of industrialists' views on this issue, see Payne, "Pragmatic Actors," chap. 7.

46. The firm's percentage of exports also proved statistically significant in analyzing industrialists' perceptions of workers' ideology. Of the industrialists who exported more than 50% of what they produced, 66% thought workers were to their left, 6% thought workers were to their right, and 28% thought they shared the same ideology. Of those who exported less than 50%, 51% considered workers to be on their left, 16% considered workers to be on their right, and 33% believed they shared the same ideology.

47. Of the industrialists who considered Medeiros to be on the extreme left, none were from the metalworking sector (Medeiros's sector). A surprisingly large percentage of these industrialists were from United States firms. (Thirty-eight percent of the industrialists from United States firms, compared with 4% of those from Brazilian firms and 2% of those from non–United States multinational firms, considered Medeiros to be on the extreme left.)

48. These state capitals were Cuiabá, Maceió, João Pessoa, Teresinha, and Rio Branco.

49. Executives from multinational firms were more likely to state that they had altered labor relations in their firms than were industrialists from Brazilian firms. See Payne, "Pragmatic Actors," chap. 7.

50. The vast majority (82%) of the industrialists who considered workers right-wing were satisfied with labor relations. The other statistically significant variables were industrialists' religion, and their relationship to the founder of the firm. See ibid.

51. These industrialists' perceptions of the ideology of the workers in their firms are also revealing. Twenty-one percent of those who classified the workers in their firms as right-wing opposed the right to strike, as compared to 7% of those who put workers in the center, and 5% of those who put them on the left. These figures are counterintuitive, since one would have expected industrialists who considered workers to be on the left to favor greater restrictions on strike activity. However, they are consistent with a conservative-paternalist vision of capital-labor relations. Industrialists who hold such a vision believe that workers in their firms share their goals and values and, therefore, that internal harmony is possible. They also perceive themselves as "protecting" workers from subversive trade union leaders who do not have the workers' best interests at heart and who lead them to carry out dangerous and self-

destructive activities only to satisfy the leaders' self-interested desire for increased political power.

52. The regulations that were being debated in the business community included controls over trade unions' freedom to call strikes (e.g., requirements for a prior vote by a majority of the membership of the trade union; for prior negotiations with employers; and for advance warning of strike activity), as well as proscriptions of certain forms of strike activity (e.g., strikes expressing solidarity, political strikes, strikes in essential or public enterprises, and strikes involving picket lines). All of the industrialists interviewed who advocated an unrestricted freedom to call strikes were Brazilian. They also tended to be Brazilian executives at non-United States foreign firms, or to be affiliated with family firms or individually owned firms. Those who advocated the most restrictions on strike declarations tended to be non-Brazilians, and executives at multinational corporations or at institutionally or publicly held firms. For more detailed information, see Payne, "Pragmatic Actors," chap. 7.

53. Nelson Letaif, "A espera do apocalipse," *Senhor,* 18 December 1985, 42; "Funaro também critica a atual onda de greves," *Estado de São Paulo,* 7 May 1986. A FIESP document stated the official view of the 1986 strikes: "To strike is a worker's right, but the calling of illegal strikes constitutes offensive and condemnable behavior, precisely at the moment when Brazil is trying to combat inflation, put the economy on its feet, and promote just social development." "Greves ilegais podem inviabilizar o Plano Cruzado, diz FIESP," *Gazeta Mercantil,* 18 July 1986.

54. Pazzianotto had been the lawyer for the São Bernardo Metalworkers' Union during the massive strikes of 1978. *Veja,* 21 May 1980, 3–6.

55. "Pazzianotto não irá intervir em sindicatos," *Jornal do Brasil,* 27 April 1985, 18.

56. Mario Amato, cited in "Pazzianotto divide em São Paulo," *Jornal do Brasil,* 26 May 1985, 7.

57. "Pazzianotto repudia o autoritarismo," *Jornal do Brasil,* 1 June 1985, 7.

58. See *Istoé,* 25 September 1985, 84–86.

59. "Proposta de estabilidade gera polémica," *Folha de São Paulo,* 7 July 1987, 19.

60. On numerous occasions, the Brazilian media and industrialists attributed this rhetorical question to Mario Amato, president of FIESP.

61. "CNI entregara propostas a Ulysses," *Folha de São Paulo,* 13 August 1987, 5. A similar petition, with thirty-eight thousand signatures, was filed by the Federation of Industries in the state of Rio Grande do Sul (FIERGS). "Os 'lobbies' se unem críticas ao governo federal," ibid., 16 August 1987, 8.

62. The television campaign had actors who played workers saying such things as, "Job security today is this: if you are a good worker, the firm will never let you leave." The actors displayed fear for the future of their children: "This security proposal in the Constitution could hurt my son's future job possibilities."

63. Skidmore, *Politics of Military Rule in Brazil,* 291–92.

64. In addition to the 37% who mentioned indemnity and the 35% who endorsed just-cause legislation, 22% of the industrialists I interviewed advocated bargained-for provisions in union contracts as protection for workers against arbitrary dismissal.

65. These percentages on alternatives to job security add up to more than 100% because interviewees provided multiple responses to the question. Those who were most strongly in favor of dismissing workers for union or political activity were from small, Brazilian firms. Payne, "Pragmatic Actors," chap. 7.

66. These individuals tended to be foreigners, immigrants, and first-generation Brazilians; they also tended to define themselves as right-wing and to work at firms with only one plant (as opposed to conglomerates or single firms with multiple plants).

67. These industrialists tended to be Brazilian and to have had no experience abroad.

68. In my interviews, antidemocratic sentiment existed primarily in the Brazilian industrial community rather than in the transnational sector.

69. The strongest support for union autonomy was among industrialists at Brazilian firms in nontraditional sectors of industry. See Payne, "Pragmatic Actors," chap. 7.

70. For more information on ideology and the issue of union autonomy, see ibid.

71. See ibid. for a detailed discussion of these issues.

72. Ibid.

73. The Interunion Department for Parliamentary Action (DIAP), the primary labor lobbying organization, had originally demanded a reduction to forty hours, but in the early drafting of the 1988 Constitution a compromise of forty-four hours was achieved.

74. The industrialists who accepted the forty-hour week tended to be from multinational firms; they also tended to be managers, and religious.

75. There were no statistically significant variables with regard to the question of the work week.

76. Most of these industrialists were from traditional and older firms, and had little experience abroad; those who worked in the modern industrial sector (i.e., newer, nontraditional firms run by industrialists with experience abroad) opposed a statutory maximum work week. Payne, "Pragmatic Actors," chap. 7.

77. Ibid.

78. Franco also mentioned that firms could accept other labor proposals, such as maternity leave for 120 days and double pay for overtime, but asserted that the job security provision would destroy firms. "Empresários pressionarão PMDB para fixar indenização para demitidos," *Folha de São Paulo,* 4 November 1987, 8.

79. They also stated that they could accept the 120-day maternity leave, and agrarian reform.

80. *Senhor,* 15 February 1988, 23–24.

81. David Fleischer, "The Brazilian Congress: From Abertura to New Republic," in *Political Liberalization in Brazil: Dynamics, Dilemmas, and Future Prospects,* ed. Wayne A. Selcher (Boulder, Colo.: Westview Press, 1986), 114.

82. Cesar Rogério Valente, of the Federation of Commercial Associations of the state of Rio Grande do Sul, quoted in "Business Funds for Congressmen," *Latin American Regional Report: Brazil,* 5 July 1985, 2.

83. David Fleischer, "O Congresso Constituinte de 1987: Um perfil sócio-econômico e político" (Brasília: Departamento de Ciências Políticas e Relações Internacionais, Universidade de Brasília, 1987, Mimeo), 8. Fleischer also provides (on p. 15) data compiled by

Semprel (a business lobbying organization) which showed that 45% of the members of the Constituent Assembly were "capitalists" (22% agrarian and 23% urban) and 12% were workers (2% rural and 10% urban). Leôncio Martins Rodrigues's survey of 487 members of the Constituent Assembly provided slightly different figures: 156 (32%) called themselves "members of the business community," and 15 (3%) called themselves "manual workers." Leôncio Martins Rodrigues, *Quem é quem na Constituinte: Uma análise sócio-política dos partidos e deputados* (São Paulo: OESP-Maltese, 1987), 79–80.

84. Compare the figures for the Constituent Assembly given in Fleischer, "O Congress Constituinte de 1987," 8, with the figures for the elections to the House of Deputies and the Senate in 1979, 1981, and 1983 given in Fleischer, "Brazilian Congress," 124–29. Of those industrialists, twenty-five were "owners of capital," and their party affiliations were as follows: 40% were in the centrist party the PMDB, and 60% were in right-wing parties (36% were in the PFL, 20% were in the PDS, and 4% were in the PL).

85. This is the average of two reliable analyses of the Constituent Assembly: Semprel placed 12% of the assembly on the left, 27% as "liberal-reformists," 35% as "liberal-conservatives," and 26% on the right; the *Folha de São Paulo* placed 9% on the left, 23% on the center-left; 32% in the center; 24% on the center-right, and 12% on the right. Fleischer, "O Congresso Constituinte de 1987," 15.

86. At first, the election was contested. Before Mario Amato had even begun his campaign, however, his liberal opponent Paulo Francini withdrew his candidacy owing to lack of support and endorsed Amato.

87. Políbio Braga, "E hora de Sarney exercer o poder," *Parlamento,* February 1986, 3.

88. Mindlin is quoted in Célia de Gouvea Franco, "Amato reflete opção conservadora do empresariado paulista," *Gazeta Mercantil,* 1 November 1985. Amato described his own vision of society as progressive capitalism: "It should be based on social justice, the antithesis of savage capitalism, but anticipate [labor] demands and transform them into capitalist conquests." "A livre empresa em primeiro lugar," *Indústria e Desenvolvimento,* October 1986, 7.

89. " FIESP vai atuar como 'lobby,' diz dirigente," *Folha de São Paulo,* 31 January 1987, 7.

90. "Empresários e Constituinte," *Folha de São Paulo,* 17 April 1987, 2.

91. The president of a very large Brazilian firm accused [23 Sept. 1987] the owners of these firms of behaving as though it were 1910.

92. However, since I could not determine the size of the firms that 20% of these directors were affiliated with, my finding that FIESP primarily represented large firms may be incorrect.

93. While primarily representing small and medium-sized industries in São Paulo, the PNBE also includes owners of firms of all sizes, located in various areas of São Paulo, Rio Grande do Sul, and Rio de Janeiro.

94. Frederico Vasconcelos, "Posição de Amato mudou conforme as circumstancias," *Folha de São Paulo,* 23 March 1988, 13.

95. None of the other twenty-four members of the 1964 FIESP directorate were still active on the 1986–89 board. Two were emeritus directors, five were consulting directors, and one was on the representative council of the 1986–89 FIESP directorate.

96. Analysis of the 28% who believed that their views were shared within the industrial community revealed four statistically relevant variables. First, 49% of the industrialists from firms with one plant thought their views were typical, compared with 21% of industrialists from firms with several plants, and 26% of industrialists from conglomerates. Second, only 19% of those industrialists with substantial experience abroad thought their views were typical, compared to 38% of those who had some experience abroad, and 33% who had none. Third, 32% of the industrialists who claimed to have supported the coup believed that their views were typical, compared to 15% who claimed that they had not supported the coup. Fourth, 34% of those who said they were religious thought their views were typical, compared to 16% of those who said they were not religious.

97. Those with few memberships in industrial associations tended to be foreign industrialists: 91% of the foreign industrialists had only weak ties to the Brazilian business community.

98. Fleischer, "Brazilian Congress," 102.

99. In addition, only about one-half (48%) of the industrialists I interviewed stated that they had affiliations with civic organizations outside the business community.

100. For more information on these industrialists, see Payne, "Pragmatic Actors," chap. 7.

101. In 1985, industrialists from two prominent firms, Villares and Probel, made separate agreements with workers despite FIESP's warning to the contrary. In 1986, Della Manna stated, "We're not against firms granting [independent wage] increases as long as these activities are spontaneous and not obtained under pressure from political movements." "FIESP instrui empresas para enfrentar os movimentos grevistas," *Gazeta Mercantil,* 22 July 1986.

102. Industrialists who opposed FIESP's intransigence with regard to labor relations even formed a group called Labor Relations Consultants to Businesses (ARTE). See "Empresários reagem em Diadema," *Estado de São Paulo,* 3 August 1986.

103. Comment made in a meeting I attended of owners of small businesses at ANAPEMEI in São Paulo on 12 May 1988. This individual argued that FIESP's intransigence with regard to wage increases had drawn out the strike in his firm and cost him more money than giving in to workers' wage demands would have.

Chapter 6. Brazilian Industrialists and Democratic Stability in Theoretical and Comparative Perspective

1. Guillermo O'Donnell, "Substantive or Procedural Consensus? Notes on the Latin American Bourgeoisie," in *The Right and Democracy in Latin America,* ed. Douglas A. Chalmers, Maria do Carmo Campello de Souza, and Atilio A. Boron (New York: Praeger Publishers, 1992), 43–47.

2. In particular, see the works by Carlos Acuña, Ernest Bartell, Guillermo Campero,

Catherine Conaghan, Francisco Durand, Blanca Heredia, and William Nylen listed in the Bibliography.

3. For more detailed information about Argentine business leaders' political attitudes and behavior, see William C. Smith, *Authoritarianism and the Crisis of the Argentine Political Economy* (Stanford, Calif.: Stanford University Press, 1989); and Jorge Niosi, *Los empresarios y el estado argentino (1955–1969)* (Buenos Aires: Siglo Ventiuno Editores, 1974).

4. Carlos H. Acuña, "Intereses empresarios, dictadura y democracia en la Argentina actual" (Paper prepared for the Fifteenth International Congress of the Latin American Studies Association, San Juan, Puerto Rico, 21–24 September 1989), 21. Forthcoming as "Business Interests, Dictatorship, and Democracy in Argentina: Why the Bourgeoisie Abandons Authoritarian Strategies and Opts for Democratic Stability," in *Business and Democracy in Latin America,* ed. Ernest Bartell and Leigh A. Payne (Pittsburgh: University of Pittsburgh Press).

5. Smith, *Authoritarianism and the Crisis of the Argentine Political Economy,* 267–97.

6. Acuña, "Intereses empresarios, dictadura y democracia," 37–38.

7. Ibid., 26.

8. Ibid., 46.

9. Guillermo Campero, *Los gremios empresariales en el período 1970–1983: Comportamiento sociopolítico y orientaciones ideológicas* (Santiago: Instituto Latinoamericano de Estudios Transnacionales, 1984), 35–61.

10. Ibid., 290–91.

11. Ernest Bartell, "Business Perceptions and the Transition to Democracy in Chile" (Paper presented at the Fifteenth International Congress of the Latin American Studies Association, San Juan, Puerto Rico, 21–24 September 1989), 4. Forthcoming in *Business and Democracy in Latin America,* ed. Ernest Bartell and Leigh A. Payne.

12. Bartell, "Business Perceptions and the Transition to Democracy," 6.

13. Campero, *Los gremios empresariales,* 298–309.

14. Bartell, "Business Perceptions and the Transition to Democracy," 8.

15. Ibid., 7.

16. Ibid.

17. Roberto Esteban Martinez, "Business Elites in Democratic Spain" (Ph.D. diss., Yale University, 1984), 482–83.

18. Víctor Pérez Díaz, *El retorno de la sociedad civil* (Madrid: Instituto de Estudios Económicos, 1987), 125–73.

19. Martinez, "Business Elites in Democratic Spain," 225.

20. Ibid., 481.

21. Ibid., 277.

22. Víctor Pérez Díaz, *Governability and the Scale of Governance: Mesogovernments in Spain,* Working Paper no. 1990/6 (Madrid: Instituto Juan March de Estudios e Investigaciones, Centro de Estudios Avanzados en Ciencias Sociales, 1990), 61.

23. Ibid., 65–66.

24. Pérez Díaz, *El retorno de la sociedad civil,* 149.

25. Ibid., 146.

26. Ibid., 162.

27. Ibid.

28. Martinez, "Business Elites in Democratic Spain," 218.

29. Acuña, "Intereses empresarios, dictadura y democracia," 11.

30. Ibid., 7–8.

31. Bartell, "Business Perceptions and the Transition to Democracy," 10.

32. Scott Mainwaring, "Political Parties and Democratization in Brazil and the Southern Cone," *Comparative Politics* 21, no. 1 (1988): 92–100.

33. Bartell, "Business Perceptions and the Transition to Democracy," 14.

34. Pérez Díaz, *El retorno de la sociedad civil,* 151–52.

35. Also, as in Brazil, they were critical of many provisions in the Constitution. In Spain, business leaders failed to defeat the job security measure and the right-to-strike provision.

36. Martinez suggests that business leaders were uninvolved in these business associations because of the presumed Spanish cultural characteristic of nonassociability. Martinez, "Business Elites in Democratic Spain," 115–200. However, given the distrust and fragmentation I have noted in the other case studies, I question his attributing these attitudes to a unique cultural or situational context.

37. Pérez Díaz, *El retorno de la sociedad civil,* 173.

38. Pérez Díaz, "Governability and the Scale of Governance," 59.

39. For more information on these pacts, see Robert M. Fishman, *Working-Class Organization and the Return to Democracy in Spain* (Ithaca, N. Y.: Cornell University Press, 1990), 214–46.

40. Pérez Díaz, "Governability and the Scale of Governance," 78.

41. Unfortunately I cannot evaluate how successful these diverse forms of political action are, because success depends on highly inconstant factors such as consensus within the business community on particular issues, and the compatibility of the business community's interests with those of other social sectors or the state.

Appendix

1. Four interviews were eliminated from the data base because they did not provide enough information to merit inclusion.

2. One recent exploration of Brazilian financial elites is Wendy Joan Barker, "Banks and Industry in Contemporary Brazil: Their Organization, Relationship, and Leaders" (Ph.D. diss., Yale University, 1990). I am currently engaged in research on the political action of rural elites in Brazil.

3. In addition to interviewing industrial leaders, I also interviewed the top eight labor leaders in São Paulo, the primary labor lobbyist in the Constituent Assembly of 1987–88, and the director of DIEESE, the labor union statistics-gathering group.

4. Albert O. Hirschman, "The Political Economy of Import-Substituting Industrialization in Latin America," in *A Bias for Hope: Essays on Development in Latin America,* ed. Albert O. Hirschman (New Haven: Yale University Press, 1971), 96–98.

5. One industrialist, Paulo Ayres Filho, voluntarily gave me permission to quote him in the text.

Bibliography

Scholarly Sources

Acuña, Carlos H. "Intereses empresarios, dictadura y democracia en la Argentina actual." Paper prepared for the Fifteenth International Congress of the Latin American Studies Association, San Juan, Puerto Rico, 21–24 September 1989. Forthcoming as "Business Interests, Dictatorship, and Democracy in Argentina: Why the Bourgeoisie Abandons Authoritarian Strategies and Opts for Democratic Stability." In *Business and Democracy in Latin America,* edited by Ernest Bartell and Leigh A. Payne. Pittsburgh: University of Pittsburgh Press, forthcoming.

Affonso, Almino. *Raizes do golpe: Da crise da legalidade ao parlamentarismo (1961– 1963).* São Paulo: Marco Zero, 1988.

Alves, Maria Helena Moreira. *State and Opposition in Military Brazil.* Austin: University of Texas Press, 1985.

Ayres Filho, Paulo. "The Brazilian Revolution." Paper presented at the Georgetown University Center for Strategic Studies, Washington, D.C., July 1964. Published (in condensed form) in *Latin America: Politics, Economics, and Hemispheric Security,* edited by Norman A. Bailey, 239–60. New York: Frederick A. Praeger, 1965.

Bandeira, Moniz. *Cartéis e desnacionalização: A experiência Brasileira, 1964–1974.* Rio de Janeiro: Civilização Brasileira, 1975.

———. *O governo João Goulart: As lutas sociais no Brasil (1961–1964).* Rio de Janeiro: Civilização Brasileira, 1977.

Barker, Wendy Joan. "Banks and Industry in Contemporary Brazil: Their Organization, Relationship, and Leaders." Ph.D. diss., Yale University, 1990.

Bartell, Ernest. "Business Perceptions and the Transition to Democracy in Chile." Paper presented at the Fifteenth International Congress of the Latin American Studies Association, San Juan, Puerto Rico, 21–24 September 1989. In *Business and Democracy in Latin America,* edited by Ernest Bartell and Leigh A. Payne. Pittsburgh: University of Pittsburgh Press, forthcoming.

Bartell, Ernest, and Leigh A. Payne, eds. *Business and Democracy in Latin America.* Pittsburgh: University of Pittsburgh Press, forthcoming.

Bauer, Raymond A., Ithiel de Sola Pool, and Lewis Anthony Dexter. *American Business and Public Policy: The Politics of Foreign Trade.* New York: Atherton Press, 1964.

Becker, David G. "Development, Democracy, and Dependency in Latin America: A Post-Imperialist View." *Third World Quarterly* 6, no. 2 (1984): 411–31.

————. *The New Bourgeoisie and the Limits of Dependency: Mining, Class, and Power in "Revolutionary" Peru.* Princeton: Princeton University Press, 1983.

Black, Jan Knippers. *United States Penetration of Brazil.* Philadelphia: University of Pennsylvania Press, 1977.

Block, Fred. "The Ruling Class Does Not Rule: Notes on the Marxist Theory of the State." In *The Political Economy: Readings in the Politics and Economics of American Public Policy,* edited by Thomas Ferguson and Joel Rogers, 32–46. Armonk, N.Y.: M. E. Sharpe, 1984.

Boschi, Renato Raul. "National Industrial Elites and the State in Post-1964 Brazil: Institutional Mediations and Political Change." Ph.D. diss., University of Michigan, 1978. Published in Portuguese as *Elites industriais e democracia: Hegemonia burguesa e mudança política no Brasil,* translated by Patrick Burglin. Rio de Janeiro: Edições Graal, 1979.

————. *Empresariado nacional e estado no Brasil.* Rio de Janeiro: Editora Forense Universitária, 1978.

Brasil, nunca mais. Petrópolis: Vozes, 1985.

Cameron, David R. "Social Democracy, Corporatism, Labour Quiescence, and the Representation of Economic Interest in Advanced Capitalist Society." In *Order and Conflict in Contemporary Capitalism,* edited by John H. Goldthorpe, 143–78. Oxford: Clarendon Press, 1984.

Campanhole, Adriano, and Hilton Lobo Campanhole, eds. *Consolidação das leis do trabalho e legislação complementar.* São Paulo: Editora Atlas, 1983.

Campero, Guillermo. *Los gremios empresariales en el período 1970–1983: Comportamiento sociopolítico y orientaciones ideológicas.* Santiago, Chile: Instituto Latinoamericano de Estudios Transnacionales, 1984.

Cardoso, Fernando Henrique. "Associated-Dependent Development: Theoretical and Practical Implications." In *Authoritarian Brazil: Origins, Policies, and Future,* edited by Alfred Stepan, 142–76. New Haven: Yale University Press, 1973.

————. *Autoritarismo e democratização.* Rio de Janeiro: Paz e Terra, 1975.

————. "Entrepreneurs and the Transition Process: The Brazilian Case." In *Transitions from Authoritarian Rule: Comparative Perspectives,* edited by Guillermo O'Donnell, Philippe C. Schmitter, and Laurence Whitehead, 137–53. Baltimore: Johns Hopkins University Press, 1986.

————. "O papel dos empresários no processo de transição." *Dados* 26, no. 1 (1983): 9–27.

Cardoso, Fernando Henrique, and Enzo Faletto. *Dependency and Development in Latin America.* Berkeley and Los Angeles: University of California Press, 1979.

Castello Branco, Carlos. "Da conspiração á revolução." In *Os idos de março: A queda em abril,* edited by Alberto Dines et al., 277–306. Rio de Janeiro: José Alvaro Editor, 1964.

Cohen, Youssef. *The Manipulation of Consent: The State and Working-Class Consciousness in Brazil.* Pittsburgh: University of Pittsburgh Press, 1989.

Collier, David, ed. *The New Authoritarianism in Latin America.* Princeton: Princeton University Press, 1979.

————. "Overview of the Bureaucratic-Authoritarian Model," In *The New Authoritarianism in Latin America,* edited by David Collier, 19–32. Princeton: Princeton University Press, 1979.

Conaghan, Catherine M. "The Private Sector and Public Transcript: The Political Mobilization of Business in Bolivia." In *Business and Democracy in Latin America,* edited by Ernest Bartell and Leigh A. Payne. Pittsburgh: University of Pittsburgh Press, forthcoming.

————. *Restructuring Domination: Industrialists and the State in Ecuador.* Pittsburgh: University of Pittsburgh Press, 1988.

Dahl, Robert. *Polyarchy: Participation and Opposition.* New Haven: Yale University Press, 1971.

Dassin, Joan, ed. *Torture in Brazil: A Report by the Archdiocese of São Paulo,* translated by Jaime Wright. New York: Vintage Books, 1986.

Diamond, Larry, and Juan J. Linz. "Introduction: Politics, Society, and Democracy in Latin America." In *Democracy in Developing Countries: Latin America,* edited by Larry Diamond, Juan J. Linz, and Seymour Martin Lipset, 1–58. Boulder, Colo.: Lynne Rienner Publishers, 1989.

Diniz, Eli. *Empresário, estado e capitalismo no Brasil, 1930–1945.* Rio de Janeiro: Paz e Terra, 1978.

————. "Post-1930 Industrial Elites." Rio de Janeiro: Instituto Universitário de Pesquisas do Rio de Janeiro (IUPERJ), n.d. Mimeo.

Diniz, Eli, and Renato Raul Boschi. *Empresariado nacional e estado no Brasil.* Rio de Janeiro: Forense Universitária, 1978.

Dreifuss, René Armand. *1964: A conquista do estado (Ação política, poder e golpe de classe).* Petrópolis, Rio de Janeiro: Vozes, 1986.

Durand, Francisco. "From Fragile Crystal to Solid Rock: The Formation and Consolidation of a Business Peak Association in Peru." In *Business and Democracy in Latin America,* edited by Ernest Bartell and Leigh A. Payne. Pittsburgh: University of Pittsburgh Press, forthcoming.

Dutra, Eloy. *IBAD: Sigla da corrupção.* Rio de Janeiro: Civilização Brasileira, 1963.

Elster, Jon. "Introduction." In *Rational Choice,* edited by Jon Elster, 1–33. Oxford: Basil Blackwell, 1986.

————. *Sour Grapes: Studies in the Subversion of Rationality.* Cambridge: Cambridge University Press, 1983.

————. *Ulysses and the Sirens: Studies in Rationality and Irrationality.* Cambridge: Cambridge University Press, 1984.

Erickson, Kenneth Paul. *The Brazilian Corporative State and Working-Class Politics.* Berkeley and Los Angeles: University of California Press, 1977.

Evans, Peter. *Dependent Development: The Alliance of Multinational, State, and Local Capital in Brazil.* Princeton: Princeton University Press, 1979.

Farneti, Paolo. *Imprenditore e società.* Turin: Editrice L'imprensa, 1970.

Fernandes, Florestan. *Reflections on the Brazilian Counter-Revolution,* edited by Warren Dean. Armonk, N.Y.: M. E. Sharpe, 1981.

Figueiredo, Angelina Maria Cheibub. "Política governamental e funções sindicais." M.A. thesis, Universidade de São Paulo, 1975.

Fishman, Robert M. *Working-Class Organization and the Return to Democracy in Spain.* Ithaca: Cornell University Press, 1990.

Fleischer, David. "The Brazilian Congress: From Abertura to New Republic." In *Political Liberalization in Brazil: Dynamics, Dilemmas, and Future Prospects,* edited by Wayne A. Selcher, 97–133. Boulder, Colo.: Westview Press, 1986.

———. "O Congresso Constituinte de 1987: Um perfil sócio-econômico e político." Brasília: Departamento de Ciências Políticas e Relações Internacionais, Universidade de Brasília 1987. Mimeo.

Flynn, Peter. *Brazil: A Political Analysis.* Boulder, Colo.: Westview Press, 1978.

———. "Brazil: The Politics of the Cruzado Plan." *Third World Quarterly* 8, no. 4 (1986): 1151–94.

Fon, Antonio Carlos. *Tortura: A história da repressão política no Brasil.* São Paulo: Global, 1979.

Heredia, Blanca. "Mexican Business and the State: The Political Economy of a 'Muddled' Transition." In *Business and Democracy in Latin America,* edited by Ernest Bartell and Leigh A. Payne. Pittsburgh: University of Pittsburgh Press, forthcoming.

Hirschman, Albert O. "The Political Economy of Import-Substituting Industrialization in Latin America." In *A Bias for Hope: Essays on Development in Latin America,* edited by Albert O. Hirschman, 85–123. New Haven: Yale University Press, 1971. Reprinted from *Quarterly Journal of Economics* 82 (February 1968): 2–32.

Humphrey, John. *Capitalist Control and Workers' Struggle in the Brazilian Auto Industry.* Princeton: Princeton University Press, 1982.

Keck, Margaret Elizabeth. "From Movement to Politics: The Formation of the Workers' Party in Brazil." Ph.D. diss., Columbia University, 1986.

———. *The Workers' Party and Democratization in Brazil.* New Haven: Yale University Press, 1992.

Kucinski, Bernardo. *Abertura, a história de uma crise.* São Paulo: Brasil Debates, 1982.

Lamounier, Bolivar, and Alkimar R. Moura. "Política econômica e abertura política no Brasil, 1973–1983." *Textos* 4 (1984): 1–48.

Lange, Peter. "Unions, Workers, and Wage Regulation: The Rational Bases of Consent." In *Order and Conflict in Contemporary Capitalism,* edited by John H. Goldthorpe, 98–123. Oxford: Clarendon Press, 1984.

Langguth, A. J. *Hidden Terrors.* New York: Pantheon Books, 1978.

Leff, Nathaniel H. *Economic Policy-Making and Development in Brazil, 1947–1964.* New York: John Wiley and Sons, 1968.

Leme, Marisa Saens. *A ideologia dos industriais brasileiros, 1919–1945.* Petrópolis: Vozes, 1978.

Leopoldi, M. Antonieta P. "Industrial Associations and Politics in Contemporary Brazil." Ph.D. diss., St. Antony's College, 1984.

Lindblom, Charles E. "The Market as Prison." In *The Political Economy: Readings in the Politics and Economics of American Public Policy,* edited by Thomas Ferguson and Joel

Rogers, 3–11. Armonk, NY: M. E. Sharpe, 1984. Reprinted from *Journal of Politics* 44, no. 2 (1982): 324–36.

———. *Politics and Markets: The World's Political-Economic Systems.* New York: Basic Books, 1977.

Linz, Juan J. *Crisis, Breakdown, and Reequilibration.* In *The Breakdown of Democratic Regimes,* edited by Juan J. Linz and Alfred Stepan. Baltimore: Johns Hopkins University Press, 1978.

Linz, Juan J., and Amando de Miguel. *Los empresarios ante el poder público: El liderazgo y los grupos de intereses en el empresariado español.* Madrid: Instituto de Estudios Políticos, 1966.

Mainwaring, Scott. "Political Parties and Democratization in Brazil and the Southern Cone." *Comparative Politics* 21, no. 1 (1988): 91–120.

———. "The Transition to Democracy in Brazil." *Journal of Interamerican Studies and World Affairs* 28, no. 1 (1986): 149–79.

Makler, Harry Mark. *A elite industrial portuguesa.* Lisbon: Centro de Economia e Finanças, 1969.

March, James G., and Johan P. Olsen. *Rediscovering Institutions: The Organizational Basis of Politics.* New York: Free Press, 1989.

Martinez, Roberto Esteban. "Business Elites in Democratic Spain." Ph.D. diss., Yale University, 1984.

Mericle, Kenneth S. "Conflict Regulation in the Brazilian Industrial Relations System." Ph.D. diss., University of Wisconsin, 1974.

———. "Corporatist Control of the Working Class: Authoritarian Brazil since 1964." In *Authoritarianism and Corporatism in Latin America,* edited by James M. Malloy, 303–38. Pittsburgh: University of Pittsburgh Press, 1977.

Miliband, Ralph. *The State in Capitalist Society.* New York: Basic Books, 1969.

Moraes, Dênis de. *A esquerda e o golpe de 64.* Rio de Janeiro: Espaço e Tempo, 1989.

Niosi, Jorge. *Los empresarios y el estado argentino, 1955–1969.* Buenos Aires: Siglo Ventiuno Editores, 1974.

Nylen, William R. "Liberalismo para todo mundo, menos eu: Brazil and the Neo-Liberal Solution." In *The Right and Democracy in Latin America,* edited by Douglas A. Chalmers, Maria do Carmo Campello de Souza, and Atilio A. Boron, 259–276. New York: Praeger Publishers, 1992.

O'Donnell, Guillermo. *Modernization and Bureaucratic-Authoritarianism.* Berkeley and Los Angeles: University of California Press, 1973.

———. "Reflections on the Patterns of Change in the Bureaucratic-Authoritarian Regimes in Latin America." *Latin American Research Review* 13, no. 1 (1978): 3–38.

———. "Substantive or Procedural Consensus? Notes on the Latin American Bourgeoisie." In *The Right and Democracy in Latin America,* edited by Douglas A. Chalmers, Maria do Carmo Campello de Souza, and Atilio A. Boron, 43–47. New York: Praeger Publishers, 1992.

————. "Tensions in the Bureaucratic-Authoritarian State and the Question of Democracy." In *The New Authoritarianism in Latin America*, edited by David Collier, 285–318. Princeton: Princeton University Press, 1979.

O'Donnell, Guillermo, and Philippe C. Schmitter. *Transitions from Authoritarian Rule: Tentative Conclusions about Uncertain Democracies*. Baltimore: Johns Hopkins University Press, 1986.

Offe, Claus, and Helmut Wiesenthal. "Two Logics of Collective Action: Theoretical Notes on Social Class and Organizational Form." *Political Power and Social Theory* 1 (1980): 67–115.

Olson, Mancur, Jr. *The Logic of Collective Action: Public Goods and the Theory of Groups*. Cambridge: Harvard University Press, 1965.

————. *The Rise and Decline of Nations: Economic Growth, Stagflation, and Social Rigidities*. New Haven: Yale University Press, 1982.

Parker, Phyllis R. *Brazil and the Quiet Intervention, 1964*. Austin: University of Texas Press, 1979.

Payne, Leigh Ann. "Pragmatic Actors: The Political Attitudes and Behavior of Brazilian Industrial Elites." Ph.D. diss., Yale University, 1990.

————. "Working Class Strategies in the Transition to Democracy in Brazil." *Comparative Politics* 23, no. 2 (1991): 221–38.

Pereira, Luiz Carlos Bresser. *O colapso de uma aliança de classes: A burguesia e a crise do autoritarismo tecnoburocrático*. São Paulo: Editora Brasilense, 1978.

Pérez Díaz, Víctor. *Governability and the Scale of Governance: Mesogovernments in Spain.* Working Paper no. 1990/6. Madrid: Instituto Juan March de Estudios e Investigaciones, Centro de Estudios Avanzados en Ciencias Sociales, 1990.

————. *El retorno de la sociedad civil*. Madrid: Instituto de Estudios Económicos, 1987.

Poulantzas, Nicos. *Political Power and Social Classes*. Translated by Timothy O'Hagen. London: Verso Editions, 1968.

Przeworski, Adam. *Capitalism and Social Democracy*. Cambridge: Cambridge University Press, 1985.

————. *Democracy and the Market: Political and Economic Reforms in Eastern Europe and Latin America*. Cambridge: Cambridge University Press, 1991.

Rodrigues, Leôncio Martins. *Quem é quem na Constituinte: Uma análise sócio-política dos partidos e deputados*. São Paulo: OESP-Maltese, 1987.

————. "Sindicalismo e classe operária (1930–1964)." In *História geral da civilicação brasileira*, vol. 3, *O Brasil republicano: Sociedade e política (1930–1964)*, edited by Boris Fausto, 508–55. Rio de Janeiro: Difusão Editorial, 1981.

Schmitter, Philippe C. *Interest Conflict and Political Change in Brazil*. Stanford, Calif.: Stanford University Press, 1971.

————. "Still a Century of Corporatism?" *Review of Politics* 36, no. 1 (1974): 85–121.

Schneider, Ben Ross. *Politics within the State: Elite Bureaucrats and Industrial Policy in Authoritarian Brazil*. Pittsburgh: University of Pittsburgh Press, 1991.

Scott, James C. *Domination and the Arts of Resistance: Hidden Transcripts*. New Haven: Yale University Press, 1990.

Sikkink, Kathryn. *Ideas and Institutions: Developmentalism in Brazil and Argentina.* Ithaca: Cornell University Press, 1991.

Simões, Solange de Deus. *Deus, patria e familia: As mulheres no golpe de 1964.* Petrópolis: Vozes, 1985.

Skidmore, Thomas E. "Brazil's Slow Road to Democratization: 1974–1985." In *Democratizing Brazil,* edited by Alfred Stepan, 5–42. New York: Oxford University Press, 1989.

————. *Politics in Brazil, 1930–1964: An Experiment in Democracy.* London: Oxford University Press, 1967.

————. *The Politics of Military Rule in Brazil, 1964–85.* New York: Oxford University Press, 1988.

Skocpol, Theda. "Political Responses to Capitalist Crisis: Neo-Marxist Theories of the State and the Case of the New Deal." *Politics and Society* 10, no. 2 (1980): 155–201.

Smith, William C. *Authoritarianism and the Crisis of the Argentine Political Economy.* Stanford, Calif.: Stanford University Press, 1989.

————. "Heterodox Shocks and the Political Economy of Democratic Transition in Argentina and Brazil." Paper presented at the Fourteenth International Congress of the Latin American Studies Association, New Orleans, La., 17–19 March 1988.

————. "The 'New Republic' and the Brazilian Transition: Elite Conciliation or Democratization?" Paper presented at the Eighth International Congress of the Latin American Studies Association, Boston, Mass., 23–26 October 1986.

Stepan, Alfred. "Civil Society and the State: Patterns of Resistance to Domination in the Southern Cone." Paper presented at the Social Science Research Council Conference on States and Social Structures: Research Implications of Current Theories, Mount Kisco, N.Y., 25–27 February 1982.

————, ed. *Democratizing Brazil.* New York: Oxford University Press, 1989.

————. *The Military in Politics: Changing Patterns in Brazil.* Princeton: Princeton University Press, 1971.

————. "On Redemocratization and the Functions of the Opposition: Relationships and Processes." *Journal of Democracy* 1, no. 2 (1990): 41–49.

————. "Paths towards Redemocratization: Theoretical and Comparative Considerations." In *Transitions from Authoritarian Rule: Comparative Perspectives,* edited by Guillermo O'Donnell, Philippe C. Schmitter, and Laurence Whitehead, 64–84. Baltimore: Johns Hopkins University Press, 1986.

————. "Political Leadership and Regime Breakdown: Brazil." In *The Breakdown of Democratic Regimes: Latin America,* edited by Juan J. Linz and Alfred Stepan, 110–37. Baltimore: Johns Hopkins University Press, 1978.

————. *Rethinking Military Politics: Brazil and the Southern Cone.* Princeton: Princeton University Press, 1988.

Syrkis, Alfredo. *Os carbonários: Memórias da guerrilha perdida.* São Paulo: Global, 1980.

Therborn, Goran. "The Travail of Latin American Democracy." *New Left Review* 113/114 (1979): 71–109.

Tsebelis, George. *Nested Games: Rational Choice in Comparative Politics.* Berkeley and Los Angeles: University of California Press, 1990.

Vogel, David. "The Power of Business in America: A Re-Appraisal." *British Journal of Political Science* 13 (1983): 19–43.

———. "Why Businessmen Distrust Their State: The Political Consciousness of American Corporation Executives." *British Journal of Political Science* 8 (1978): 45–78.

Weber, Max. *The Theory of Social and Economic Organization,* edited and with an introduction by Talcott Parsons, and translated by A. M. Henderson and Talcott Parsons. New York: Free Press, 1947.

Weffort, Franciso. "Participação e conflito industrial: Contagem e Osasco, 1968." *Cadernos do CEBRAP,* no. 5 (1972): 6–93.

Interviews

Industrial Leaders

The following list of the industrial leaders interviewed for this project is organized in alphabetical order. The interviews occurred between July 1987 and June 1988.

Arthur Ricardo Alicke Júnior, Director, Alcan do Brasil
Mario Amato, Director, Springer
Salvador Arena, President, Termomecânica
Jamil Nicolau Aun, Director, Papel Simão
Paulo Ayres Filho, Director, Universal Consultores
René Baldacci, Director, Casa da Prateleria
Cláudio Bardella, President, Grupo Bardella
Elizir Batista, Chairman, Vale do Rio Doce
André Beer, Vice-President, General Motors do Brasil Ltda.
Alain Belda, President, Alcoa do Brasil
Abram Berland, President, Grupo Adela
Pietro Biselli, Director, Sistema
W. Wayne Booker, President, Ford Brasil S.A.
Herbert Brenner, Director, General Motors do Brasil
Wagner Brunini, Manager, BASF Brasileira S.A.
Sebastião Burbulhan, Director, Babuche and Novomocassin
Keith Bush, Director, São Paulo Alpargatas S.A.
Paulo Roberto Rodriques Butori, Director, Fupresa-Hitchinir S.A.
Oscar Augusto de Camargo, Director, Fiação e Tecelagem
Aguinaldo M. Carvalho, Manager, Zadra Indústria Mecânica Ltda.
Francisco de Castro Netto, Director, Indústrias Gessy Lever Ltda.
Alberto Cavalcanti de Figueiredo, Vice-President, S.A. Indústrias Reunidas Francisco Matarazzo
Diogo Alarcon Clemente, Director, Ford Brasil S.A.
Mario Rubens Costa, Director-President, Costume Firmino Costa S.A.

Paulo Roberto Perreira da Costa, Director, Brastemp S.A.
Joseph M. Couri, Director, Fundição Balancins Ltda.
Paulo Gulherme Aguiar Cunha, Director, Companhia Ultragas, S.A.
Valdemar Davini, Director, Companhia Industrial de Conservas de Alimentos
Roberto Della Manna, Director, Tubozin
Clovis Dutra, Manager, Dow Química
Pedro Armando Eberhardt, Director, Artebi
Zenon Flórido Espim, President, Metalúrgica Rio S.A.
Salvador Evangelista Júnior, Director, Coca Cola Indústrias Ltda.
Carlos Eduardo Uchôa Fagundes, Director, Comlux
Said Farhat, President, Semprel
Max Feffer, Vice-President, Companhia Suzano
Nelson Fernandes, Manager, Caterpillar Brasil S.A.
Roberto Ferraiuolo, Director, Ideal and Adrizyl
Joaquim Romeu Teixeira Ferraz, Director, Antártica
Ana Maria Ferreira, Manager, Cargill Agrícola S.A.
Carlos Eduardo Moreira Ferreira, Director-President, Companhia Paulista de Energia
    Elétrica
José Roberto G. Ferreira, Director, Cargill Agrícola S.A.
Paulo de Toledo Ferreira, Director, Indústrias Romi S.A.
João Batista Leopoldo Figueiredo, Director, Banco Itaú S.A.
Salvador Firace, Manager, Proteindus
Fábio Starace Fonseca, Director, Friozem
Paulo Francini, Director, Coldex Frigor
Edson Fregni, Director-President, Scopus Tecnologia
Alfredo Guenther Fuchs, President, Brazaço-Mapri Indústrias Metalúrgicas S.A.
Luciano S. Gaino, Director, Eucatex S.A.
José Gelazio da Rocha, President, Indústria de Material Bélico do Brasil–IMBEL
Waldyr Antonio Giannetti, Vice-President, M. Dedini S.A.
Jorge D. Giganti, Vice-President, Coca Cola Indústrias Ltda.
Norbert Gmur, President, Ciba-Geigy Química S.A.
Szymon Goldfarb, President, Itapuã
Severo Fagundes Gomes, President, Tecelagem Parahyba
José Dimas Gonçalves, Manager, Companhia Cacique
Oded Grajew, President, Grow Jogos e Brinquedos
Henrique Sérgio Gregori, President, Xerox do Brasil S.A.
Sergio Haberfeld, Executive Director, Toga
Hiroshi Hashimoto, Director, Proton S.A.
Fernando Braga Hilsenbeck, Vice-President, Indústrias Villares S.A.
Gilberto Huber, Director, Grupo Gilberto Huber
Nobuya Ishii, Director, Toyobo do Brasil S.A.
Roberto Nicalau Jeha, President, Indústria de Pape le Papelão São Roberto S.A.
Emerson Kapaz, Director, Elka Plásticos Ltda.

Abraham Kasinsky, Executive President, COFAB
Roberto Kasinsky, Director, COFAB
Geraldo Adolpho Kielwagen, Vice-President, Tupy S.A.
Hans Rudolf Kittler, President, Presstécnica
Edmundo Klotz, Director, Liotécnica
Einar Alberto Kok, Director, Indústrias Romi S.A.
Celso Lafer, Director, Metal Leve S.A.
Luis Carlos Delben Leite, Director, Manig
Bettina Lenci, President, Translor
Fernando Ulhôa Levy, President, Kentinha S.A.
Wolfgang Anton Lieb, Manager, Hoechst do Brasil
Adolpho Lindenberg, President, Construtora Adolpho Lindenberg S.A.
Aldo Lorenzetti, President, Lorenzetti S.A.
Braulio Cesar Jordão Machado, Director, Wolff
Mauro Marcondes Machado, Director, Saab-Scania do Brasil Ltda.
Chico Maia, Director, Apoio Video
Henry Maksoud, Director, Hidroservice
Helio B. Marçon, Director, H. B. Marçon e Companhia Ltda.
Dante Ludovico Mariutti, Director, Pedreira Mariutti Ltda.
Nildo Masini, Director, Ipiranga Aços Especiais
Eliane Pinheiro Belfort Mattos, Director, B. M. Eletrônica Industrial Ltda.
Geraldo Luiz Santo Mauro, Director, Retífica Motolux
Edigimar Antonio Maximiliano, Manager, Pirelli S.A.
Luiz Américo Medeiros, Director, Comexport
Jacy de Souza Mendonça, Director, Volkswagen do Brasil and Autolatina
Laerte Michielin, Director-President, Torque S.A.
José Mindlin, President, Metal Leve S.A.
Enrico Misasi, Director-President, Olivetti do Brasil
Alfeu Bruno Monzani, Manager, Refinações de Milho, Brasil Ltda.
Mario Mugnaini Júnior, Director Superintendent, Degrémont
Sidnei Roberto Ladessa Muneratti, Manager, Pirelli S.A.
Edson Vaz Musa, President, Rhodia S.A.
Bruno Nardini Feola, Director, Indústrias Nardini S.A.
Carmelino de Oliveira, Manager, Cascadura Industrial S.A.
Antonio Gonçalves Pacheco, Manager, Goodyear do Brasil
José Papa Júnior, Director, Grupo Empresarial Lavra
Ulrich M. Parnitzke, Director, Telefunken Rádio e Televisão Ltda.
Cláudio Rubens Ribeiro Pereira, Director, Rowamet
Carlos Perez, President, Goodyear do Brasil
José de Freitas Picardi, Director, Johnson and Johnson
Leda Chiarotto Pierro, Director, Porcelana Chiarotti Ltda.
Lawrence Pih, Director Superintendent, Moinho Pacífico S.A.
Roberto Pinto de Souza, Director, Sarabor S.A.

Adauto P. Ponte, Director, Metal II Indústria Metalúrgica Ltda.
Ilma Cauduro Ponte, Director, Metal II Indústria Metalúrgica Ltda.
João Carlos Prada, Director, Companhia Metalúrgica Prada
Jorge Prada, Director, Companhia Metalúrgica Prada
Antonio Alberto Prado, Manager, Bayer do Brasil S.A.
Pedro Proscurcin, Director, Mercedes-Benz do Brasil S.A.
Mario Pugliese, President, Pugliese S.A.
Jacks Rabinovich, Director-President, Campo Belo
Franciso Ramalho Alge Júnior, Director, Inabra
Paulo Reis de Magalhães, President, Phillips do Brasil and Champion Papel e Celulose Ltda.
James Ian Robertson, President, Companhia Atlantic de Petróleo
Firmino Rocha de Freitas, President, Bravox S.A.
Antonio Carlos F. Rosa, Manager, São Paulo Alpargatas S.A.
Luiz Rodovil Rossi, President, Auto Comércio e Indústria ACIL Ltda.
Kamal Saad, President, Saad e Companhia Ltda.
Walter Sacca, Director, Holstein-Kappert
Daniel Sahagoff, Director, Orion S.A.
Antonio Sergio Salles, President, Exxon do Brasil
José Carlos V. Santi, Manager, Union Carbide do Brasil S.A.
Domício dos Santos Júnior, Director, Volkswagen do Brasil S.A. and Autolatina
Manoel da Costa Santos, President, ANIP
Wolfgang F. J. Sauer, Director, Volkswagen do Brasil and Autolatina
Nelson Savioli, Manager, Rhodia S.A.
Robert Schoueri, Director, Fábrica de Fios e Linha Marte S.A.
Ricardo Frank Semler, Director-President, Semco S.A.
Emanuele Sessarego, Manager, Pirelli S.A.
Laerte Setubal Filho, President, Duratex S.A.
Olavo Egydio Setubal, President, Banco Itaú S.A.
Ichiu Shinohara, Executive Director, National do Brasil Ltda.
Ruy Martins Altenfelder Silva, Director, S.A. Moinho Santista Indústrias Gerais
Ozilio Carlos da Silva, President, EMBRAER–Empresa Brasileira de Aeronáutica S.A.
Ozires Silva, Director, PETROBRÁS S.A.
Alexandre Rodolfo Smith de Vasconcellos, President, SIFCO S.A.
Geo Albert Stammer, President, SKF do Brasil Ltda.
Eugenio Emilio Staub, Director-President, Indústrias Gradiente Brasileiras S.A.
Jacob Tabacow, Director, Textil Tabacow S.A.
Walter Torres, Director, Cerv n
Sergio Roberto Ugolini, President, Companhia Industrial Roberto Ugolini
Décio Fernandes Vasconcellos, President, D. F. Vasconcellos, S.A.
Alberto Vassoler, Director, Irmãos Vassolér Ltda.
Everaldo Veiga, President, MEGA
Luis Eulálio Bueno Vidigal Filho, Director, Cobrasma
Roberto Caiuby Vidigal, Director, Confab Indústria S.A.

Antonio A. Vieira, Manager, General Electric do Brasil S.A.
Antônio de Jesus Vieira, Director, Indústria de Pneumáticos Firestone S.A.
Carlos Villares, Director, Indústrias Villares
Walcyr Villas Bôas, Director, Indústrias Gessy Lever Ltda.
José Villela de Andrade Neto, Director, Companhia Metalgráfica Paulista
Armando Luiz Viviani, Director, S.A. Moinho Santista Indústrias Gerais
Hermann H. Wever, President, Siemens S.A.

Labor Leaders, Labor Lobbyists, and Labor Consultants

The following list of interviewees is organized in alphabetical order. The interviews occurred between July 1987 and June 1988.

Joaquim dos Santos Andrade, President, Central Geral dos Trabalhadores (CGT)
Walter Barelli, Director, Departamento Intersindical de Estatística e Estudos Sócio-Econômicos (DIEESE)
Antonio Pereira Magaldi, President, Federação dos Empregados no Comércio do Estado de São Paulo
Antonio Rogério Magri, President, Sindicato dos Trabalhadores nas Indústrias da Energia Elétrica de São Paulo
Luiz Antonio de Medeiros, President, Sindicato dos Trabalhadores nas Indústrias Metal-úrgicas, Mecânicas, e de Material Elétrico de São Paulo
Jair Menguelli, President, Central Única dos Trabalhadores (CUT)
Ulysses Riedel, Lobbyist, Departamento Intersindical de Assessoria Parlamentar (DIAP)
Argeo Egídio dos Santos, President, Federação dos Trabalhadores nas Indústrias Metal-úrgicas, Mecânicas, e de Material Elétrico de São Paulo
Vicente Paulo da Silva, President, Sindicato dos Trabalhadores nas Indústrias Metalúrgicas, Mecânicas, e de Material Elétrico de São Bernardo do Campo e Diadema
Antonio Toschi, Vice-President, Sindicato dos Trabalhadores nas Indústrias Metalúrgicas, Mecânicas, e de Material Elétrico de Osasco

Index

AAB, 48, 49, 50, 171
Abertura. *See* Transitions from authoritarian rule, in Brazil
ABI, 49, 171
Accident prevention committees. *See* CIPA
Acuña, Carlos, 138, 146
Adaptive actor approach, xiv–xvi, xxii, 1–15, 135–51; and Brazilian business elites, 13–15, 124–35; in 1964, 36–38, 126–27; during military regime, 53–55, 127–28; during early transition, 82–83; during New Republic, 120–22, 128–29
ADCE, 58, 171
ADEP, 19, 171
ADP, 171, 176n.4
AFL-CIO, 20
AIFLD, 20
Alfonsín, Raul, 137, 138, 146, 147
Allende, Salvador, 138–39, 141, 146
Alliance for National Renovation. *See* ARENA
Amato, Mario, 88, 112, 114, 116, 191n.60, 193nn.86 and 88
Amazonas, 18
American Chamber of Commerce, 18, 24, 47, 176n.4
American Institute for Free Labor Development. *See* AIFLD
Amnesty, 57, 96, 129
ANAPEMEI, 76, 171, 194n.103
ANFAVEA, 70, 76, 171
Anticommunist movement. *See* MAC
Anticommunist Organization of Paraná. *See* OPAC
AP, 144, 171
Araguaia, 47
ARENA, xix, xxi, 57, 171, 181n.2
Argentine, xiii, xxii, 123, 135–38, 140, 141, 142, 143, 145, 146–48
Armed forces. *See* Military

Arraes, Miguel, 177n.38
ARTE, 171, 194n.102
Association of Christian Entrepreneurs. *See* ADCE
Ayres, Paulo Filho, 16, 17, 18, 20, 21, 23, 30, 32, 48, 50, 60, 96, 175n.1, 196n.5

Balance-of-payments deficits, xviii, 9, 34, 143
Bank for National Economic Development. *See* BNDE
Bardella, Cláudio, 58, 114
Bartell, Ernest, 141, 142, 148
Belo Horizonte, 58
BNDE, 171, 179n.3
Boilesen, Henning Albert, 49, 50, 59, 180n.14
Bolivia, xiii
Braço cruzado, 71, 184n.59
Brasília, xviii, 80, 87
Brazilian Anticommunist Alliance. *See* AAB
Brazilian Communist Party. *See* PCB
Brazilian Democratic Institute. *See* IDB
Brazilian Democratic Movement. *See* MDB
Brazilian Institute for Democratic Action. *See* IBAD
Brazilian Press Association. *See* ABI
Bresser Pereira, Luiz Carlos, 67, 87, 89
Bresser Plan, 87, 89, 91
Brizola, Leonel, 22, 28, 96, 126, 177n.38
Bureaucratic-authoritarian state, theory of, xiv, 2, 3, 4, 8, 9, 12, 16, 23, 26, 28, 34, 36, 37, 39, 124, 125, 152, 153, 157
Bureaucratic rings, 52, 174n.24
Business: characteristics, xv, 6, 46, 54, 81, 82, 83, 91–92, 107, 112–13, 116–17, 120, 121–22, 124, 125, 127, 130, 132, 136, 147, 157–59, 160, 162; associations, xvii–xviii, xx, 5, 52, 58, 59, 69, 83, 88, 91, 112, 118–19, 130, 131, 132, 135, 137, 139, 146–51, 158, 160, 161, 162, 168, 169, 177n.34; relations with state, 6, 130–32, 158–60; representation of, 68, 89, 90,

209

212   Index

General Workers' Command. *See* CGT
General Workers' Union. *See* UGT
Golbery do Couto e Silva, 19, 179n.5
Gomes, Severo, 63, 78
González, Filipe, 144
Goulart, João, xiii, xvi, xviii, xix, xxi, 13, 16, 17,
   20, 21, 22, 27–29, 31, 32, 34, 35, 36, 37, 42,
   46, 51, 52, 53, 54, 56, 84, 85, 92, 93, 96, 120,
   124, 126, 127, 132, 133, 138, 178n.46,
   180n.14
Government. *See* Competence; Legitimacy; Sta-
   bility; State intervention; State investment in
   business
Group of Fourteen, 69, 76, 119
Grupos de onze, 28
Guarulhos Metalworkers' Union, 69
Guerrilla movements, xix, 21, 47, 48, 50, 136,
   138

Haiti, 154
Hegemony, 5
Herzog, Vladimir, 182n.13
Hirschman, Albert, 6–7, 165–68
Huber, Gilberto, Jr., 17
Human rights, abuses of, 47, 57, 58, 79, 127, 128,
   137. *See also* Repression; Torture

IBAD, 17, 19, 172
IDB, 172, 176n.4
Ideology, 17, 20–21, 26, 27, 30, 31, 32, 33, 36,
   84, 87, 95, 96–102, 113, 115, 121, 132, 139,
   145, 148, 150, 159, 167, 168, 169, 178n.46,
   189n.35, 190nn.46, 47, and 50, 192n.66
Illía, Arturo, 135–36
Import-substitution industrialization, 8–9, 64,
   174n.26
Individualism. *See* Business characteristics
Industrialists quoted: from multinational corporations, 16, 21, 22–23, 34, 47, 48, 61, 63,
   65–66, 72, 74–76, 98, 100, 101, 106, 109–10;
   from large and very large firms, 27, 32–33,
   50–51, 65, 74–77, 81, 92, 94, 97, 98, 99–101,
   108, 109, 115, 117, 185n.61; from medium-
   sized firms, 27, 32, 57, 58, 62–63, 72–75, 77,
   88–89, 93, 96, 106, 113, 183n.42; 193n.93;
   from small firms, 31, 33, 50–51, 61, 62–63,
   65, 72, 77, 94, 95, 100, 101, 106, 110, 112,
   116, 119, 120, 185n.61
Inflation, xviii, 9, 34, 35, 40, 41, 61, 62, 85, 86,
   88, 90, 121, 143, 181n.8, 183n.43
Information Operations Detachment—Center for
   Internal Defense Operations. *See* DOI-CODI

Institute for Economic and Social Research. *See*
   IPES
Institutional Acts, xix, 47, 48, 180n.14
International Labor Organization, 108
International Organizations, 57, 80, 174n.27
International trends, xiii, xv–xvi, xxi–xxii, 1,
   125, 130, 134, 137, 138, 142, 154, 156, 157,
   159, 160; in 1964, 15, 16, 32, 34, 36–37, 94–
   95, 126, 127; during early transition, 60, 82–
   83, 128; during New Republic, 84, 94–95,
   120, 128. *See also* Cold War; Cuban Revolu-
   tion; Human rights, abuses of
International Union of Christian Entrepreneurs.
   See UNIAPAC
Interunion Department for Parliamentary Action.
   See DIAP
Interunion Department of Statistical and Socioeconomic Studies. *See* DIEESE
Interviews, xvi, 130, 161–69, 175n.1, 208–12
Investment stability, xv, xix, 10–12, 46, 123,
   125, 129, 138, 153, 157, 159; in 1964, 13–14,
   16, 30; during military regime, 51, 54, 127;
   during early transition, 67, 68, 82, 127; during
   New Republic, 87, 88, 120, 128
IPES, 16–23, 36, 40, 42, 47, 60, 172, 176n.9,
   177n.21, 178n.39

João Pessoa, 190n.48
Job security, xxi, 103, 105–8, 111, 114, 121, 133,
   134, 191nn.62 and 64, 192n.65
Julião, Francisco, 177n.38

Kok, Einar, 58
Krieger Vasena, Adalberto, 136
Kruel, Amaury, 23
Kubitschek, Juscelino, xviii, 44, 45, 46, 48, 54,
   125, 180n.14

Labor, xviii, xix, 9, 79. *See also* Labor conflict;
   Unions; Workers
Labor conflict: in 1964, 26–27, 32–34, 35, 86;
   during military regime, 40, 42, 53; during early
   transition, 56, 68–78, 81, 82; during New Re-
   public, xxi, 15, 84, 85, 86, 102–12, 120. *See
   also* Strikes
Labor courts, xvii, 68, 70, 71, 75, 103
Labor Relations Consultants to Business. *See*
   ARTE
Lanusse, Alejandro A., 136
Late-late development. *See* Delayed
   development
Lawyers, 57. *See* also OAB

São Bernardo Metalworkers' Union, 113, 183n.48, 194n.54
São Caetano Metalworkers' Union, 183n.48, 184n.56
São Paulo, xvii, 16, 17, 18, 23, 32, 58, 59, 60, 63, 68, 70, 73, 77, 80, 81, 102, 103, 116, 145, 147, 156, 162, 176n.9, 178n.39, 179n.3, 183n.48, 193n.93, 194n.103
São Paulo Metalworkers' Union, xvii, 69, 101, 108
São Paulo Union of Electrical Energy Workers, 101
Sarney, José, xxi, 84, 85, 86, 87, 88, 91, 92, 93, 112, 129, 172n.12, 187n.11
"Satisficing," 174n.32
Second-best alternative calculation, 13
Shop-floor representation. See Plant committees
Sindicato de resultados, 101
Sindicatos. See Unions
SINFAVEA, 76, 172, 185n.68
Slumdwellers, 57
SNI, 58, 60, 172, 179n.5
Social Democratic Party. See PDS
Social movements, 1, 5. See also Catholic Church; Slumdwellers; Students
Social Order, 9, 16, 37, 40, 46, 124, 125, 135
Social pact, 86, 87, 89–91, 150, 151, 181n.8, 188n.26
Southern Cone, xiii, xiv, 1, 9
Spain, xxii, xxiii, 123, 135, 143–46, 149–51, 156
Spanish Confederation of Business Organizations. See CEOE
Spanish Socialist Party. See PSOE
Stability, xv, xix, 1, 11, 37, 51, 53, 68, 74, 83, 97, 120, 143, 155, 159–60. See also Democratic stability; Investment stability; Political instability
State intervention: in economy, xiii, 2, 62, 114, 123, 127, 131, 137, 140, 142, 154, 155, 157, 158 (see also Desestatização); in labor relations, xxi, 70, 71, 72, 74, 75, 77, 81–82, 83, 89, 103–5, 108, 119, 121 (see also Unions, state control of)
State investment in business, xvii, xx, 63, 64, 67, 78, 94, 127, 137. See also Business
Strikes, xxi, 61, 71, 75, 76, 77, 83, 89, 103–5, 128, 129, 143, 191n.52; legal restrictions regarding, xvii, 103, 111, 121, 133; before 1964 coup, 32–34; 1963–77, 42–43, 48, 68; in 1978, 69, 74, 77, 184n.54, 191n.54; in 1979, 70, 75, 76, 183n.48; in 1980, 70, 76, 184n.49, 184n.56; in 1982, 70; in 1983, 71; in 1985,

103; in 1986, 103, 190n.53; in 1987, 102. See also Labor conflict; State intervention, in labor relations
Structuralist approach, 5
Students, 19, 30, 35, 57, 58, 136
Suárez, Adolfo, 144
Summer Plan, 87, 186n.2
Superior War College. See ESG
Syndicates. See Business associations; Unions

Technocrats, 1, 2, 8, 9, 14, 19, 63, 133
Teresinha, 190n.48
TFP, 49, 60, 173
Torture, xix, 7, 39, 42, 48, 49, 50, 59, 182n.12
Tradition, Family, and Property. See TFP
Transitions from authoritarian rule, xiii–xiv, 1–2, 135, 138, 140, 142, 143, 144, 145, 152, 156, 157, 158; theoretical approaches to, xiv, 2, 4, 9, 56, 120, 153, 157; in Brazil, xvi, xx–xxii, 15, 53, 56–122, 127, 128, 162
Transnational corporations. See Multinational corporations

UBE, 106, 114, 173
UCD, 144, 173
UDR, 114, 173
UGT, 144, 173
Uncommitted, the, 124; and 1964 coup, 50, 54, 127; during military regime, 50–53, 54, 128; during early transition, 57, 60–61, 66–67, 75–77, 78, 80, 81–82, 128; during New Republic, 108
UNIAPAC, 58, 173
Union of Brazilian Businesses. See UBE
Union of the Democratic Center. See UCD
Unions, xvii, xix, 20, 32, 65, 69, 72, 73, 74, 75, 76, 77, 97–102, 107, 108–10, 128, 131, 137, 138, 142, 143, 144, 146, 168, 169, 178n.48; state control of, xvii, xix, 71
United States, 20, 23, 47, 51, 74, 77, 178n.55; government of, xviii, 23, 34, 37, 57
Uruguay, 28

Valente, Cesar Rogério, 192n.82
Vargas, Getúlio, xvi–xviii, 44
Vellinho, Paulo D'Arrigo, 60
Velloso, João Reis, 183n.43
Veloso da Silveira, Domício, 182n.25
Venezuela, 1, 154
Veto, 12–13, 107, 134. See also Business characteristics
Videla, Jorge Rafael, 137